# STAR TRACKS

## PRINCIPLES FOR SUCCESS IN THE
## MUSIC & ENTERTAINMENT BUSINESS

# LARRY E. WACHOLTZ, Ph.D.

**Thumbs Up Publishing**
A Division of Entertainment Media Research, 123 Hillsboro Place, Nashville TN 37215
1-888-STAR TKS (1-888-782-7857 Toll Free); 1-615-386-0407 fax

123 Hillsboro Place
Nashville TN 37215

Library of Congress Catalog Card Number 96-90594

Wacholtz, Larry E. Ph.D. 1947-

Inside Country Music, Billboard Books, 1986

STAR TRACKS; Principles for Success in The Music &
Entertainment Business, 1996

ISBN # 0-9652341-0-X

Product # LEW 001249

Printed in the United States of America

## Acknowledgments: Photographs

*B.B. King*, courtesy of Sidney A. Seidenberg, Inc.,
New York, NY. Photograph by Guido Harari.

*Robert Deaton*, courtesy of Deaton Flanigen,
Nashville, TN.

*Vince Gill*, courtesy of The Fitzgerald Hartley
Company, Nashville, TN. Photograph by Victoria
Pearson.

*Whitney Houston*, courtesy of Nippy, Inc., Fort Lee,
NJ. Photograph by Neal Preston.

*Walt Lederle*, courtesy of Walt Lederle/Mid-South
Concerts, Memphis, TN.

*Kathy Mattea*, courtesy of Bob Titley and
Associates, Nashville, TN. Photograph by Randee
St. Nicholas.

*Reba McEntire*, courtesy of Starstruck
Entertainment, Nashville, TN. Photograph by Peter
Nash.

*Bill Monroe*, courtesy of Buddy Lee Attractions,
Nashville, TN. Photograph courtesy of The
Tennessean, Nashville, TN.

*Michael Omartian*, Courtesy of Michael Omartian
Productions, Nashville TN. Photograph by Harry
Langdon.

*Kenneth Schermerhorn*, courtesy of The Nashville
Symphony, Nashville, TN. Photograph by Nina
Long; courtesy of The Tennessean, Nashville, TN.

*Susan Shurtz*, courtesy of Reunion Records,
Nashville, TN. Photograph by Norman Jean Roy.

*Grant Smith*, courtesy of Grant Smith, Attorney,
Nashville, TN.

*Tag Team*, courtesy of Pam Browne, Nashville, TN.

*KoKo Taylor*, courtesy of Alligator Records &
Alligator Artist Management, Chicago IL. Photograph courtesy of The Tennessean, Nashville, TN.

*S. Tyler* (Aerosmith) courtesy of Collins
Management, New York. Photograph by Todd
Kaplan.

*Wynonna*, courtesy of John Unger, The Judd House,
Franklin, TN. Photograph by Randee St. Nicholas.

## Acknowledgments: Industry Contributions

NSAI Song Evaluation Form
NSAI Critique Checklist

NSAI information courtesy of The Nashville
Songwriters Association International, Nashville, TN.

*Thank you good friends, industry acquaintances, and mother and father for your gifts of love. My faith in God and your invaluable help have made this book possible.*

# CONTENTS

# PREFACE

This summer, on a plane ride to Berlin, I sat next to a tall, attractive woman in her late twenties. I was surprised to discover that she was flying to Germany to sing as the featured artist with the Berlin Opera. As we exchanged pleasantries, she was surprised to learn that my area of expertise is teaching and researching the music industry. It was one of those magical occasions when you meet someone from another part of the country and you find out how much you have in common.

As I congratulated her on her success, she told me about how her college professors *didn't* teach her about the music business. They had taught her how to sing, but not how to make a living as an artist in the music business - she had to do that on her own. Accordingly, she taught herself about the legal, marketing, promotion, management, and accounting aspects, as well as the importance of networking. She found that to be successful as an artist, she first had to become an entrepreneur, own her own business, and learn how to manage and market herself. It had been a hard lesson to learn, and it had taken years away from her singing career.

## Missed Opportunities

The music business is a fun, glamorous, energetic, and sometimes crazy business. Teaching it can be the same, yet it is not easy. Current text books often emphasize copyright and legal issues but fail to provide a broad and current overview of the music business. According to Michael Green, President of NARAS (the National Academy of Recording Arts and Sciences, the organization which awards the Grammy's):

*The long-term player needs to be a talented specialist and, equally important, a dedicated generalist. Our industry is so diversified that you must understand both the broad overview and how your particular discipline fits into it. That's the best route to personal satisfaction, creative innovation, and most importantly, the options that enable you to advance your career.*[1]

Accordingly, this text is designed to offer students a generalist's overview of the entire music industry with a comprehensive specific review of professional opportunities, responsibilities and legal aspects.

## Vital Features

Features detailed, revealed, and explained in this book include:

- Facts, figures and original graphs which have been developed to depict the *history, size, creative and business processes* of the music industry

- *BMG, EMI, MCA, Polygram, Sony, Time Warner and DreamWorks*, the dominant global music and entertainment companies

• The major, secondary, and emerging *world music markets*

• Hot topics, such as *Internet marketing* and *DART royalties*

• *Key industry terminology*

• The *recording process*, which is illustrated from budgetary, technical and professional perspectives, including qualifications and duties of the recording artists, studio musicians, session producer, and audio engineer

• *Publishing and label deals*

• Methods and examples of *music industry entrepreneurship*

• *The music video production process*

• The *creative process* from songwriting to recording

• The *business process* from song and artist selection to budgeting, marketing, promoting, publicity, and distribution

• The *synergy* between the creative and business systems

• *Professional opportunities* found in the *creative side* of the industry which includes songwriters, musicians, vocalists, recording artists, record producers, audio engineers, graphic artists, music video producers, directors, actors and actresses

• *Professional opportunities* found in the *business side* of the industry which include music publishers, record labels, artist managers, concert promoters, booking agents, promotion, marketing, distribution, symphonies, opera companies and corporate sponsors

• The *distribution processes* of direct marketing, rack jobbers, one-stops, record clubs, mass merchandising, and computer Internet home pages

• The *promotion process* and *relationship* between the music business and the mass media (radio, TV, films, and print)

• *AF of M and AFTRA union scales* are offered and students are given the opportunity to *figure recording budgets* for a master, limited pressing and demo project

• *Sage windows* consisting of interviews with successful *industry insiders*, which provide unique perspectives to the internal workings of the industry

• The 1995 Copyright Act and Digital Transmission Exclusive Right

• The *role of the music publisher,* and the difference between co-publishing and sub-publishing

The *creative systems* of songwriters, musicians, producers, audio engineers, etc., rely on the music industry's business system, which is composed of music publishers, record labels, mangers, concert promoters, and the mass media to finance, promote, and market images and creative products.

What is being created and sold are the artists and their images as communicative pop-culture icons. The industry's *currency* is the number of units of CDs, cassettes, etc., that are sold. Profits from the successful recordings are used to cover recordings that fail to break even. Profits are frequently reinvested to finance the development of new acts and other products. The *serious music market* offers live symphony and operatic performances, which are usually supported by corporate sponsors and memberships.

## Purpose of the Text

The purpose of this book is to illustrate the complexity and synergy of the creative and business aspects of the music industry. The recording business is offered in detail. Live performance careers and many associated professional careers are explored. The music business is a tough business. It is competitive and a place where only the most talented or business-minded individuals sustain long-term careers. Use this book to help you and your colleagues gain the information you need to become a successful part of one of the most rewarding careers anyone could ever want to be a part of, *the music business.*

*Chapter One* provides an overview. *Chapter Two*: The **Copyright Law** examines the rules of the game. *Chapter Three*: **Songwriting** illustrates the importance of songs and provides some songwriting tips and information on professional organizations. *Chapter Four:* **Music Publishing** provides the historical perspective of Tin Pan Alley and the functions of music publishers. *Chapter Five*: **Exploiting Copyrights** depicts how songwriters and music publishers work together to exploit a song's copyright, including revenue sources, such as mechanical, performance, foreign, sync, commercial advertisement, and dramatic or grand licenses. *Chapter Six:* **Mega Entertainment Organizations** portrays the macro structure of the six global mega entertainment industry organizations. *Chapter Seven:* **Record Labels** supplies a micro prospective of a typical record label, its departments, and common recording contract jargon. *Chapter Eight:* **The Recording Process** details the recording session process required to complete an album. *Chapter Nine:* **The Recording Team** depicts the careers and responsibilities of the recording artists, studio musicians, the audio engineer and producers who, together, create magic in the recording studio. *Chapter 10:* **Marketing Music** reviews the distribution of recorded music to retail outlets including rack jobbers, one-stops, and record clubs. *Chapter Eleven:* **Promotion** illustrates promotion of the recorded product through the mass media, (radio, TV, videos, movies, and print) and trade magazines. *Chapter Twelve:* **Artist Management** reviews the hierarchical organization, supervision and the methods of talent and product imaging through artist management. *Chapter Thirteen:* **Concerts** looks at concert promoters, bid sheets, and the gamble of the live concert and serious music business scenes. *Chapter*

and the gamble of the live concert and serious music business scenes. *Chapter Fourteen:* **Music Business Economics** explores the bottom line; what it costs to produce master, limited pressing, and demo tapes, plus marketing and promotion expenditures and break-even points. *Chapter Fifteen:* **Creating a Successful Career** concludes the text by offering advice and suggestions for building a successful business and career in the music industry.

This book helps readers see the "bigger picture" and how the "pieces of the puzzle" fit together. It helps each person to define their music business career interests and goals. Once the students have a grasp of the industry and of their career interests, instructors are usually freed from answering most of the generalist's questions beginning students often ask. Students already know the answers from the reading. It allows the instructor to move the class forward and to answer educated questions about more specific facets of the industry.

## Acknowledgments

Many thanks to the over 200 students and professional faculty members who have reviewed this manuscript. Your comments and suggestions *are* included in the final draft. Thank you to all of the industry insiders who contributed to the text. Praise to the late David Baskerville Ph.D., for his ground breaking text, The Music Business Handbook and Career Guide. To my proof readers, Jennie Bowman, Paula Bienvenu, Renee Copeland, and April Higuera - God bless you! To my former editor, Ms. Kathy Hartlove, I can only express gratitude, appreciation and admiration for your support, suggestions, guidance, poise, intelligence, patience, and passion for the music industry. Kudos to my text and cover designer, Quark expert Marian Eichelman. To my colleagues at Belmont University and in The Music & Entertainment Industry Educators Association (MEIEA), thank you for your advice and collegiate support. To the Coleman Foundation, Dr. Harold Welsch, and the Kauffman Foundation, many thanks for your support. To my friends and family, mother Midge, father, Aunt Ada, Lyle, Michelle DeStefano, and brothers - love you. To my mentors, Dr. Robert Monaghan, Dr. Elgabri, Dr. Don and Carol Sexton, Dr. Cliff Eubanks, Don Cary, Bill Turner, Bruce Hinton, Walt Wilson, Harold Streibich, Dr. Jay Collins, Dr. Walter Kirkpatrick, Jim Mosley Esq., Gloria Hendricks, Art Smith, the late Dr. James Harless, and Dr. Howard E. Hopf, I am truly grateful. Finally, to my students, both past and present, thanks for *taking the risk* to be a part of the music and entertainment industry and thank you for asking those great questions that tend to keep me young at heart. God Bless!

---

[1] "Surviving and Succeeding In Today's Music Industry," by Michael Green The Recording Industry

# 1

# THE BUSINESS OF MUSIC

**The Creative and Business Sides of the Industry**
**The Entertainment Economy**
**Music Business Careers**

Many years ago, a young man walked into a Memphis recording studio, cut a record for his mother, and became the biggest rock star ever to grace the planet. Elvis Presley made it happen by having the talent to sing, a passion to entertain, the initiative to learn from others through listening, watching, and asking questions, and, most importantly, by being in the right place at the right time.

Elvis didn't, however, become a world famous recording artist by himself. He used his vocal talents, good looks, and assertiveness to get his foot into the door of the music business, and it was the music business, or more precisely, the people who make up the music business, that helped make Elvis "the king" of rock and roll.

## Creative and Business Systems

The music business is a complex industry. It is a collection of artists, entrepreneurs, record labels, and the mass media (radio, television, and print organizations) who together form the industry. The *creative side* (or system) is composed of songwriters, musicians, producers, and audio engineers who create the albums and videos we use, rent, or buy. The supporting *business side* (business system) consists of entrepreneurs and business persons who publish songs, finance recordings, distribute, market, and promote the albums through the mass media and other outlets. Sales of the recordings, concert tickets, and the public and private use of music by the mass media and businesses provide revenues and profits to both sides of the music industry.

## Major Players

Songs are the foundation of the music business. They bring the song-writers, producers, musicians, and the business world together. *Songwriters* are customarily creative and energetic, and they appear to be consistently seeking a better way to express a catchy idea or *hook*. They are poets who use music to enhance their messages. They ingeniously combine words (*lyrics*) and music (*chords and melody)* to create emotionally-charged messages (*songs*).[1&2]

## Music Publishers

Music Publishers bridge the *creative* and *business systems.* On the creative side, they *screen new songs* from independent songwriters, hire *staff writers* to write new songs, *demo record* accepted songs, print or have *sheet music printed*, and *pitch* the songs to artists, record labels, managers, and producers.

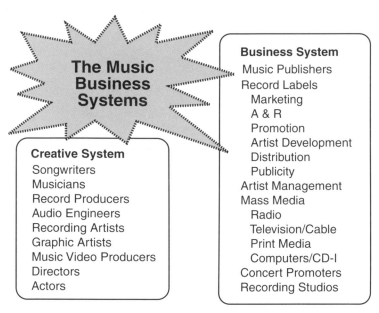

**The Music Business Systems**

**Business System**
Music Publishers
Record Labels
  Marketing
  A & R
  Promotion
  Artist Development
  Distribution
  Publicity
Artist Management
Mass Media
  Radio
  Television/Cable
  Print Media
  Computers/CD-I
Concert Promoters
Recording Studios

**Creative System**
Songwriters
Musicians
Record Producers
Audio Engineers
Recording Artists
Graphic Artists
Music Video Producers
Directors
Actors

*Figure 1.1 Music business professionals understand the marriage between art (creativity) and business. The creative system of songwriters, musicians, and others depend on the business system which is made up of music publishers, record labels, and the mass media to provide the finances and business structures required to market, promote, and distribute their songs, corresponding recordings and images.*

## Musicians

Musicians are the great interpreters of songs. They reveal their emotions and personalities through their musical instruments and performances. They are the backbone of the recording process, supporting both the lyrics of the song and the performance of the vocalists.

## Sage Window

*" If you're going to play an acoustic instrument, you have to be a really good player to work.[3] "*

**– Branford Marsalis, Recording Artist**

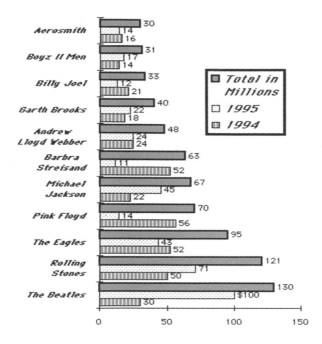

*Figure 1.2 Top recording artist and music personality gross incomes for 1994 and 1995 include: The Beatles, $130 million, thanks to a television project and recurrent album sales; The Rolling Stones, $121 million; The Eagles, $95 million; Pink Floyd $70 million; Michael Jackson (who has a profit sharing deal with Sony Music), $67 million; Barbra Streisand, $63 million; Composer Andrew Lloyd Webber, $48 million; The Grateful Dead, $42 million; Garth Brooks, $40 million; Elton John, $35 million; Billy Joel, $33 million; Boyz II Men, $31 million; Aerosmith, $30 million; and Jimmy Buffett, $26 million.[4]*

## Recording Artists

Successful recording artists breathe life into a song by conveying the song's emotional message to potential listeners. They infuse energy into lyrics and vitality into the notes printed on the sheet music. *Session* musicians and vocalists are considered recording artists. Performances must be believable, sellable, and true to the message of the song and the persona of the artists.

Prominent recording artists often create enigmatic public images, and yet, at the same time, they must be able to interact with musicians, record executives, media personalities, the public, and their fans. Major recording artists usually incorporate as businesses to systematically protect their creative efforts and employ road musicians, background singers, personal and business managers, an attorney, booking/talent agent, administrators, and others.

## Record Producers

Music producers have the ability to intelligently combine talented singers, studio musicians, and audio engineers to create potential hit recordings. In *pre-production*, producers, recording artists, managers, and record companies search to find the types of songs that will best fit the images and vocal capabilities of the artists. *In the studio*, producers are in charge of the actual recording session and responsible for the budget and "sound" quality of the final product.

## Audio Engineers

Audio engineers are considered *electronic creative artist*s because they use the studio's acoustics, microphones, consoles, tape machines, computers, and special effects outboard equipment to enhance the quality of the recording. Audio engineers are responsible for the technical quality of the recording, just as the producers are responsible for the creative quality of the recording. Their job is to make the artists and musicians sound as good as technically possible. Accordingly, they work *with* the recording artists, musicians, and producer to *capture* the artists' and musicians' best creative efforts on tape or computer hard disk.

Additional professional opportunities for audio engineers include audio production for movies, videos, television shows, radio broadcasts, jingles, and commercials. Entry level jobs are often found in night clubs, hotels, amusement parks, cruise ships, convention performance art centers, as well as government and military installations.[5]

## Additional Creative Music Business Team Members

There are additional professional creative careers. *Computer graphic artists* create computer-generated movies, television shows, images, posters, and album covers. *Music video scriptwriters, producers, directors, actors,* and *actresses* are involved in music videos, TV commercials, and advertisements which are used by record labels to market, promote, and publicize artists and album releases.[6]

Just as important as the creative major players are the individuals and companies (also considered major players) who make up the business side of the industry.

## Music Publishers (Business side)

Music publishers, in addition to being part of the creative system, operate as part of the business system. Publishers register copyrights, issue licenses, market songs, print or have sheet music printed, collect song royalties and pay writers.

## Record Labels

The consumer's personal selection, use, and enjoyment of musical recordings ultimately determines the financial success of the record industry. To launch a new act, a record label invests an average of between $500,000 and $1,000,000 for each production, marketing, promotion, and distribution of their signed recording artist albums and "images." Yet, the recordings, which the label pays for, are produced, manufactured, distributed, and promoted *before* the label knows if the album will be successful. It's a roll of the dice; often a gamble based on human emotions, assumptions and gut reactions as to which songs and artists will connect with consumers.

## Recording Studios

Recording studios frequently cost more than a million dollars to own and operate. The performance studio and control room can easily account for a couple hundred thousand dollars when designed and constructed by the best consultants and contractors in the business. Consoles, digital tape machines, special effects equipment, microphones, and monitor speakers quickly add up to between $300,000 and $700,000. Add offices, operational personnel, and a cup of coffee, and you have a million-dollar business. Studios rent for $1,000 to $1,500 a day to cover the cost of their initial investments. This also explains why record labels routinely rent studios instead of own them.

## Promotion

*Radio stations* broadcast recordings to attract audiences in order to sell airtime to businesses that want to reach those specific audiences. The larger the audience, the more they can charge for their commercial airtime. Airplay generates record sale propensity for record labels and image acknowledgment for the recording artists and albums. *Music videos* are produced by independent producers and production houses. *Concerts* are commonly produced by local entrepreneurs and promoted by radio stations, print, and television media. There are even a few "mom-and-pop" retail record outlets mixed with the *Kmart* and *Wal-Mart* rack jobbers and chain store one-stops.[7]

## Publicity

Television *talk shows* host music and entertainment celebrities to gain larger audiences in order to sell commercial airtime. The record labels and their signed artists use their appearances to promote new books, albums, movies, concerts, and other projects. The purpose of publicity is to alert the public to the artist's new products (which are for sale) and to create a buzz (a conversation or topic) consumers can talk about. The "buzz" is really word-of-mouth advertising which is commonly considered by the labels to be one of the best forms of publicity. It's free, and consumers tend to "hype" each other about the labels' artists and products, which ultimately increases the bottom-line unit sales.

*Tabloid television* also features stories about recording artists and entertainment personalities to generate commercial sales.[8] The *print media* includes information supplied by the label or artist's publicist as "news" to sell magazines, newspapers, and books. *Radio* and *television stations* contract "star" voices to promote their stations. The "star's name and voice" promote the image of the star and connect the station's image with a famous personality.

### Artist Managers

Artist managers use the albums distributed and marketed by record labels and promoted by radio station airplay to emphasize the image of their artists, which, in turn, increases record sales, concert appearances, and commercial endorsements. *Movie studios* engage the recording artist's album for soundtracks in movies. Radio station airplay promotes the movie and the movie sound track which encourages album sales. Artist managers approve the artist's personal appearances and concerts.

### Additional Business Contributors

If the label's marketing and promotional efforts are working, the recording artist's *talent* or *booking agents* will encourage *promoters* to produce their artists in concerts in various local or regional markets. *Corporate sponsors* often financially support artists, musicians, and orchestras in exchange for community service and product awareness and to increase product sales. *Business managers* hire *accountants* to balance the books, *finance advisors* to invest the profits in long-term stocks and money markets, and *attorneys* to negotiate, draft and oversee the process of executing contractual agreements.

### The Biz

The consequence of the *creative systems* and the *business systems* working together is the formation of what is called the *music business or music industry*.

**The Music Business: A Combination of Systems**

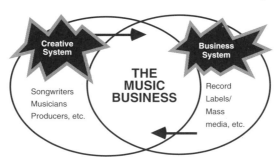

*Figure 1.3 The music industry/business is formed by the overlapping of the creative and*

*business systems. The creative system is composed of songwriters, producers, film directors, graphic artists, studio musicians, road musicians, etc. who create the recordings, symphonies, concerts, music videos, and films consumers want to watch, listen to, use, and buy. The business sub-system consists of the educated, established, experienced, individuals who manage careers, finance, promote, publicize, and distribute the records, films, videos, concerts, etc. made by the creative individuals. The two systems are interlocked. The creative side provides the products (recordings, etc.) the business side, the money, distribution, marketing, sales, and profits.*

# Recording Creative/Business Process

**Creative**
- Create songs
- Co-write with other writers
- Network with industry insiders

**Business**
- Register copyrights with Library of Congress
- Pitch songs to music publishers, artists, producers, managers
- Become an entrepreneur (form business, pay taxes)

**SONGWRITERS**

**Creative**
- Provide  a creative environment for staff writers
- Select songs to publish from independent songwriters
- Hire staff writers to create new songs
- Demo  record songs, print lyric sheets and sheet music
- Pitch songs to labels, artists, managers, music producers and film companies

**Business**
- Issue licenses to the users of music
- Collect royalties and payments
- Copyrights administration
- Pay employees, bills, taxes

**MUSIC PUBLISHERS**

**Creative (A & R)**
- Select songs and artists for the label
- Select producers, musicians, etc. for albums
- Determine and administer recording budgets

**Business  (marketing, promotion, etc.)**
- Establish marketing, promotion, distribution budget
- Market product through project manager
- Administer statements, notices, sound copyrights, etc.
- Distribute CDs, cassettes to distributers for retail, etc.
- Collect royalties from sales, pay artists/producer royalties
- Pay employees, bills, taxes

**RECORD LABELS**

- Record Chain Stores (One-Stops)
- Kmarts, Wal-Marts, Targets (Rack Jobbers)
- Record Clubs (direct from label distributors)
- TV Broadcaster and Cable Outlets
- Mass Merchandisers (direct from label distributors)
- Internet/World Wide Web (direct from label distributors)

**RETAIL OUTLETS**

## Centers of Creativity

The history of rock music provides a good example for this entertainment "business" phenomenon. Rock music evolved from the traditional slave spirituals and black music of the South and inner cities. Yet, it took the business side of the music industry to turn the spirituals and black music into *New Orleans Jazz, Memphis Beale Street Blues, Chicago Electric Blues, folk, gospel, country,* and eventually *rock 'n' roll music.*[9]

Today's recorded music originates from many of these same music genres and creative centers located in New York, Los Angeles, Nashville, Miami, Minneapolis-St. Paul, San Francisco, Chicago, Memphis, Austin, Seattle, London, Paris, Tokyo, Moscow, and even Prague.[10] Each city's creative and business systems have their own strength and personality. New York has Broadway theater, the Metropolitan Opera, giant music publishers, film, symphony, notable recording artists, studio musicians, and songwriters. Hollywood has its share of weighty writers, publishers, music video directors, producers, actors, actresses, performers, supporting music and movie business (including most of the movie studios and record labels). Nashville's creative village of songwriters, musicians, producers, recording artists, and media personalities is the equivalent of a modern Tin Pan Alley.[11] It is the center of country music, gospel music, and a surprising amount of rock, pop, and television production.

## The Process

*Songwriters, music publishers, musicians, session producers, record labels, distributors, artist managers, the mass media, marketers, publicists, concert promoters*, and the list goes on, customarily combine their knowledge and talents to assist in the development of a recording artist's career.

Great vocalists need unforgettable songs. Most are created by entrepreneurial songwriters. *Music publishers* (often small businesses) financially support songwriters and provide invaluable services and industry connections. *Record labels*, through session producers, marry the most notable songs to the appropriate recording artists. *Musicians* record the songs and perform in concerts, symphonies, movies, television shows, and commercial jingles. *Labels* usually finance, distribute, promote, and market the recording artists' careers, products, and images through the mass media.

*Record producers* supervise recording sessions. *Audio engineers* record the vocalists' and musicians' performances onto tape or computers. *Artist managers* supervise careers, images, and concert appearances. *Mass media* promote, publicize, and market the products and images. *Booking agents* line up concert promoters and schedule tour venues and dates. *Corporate sponsors* support the artists, *business managers* invest the profit, and *attorneys* negotiate and write the contractual agreements.

## Consumers

Consumers, without whom the music and entertainment industry would not exist, support both the creative and business systems by buying and using the CDs, cassettes, DCCs (digital compact cassettes), minidisks, movies, television shows, etc. and by listening to radio stations, watching television, and renting movies that use pre-recorded music. Consumer purchases or use of music and entertainment products made by the creative system and financed, marketed, and promoted by the business system, compensate the artists for their creative efforts and the record labels for their financial risk.

### The American Entertainment Economy

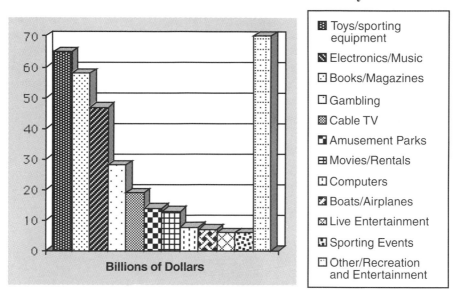

*Figure 1.4  Recorded music combined with the sale of VCRs, consumer electronics, and videotapes totaled $58 billion in 1993. Toys and sporting equipment netted $65 billion; books, magazines and newspapers, $47 billion; gambling, $28 billion; cable TV, $19 billion; amusement parks and other commercial participant of amusements, $14 billion; movie admissions and video rentals, $13 billion; home computers for personal use, $8 billion; personal boats and aircraft, $7 billion; live entertainment except sports, $6 billion; spectator sports, $6 billion; and all other recreation and entertainment, $70 billion.[12]*

## Entertainment Economy

It is the American consumers' *$340 billion* appetite for music and entertainment that provides the economic foundation for the music business. Music is all around us. It's a part of our daily lives. We listen to it as we drive to work, complete our homework, and, sometimes, as we fall asleep. We use it to structure our moods, lighten our work loads and to brighten our day. Music is enjoyed in amusement parks and performed as operas, symphonies, and in concerts. Network and cable TV utilize music in their programming, station identifications, and commercials to help attract consumers' attention. Movies add music to increase dramatic tension and personal enjoyment. Radio stations play music to build audiences to sell advertisements. Even the CD, cassette, and minidisk players that are sold (to reproduce recordings) are products of the business of music.

## Sage Window

" *I think the worst mistake an aspiring musician can make is not taking the business seriously. . . . Do your homework. Learn the business. Because there's a lot more to it than just picking up your ax and playing.*[13] "

— **George Porter, Recording Artist/Musician**

## Music Business Puzzle

This book provides a survey of scholarship on the structure, legalities, methods and goals of business operation, types of artistic and creative talents, and careers that make up *the music business*; it's the fundamental information for success in the music industry. Forget delusions of grandeur, autographs, and the show biz glitzs—it is a <u>*business*</u>, and a risky one at that. Successful businesses are ones in which the most capable people are employed. In the music business, the balance of creative and business-minded men and women determine its potential for success. Elvis had the staff of RCA Records and his manager Col. Tom Parker supporting him. This particular mix of administrative and creative personnel, along with artistic talent, was the perfect recipe for Elvis' great success.

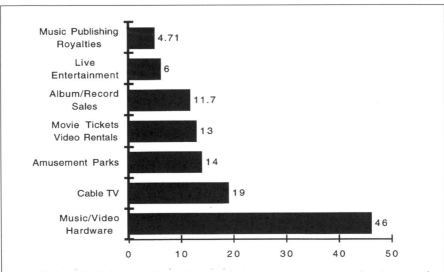

*Figure 1.5  Music is a vital part of the American entertainment economy.  American record-ed music sales for 1994 were approximated at $11.7 billion,*[14] *with live entertainment and concerts at $6 billion.  In 1992, music publishers collected $4.71 billion worldwide.*[15]

The music business is a huge and complex industry. It's the knowledge and talents its people possess that make a record sell at platinum levels. It's the people behind the stars and public personalities that make the engine run. They finance the recordings, manage the images and careers, promote, publicize, and market the products to consumers. The mass media is also heavily involved in the music industry. The recording artists have to be able to sing and play their instrument, but they are just one element (be it a very

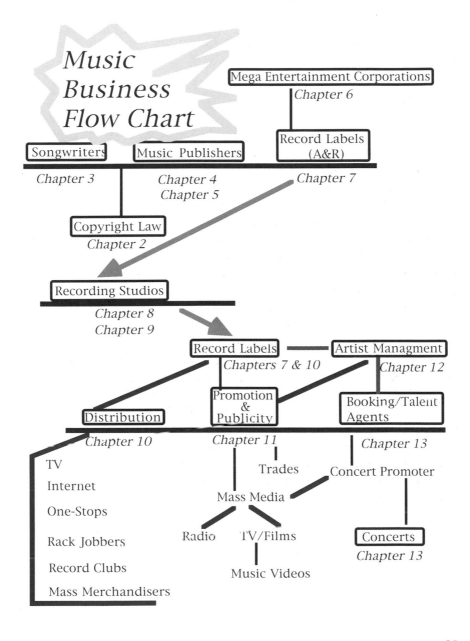

important one) of a larger team of people who create and market profitable recordings.

The music industry is a business in which the products are people (the artists packaged as icons) and their music (which is recorded and packaged for the consumer). The industry's primary purpose is to make a profit and to provide rewarding careers for its members. It is a business which usually hires or signs the brightest, most clever, positively-assertive, creatively-talented, business-minded, recording artists, musicians, songwriters, audio engineers, administrators, accountants, entrepreneurs, marketers, financial experts, publicists, artist managers, etc. The more successful the recording artists and their recordings, the more successful the label and all the individuals are who work for the artists at the label or as entrepreneurs.

## Summary

Seeking a career as an entertainment star, a studio musician, producer, audio engineer, etc. in the music business is a risk-taking opportunity; a roll of the dice; often one huge gamble. Creating a "break" can be the hardest job music business graduates will ever do for the least amount of money they will probably ever make. Yet, the individuals who succeed will find immense personal and creative satisfaction and wealth beyond their wildest dreams. *Success depends on having talent, an education (which often includes the streets as well as a formal education), networking skills, a thorough understanding of the structure of the business, an understanding of the various professions available, knowledge of the copyright law and contracts, plus a passion to be a positive part of the industry.*

Being a part of the music business is one of the greatest professions in the world, and, at the same time, one of the most competitive. Professional experience, artistry, common sense, knowledge, and wisdom are important personal attributes for any long-term career success. Understanding the political, business, legal and social complexities of the music industry are essential. However, acknowledging the fact that the music industry is truly a business which runs primarily to create profits is the most important thing to remember. This book is a great place to start the adventure. Use it as a guide or handbook to build your knowledge base about this wonderful industry we call the music business. At the same time, use the information to make yourself more valuable to all the individual businesses that make up the music industry.

## Chapter Footnotes

1 Websters New World Dictionary, p. 894 (1986).

2 Philosophy in a New Key by Susanne Langer (1951). Concerns about the emotional power of music include the Greek philosophers. Plato demanded "a strict censorship of modes and tunes, least citizens be tempted by weak or voluptuous aires to indulge demoralizing emotions." (Republic bk iii) "The legend of the sirens is based on a belief in the narcotic and toxic effects of music, as is Terpander's preventing civil war in Sparta, or of the Danish King Eric, committing murder as a result of the harpist's deliberate experiment in mood-production." Langer cites stories from "Von sonderbahrer Wilrchung und Krafft der Music," Die Musik XXIX (1937), part II, pages 625-630. It's amazing how few things really change. "Mobilizing Against Pop Music and Other Horrors" by Chris Hedges of The New York Times International (July 21, 1993) states that in Iran, "the Bassij are an army of volunteers formed by Islamic clerics to monitor and seize western popular entertainment products in an attempt to prevent western entertainment from corrupting the youth of their nation."

3 The Recording Industry Career Handbook by The NARAS Foundation (1995).

4 "Top 40" by Robert La Franco, Forbes (1995).

5 For additional information, see Chapter 7: Record Labels; Chapter 8: The Recording Process; Chapter 9 The Recording Team; and Chapter 10: Marketing Music.

6 Releases are often old recordings "repackaged" as a " Greatest Hits" album.

7 Rack jobbers are distributors who often own the racks in the Kmarts and Wal-Mart stores. The stores receive a percentage from the records sold. One-stops offer more titles than the "hits" offered by the rack jobbers. Record chain stores (as an example, Tower Records) are usually mass-marketed through the label's own distribution systems.

8 Newspapers and television shows often use the term "a reliable source" to indicate a "newsworthy leak." Many "reliable sources" are really the label or paid publicist who purposely "leak" or "plant" a story to create public interest in a new album, book, or movie that is about to be released for sale.

9 "The History of Rock & Roll Part One," Showtime Productions (Video Tape) (1985).

10 Grunge Music comes from Seattle, Latino is from Los Angeles and Miami. Rap originates from the culturally diverse neighborhoods in Los Angeles, Chicago, and New York.

11 The original Tin Pan Alley was located on 28th Street in New York City during the middle to late 1800's. Source Music Publishing: A Songwriters Guide, Randy Poe (1990).

12 "The Entertainment Economy" U.S. Commerce Department data, as reported in Business Week (March 14, 1994).

13 The Recording Industry Career Handbook, by The NARAS Foundation (1995).

14 Albums are defined as the songs and artist performances recorded and embedded into the bits (binary codes) of CDs, DCCs, mini discs, etc., and the analog recordings recorded as magnetic signals on cassettes tapes.

15 "The Entertainment Economy" U.S. Commerce Department data, as reported in Business Week (March 14, 1994). Music publishing figures are for 1992 instead of 1994 because it takes at least two to five years to collect all the money in the pipeline from foreign music publishers.

# 2

# THE COPYRIGHT LAW

**History**
**Exclusive Rights**
**Process and Forms**
**Free Use and Compulsory Licenses**
**Copyright Notice and The Berne Convention**

Copy and rights.  Two words that have specific, clear meanings.  Yet, when we combine the two words, forming the term *copyrights*, most of us just shake our heads in confusion.

Let's make this easy.  In the music business, the copyright law deals with just about everything when it comes to *the right to use* or *copy* someone's creative works.  It is a law that is continually being defined by the legal actions of copyright *owners* against individuals or companies who have failed to gain permission or make payments for their use of copyrighted songs, recordings, TV productions, musical arrangements, etc.

## Historical Perspective

The *origin* of copyright law is related to the invention of the printing press in 15th century England.  The possibility of mass-produced printed matter that might provide "Protestant religious heresy and political upheaval" threatened the English government.  To control the distribution, the government forced book publishers to obtain a "license to publish" before making *copies* of a manuscript.[1]  This *censorship law* only allowed the printing of books which contained storylines loyal or non-confrontational to the government.

## Statute of Anne

The expiration of the *license to publish law* in 1695 initiated stiff competition between entrepreneurial book publishers who were seeking to profit from books expounding a different perspective and the established autocratic publishers.[2] In defiance of the lobbying efforts of the established book publishers, the *English Parliament* passed the first known copyright law in 1710, called the *Statute of Anne*. It established the ultimate purpose of modern copyright laws, which is to *enhance public welfare by encouraging the dissemination of knowledge.*[3]

The established book publishers lost their monopoly because of the statute's stated purpose of *encouraging learned men to compose and write useful works.*[4] This important terminology *shifted the distribution rights associated with ownership from the book publishers to the authors.* For the first time, the *ownership right of distribution* was sanctioned to the inventors, discoverers, and creators of scientific and creative works. The provision helped *define ownership rights* and provided to the artists, scientists and companies, who author or invent *creative works, a* method of gaining *financial rewards.*

## United States Constitution

The Statute of Anne's inference was not missed by the authors of the United States Constitution. Article 1, Section 8 gives Congress the right to legislate copyright statute *to Promote the Progress of Science and Useful Arts, by securing for Limited Times to Authors and Investors, the Exclusive Right to their respective Writings and Discoveries.*[5]

Let's take a closer look at the statute. *Promoting the progress of science and useful arts* is accomplished by providing legal ownership and, therefore, potential financial rewards to the individuals who invest their time and money in writing songs, scripts, recording music, creating movies and other entertainment products. *By securing for limited times* means that ownership rights are not forever but only for a stated period of time. After which time, use is granted automatically to the general public.[6] *Exclusive Right* means that ownership is a monopoly right controlled solely by the creator(s) of the work. Following the instructions in the Constitution, Congress passed copyright legislation (called *acts*). The most important acts were approved in 1790, 1909, 1976, 1992 and 1995.

## Copyright Act of 1790

The *Copyright Act of 1790* gave authors *monopoly ownership rights* (for a limited period of time) of approval for the copying, displaying and performing of their creative works. The monopoly ownership rights, later called *Exclusive Rights*, were granted for one 14-year term, plus an additional 14-year *renewal term*.

## Public Domain

After the expiration of the copyright, the creative products (books, songs, etc.) were placed into *public domain*. Accordingly, creative "works" placed into public domain are owned by the public and may be used by anyone for entertainment or profitable purposes.

## Copyright Act of 1909

The *1909 act* expanded the monopoly ownership from 28 years to two terms of 28 years, for a total of 56 years. The copyright had to be *renewed* after the first 28 years for another 28 years. Think back to the year 1909. What was going through the lawmakers' heads about copyrights? Radio, TV, tape recorders, even movies as we know them today had not yet been invented. The problem for many in the entertainment business was how to adapt the old copyright law of 1909 to the modern mass media and entertainment business as it was being developed. What defined a copyrightable product? Who, how, where, and when could consumers and businesses be charged for their use *or* purchase of musical recording, the music used in concerts, movies, etc.? Although it was often discussed, it was not until 67 years later that Congress addressed many of these issues in a new copyright act.

## Copyright Act of 1976

Prior to the 1976 law, copyrights were granted under two sets of laws: *federal protection* for published works and *state common law protection* for unpublished or non-distributed materials. The 1976 law terminated this dual copyright system. The 1976 law, which became effective January 1, 1978, provides federal copyright protection for all published and non-published works.[7]

Some of our greatest songwriters, including the late Irving Berlin, were outliving their copyrights, so the 1976 act extended the *term of a copyright to life plus 50 years.*[8] Joint authorship works have copyright protection for *50 years after the surviving author's death.* Pseudonymous, anonymous, and works for hire (for example, songs written by a staff writer at a publishing company) are now protected for *75 years from the date of first publication or 100 years from the date of creation*, whichever expires first.[9] Finally, the 1976 act required juke box owners to obtain a *compulsory performance license* for each of their juke boxes. Previously, juke boxes were exempt from royalty payments.[10]

## Copyright Act of 1992

Until recently, songs written prior to January 1, 1978 were still under the 1909 copyright law and were, therefore, receiving protection for only 56 years (28 years plus another 28 years if the copyright had been renewed). In 1978, Congress extended the copyright duration to 75 years (*called transitional copyrights*) for the songs that had not yet gone into public domain. The *1992 act* makes the renewal automatic for all works written between January 1, 1964 and December 31, 1977.[11]

## Copyright Act of 1995

Cyberspace appears to be the wave of the future for the distribution of entertainment products to the general public. It is already possible to download music and short clips of video to your home computer. Soon, entire music CDs, TV shows, movies, books, magazines and other forms of popular culture entertainment will be accessible to your computerized telephone/digital high-definition television. The *1995 act* provides copyright protection by defining audio digitized transmissions as a public performance. The motion picture industry has submitted similar legislation to Congress, however, it has not yet been discussed.

## What Can Be Protected By Copyrights

The 1976 act defined copyrightable works as:
> *(1) literary works;*
> *(2) musical works, including any accompanying words;*
> *(3) dramatic works, including any accompanying music;*
> *(4) pantomimes and choreographic works;*
> *(5) pictorial, graphic, and sculptural works;*
> *(6) motion pictures and other audiovisual works;*
> *(7) sound recordings; and*
> *(8) architectural works.*[12]

## Process

The copyright law provides *copyright protection at the moment an original work is "fixed" into a tangible medium.*[13] The work must be original (not a copy or derived from another source), and it must be placed into a tangible (physical) form such as written onto a piece of paper or recorded onto a cassette tape. Therefore, copyrights (ownership) are considered inherent, intrinsic rights based on our Constitutional rights. *Copyrights are not granted from The Library of Congress in D.C. They are ownership rights we automatically gain by creating an original work and by placing that song, etc. into a tangible medium.*

We cannot copyright an idea. However, we can copyright the way we *express our original ideas* in songs, motion pictures, etc. Here is an example. Let's say that you have a great song that you've made up in your mind. You composed it and sing it to yourself all day. Is it copyrighted? No. However, the instant you complete writing the lyrics and musical notations on a piece of paper or you record the song (even into an inexpensive cassette tape recorder), your original song is copyright protected. You have, in effect, "placed and fixed" your original idea into a tangible form, in this case, a piece of paper or a cassette. The copyright is automatic. By making a copy of your original creative ideas in the form of a song, and by placing the song on paper or some other tangible medium, you have protected it through the copyright law. You own the song, and more importantly, you control the corresponding rights of ownership, which are called *the exclusive rights*.

## Exclusive Rights

Copyright ownership provides *six exclusive rights*. They include the right to:

### (1) Reproduce the copyrighted work in copies or phonorecords.

Let's say that you've written a great song. You have recorded the song onto your dad's old Radio Shack cassette player. This exclusive right means that <u>no one</u> can legally record or make any type of copy of your song (including writing the lyrics on paper or recording the song onto another tape) without your permission.

### (2) Prepare derivative works based upon the copyrighted work.

A derivative work is one that is based on a previous work. Let's say that your father is stuck in traffic on the freeway. He pulls your cassette out of the glove compartment and lets his boss hear your song. The boss loves the song and borrows the tape. Later, he schmoozes with a bunch of Hollywood types who hear the tape. Two days later, you get a phone call from a movie producer in LA. who wants to use your song as a basis for a movie script. The movie would then be derived from your original copyrighted song and recording. Honesty is important. People who steal, borrow, or use, another person's creative works without paying for it and giving authorship credits are in violation of the copyright law. In this example, the movie producer is requesting permission for a derivative use of your copyright. Which means that it is of value, and that if he wants to produce a movie (based on the theme of your song), he needs to negotiate permission from you.

### (3) Distribute copies or phonorecords of the copyrighted work to the public by sale or other transfer of ownership, or by rental, lease, or lending.

Assume you get your tape back. Your girlfriend borrows the tape. She's impressed. You're glad. However, without your knowledge or permission, she makes a hundred copies of the tape at Mr. Cheapo's Cassette Duplicators. She sells them to your classmates and decides to keep the money. She's infringed upon your copyright.

The *reproduction exclusive right* gives you, as the copyright owner, *control of who can first commercially record your song*. However, once someone has recorded the song with your permission and it's been commercially released to the public, you lose control of who can record it. Therefore, anyone can record a *cover version* of a song once it has been recorded and released to the public for sale, provided they secure the proper license or permission. Money called *mechanical royalties* is still owed by the record label that distributes the cover version, or whomever is responsible for the project if it is an independent production, for each unit (record, CD, cassette, DAT, etc.) sold.[14]

If your tape had been commercially released for sale or distribution and your girlfriend had recorded her own version of it, paid you the mechanical royalty (*currently 6.95¢ per copy*), she would not have infringed your copyright. You, as the song's author, and your publisher (if you had one) would split the collected mechanical royalties. Record labels usually get back the money they paid as mechanical royalties to the publisher (for the use of the publisher's songs) from the price of the albums when purchased by consumers.[15]

**(4) In the case of literary, musical, dramatic and choreographic works, pantomimes, motion pictures and other audiovisual works, perform the copyrighted work publicly.**

A recording is considered *a delayed or captured performance.* Consumers gain the right to use songs by buying a recording. Labels have no control over how often consumers play a recording they bought for personal enjoyment. As a result, consumers can play it a million times (in a non-public setting), yet they have to only pay a few extra cents (included in the purchase price of a recording) to cover the label's cost of the songs which are paid as mechanical royalties to the music publisher.[16]

Businesses are a different story because of the *public performances* of music. *Accordingly, businesses that use music must pay a performance royalty for using music as a part of its business.* For example, radio stations play recordings to gain an audience, restaurants may want to use it to set a mood, and if it's a hit recording, night club bands may perform a cover version.[17] The songwriters and music publishers are owed monies for the use of their song by these radio stations, restaurants, and nightclub owners. Performance Rights Organizations (ASCAP, BMI, and SESAC) collect the royalties owed to and on behalf of the songwriters and music publishers by selling blanket licenses to the businesses which use the music.[18]

The copyright owners of literary, musical, or dramatic works retain control of who can use or perform their creative works in public. *This includes plays after they have been released to the public for the first time.* For example, if your school wanted to put on the Broadway play <u>A Chorus Line</u>, it would have to obtain permission from the copyright holder or assignee.[19]

**(5) In the case of literary, musical, dramatic, and choreographic works, pantomimes, and pictorial, graphic, or sculptural works, including the individual images of a motion picture or other audiovisual work, display**

*the copyrighted work publicly.*

In the entertainment business, the exclusive display right protects items used for promotion, such as posters, still frames captured from a movie, paintings of artists' images, and non-musical creative copyrights.

*(6) In the case of sound recordings, to perform the copyrighted work publicly by means of a digital audio transmission.*

Large entertainment media companies who want to sell their music CDs and recordings through the typical computer digital transmission and down-loading process are now protected by the copyright law. Access and down-loading of copyrighted materials (without payment when required) is a vio-lation of the digital transmission exclusive right of the copyright law. *Entertainment products will soon be encoded with digital watermarks and embedded tags.* They will be encrypted or have their digital signals scram-bled, which will need to be de-scrambled by the consumer's software once the downloading fee has been paid. The *European Commission is develop-ing the Intellectual Multimedia Property Rights Model & Terminology for Universal Reference Metering System*, that may provide a pay-per-use billing system.[20]

## Exceptions to the Exclusive Rights

One of the great lessons in life is that there is an exception to everything. Individuals and companies (labels) *pay* for the use of songs, recorded music, etc. created by or leased to them by the copyright holder. *Fair Use Rights* are the exception to the exclusive rights of the copyright law. They allow for *free use* of copyrighted works in criticism or commentary, news reporting, teaching, academic scholarship, and research. *No payment for the use of the materials in these situations is required.* However, there are some deter-mining factors, including nonprofit purpose, the type of copyrighted mater-ial used, the amount used, and the effect of the used portion on the com-mercial market or value of the original source. The law uses the following components to determine fair use approval:

1. *Whether the use is for commercial use or nonprofit education purposes.*
2. *The nature of the copyrighted work.*
3. *The amount and substantiality of the portion used in relation to the copyrighted work as a whole.*
4. *The effect of the use upon the potential market or value of the copyrighted work.*[21]

## Compulsory License

The copyright owner (through the exclusive rights) can determine who may use their creative works. However, the government has determined that the copyright owner *must grant permission* for use of their creative work in the following *six areas*, when requested. *Compulsory Licenses* are only available *after* the initial release (publication) of a composition or creative work. Compulsory licenses still require music users to pay for their use of the music, songs, and compositions they re-record, download, play or re-transmit. Examples include:

1. *Cable television stations*
2. *Jukebox owners*[22]
3. *Public broadcasting, including PBS-TV and PBS-Radio*
4. *Satellite re-transmission operators*[23]
5. *Music producers and user*[24]
6. *Digital Transmissions*

## Digital Transmissions

The 1995 Digital Transmission Act expands compulsory licenses to include audio digital transmissions. Computer subscription companies, such as America Online, are now required to collect a *3% transfer royalty fee* on all audio recorded transmissions. Manufacturers are required to collect a *2% fee* (ranging from $1-$12) for any digital audio recording devices sold in the U.S. market.

## Publication

The term "publication" in the music business often means acquiring a music publisher to "publish" your songs. However, in copyright language, publication means *distribution* of the product to the public:

> . . . *the distribution of copies or phonorecords to the public by sale or other transfer of ownership, rental, lease, or lending. The offering to distribute copies or phonorecords to a group of persons for purposes of further distribution, public performance or public display, constitutes publication. A public performance or display of a work does not of itself constitute publication.*[25]

## Collective Works

A single copyright is sufficient to protect a collection of songs recorded onto a cassette or album. Each song may also have its own copyright, however, the individual copyrights are not required, as the collective copyright protects all the songs embodied on the tape or album. The copyright, in this case, is limited to the collective work. Individual songs recorded and released from a copyrighted collective work require their own copyright.

## Collaboration

Collaborative works are songs that are created by *lyricists* and music *composers.* The lyricists provide the words, the composers the musical notations. Collaborations allow lyricists to work with composers who are better at creating the music than the lyrics and vice versa. Successful collaboration teams include Rodgers and Hammerstein, the Gershwins, Irving Berlin, and many of today's famous recording artists. Copyright ownership is divided into *shares* which are negotiated in legal written form before the collaboration work begins. The shares are not always split 50/50, as some partners may only contribute a small amount of work or there may be more than two individuals working on the project. Therefore, it is important to agree *before* the project (writing of a song), if possible, on the amount of copyright ownership.[26]

## Co-songwriting

Co-writing means writing with one or more other writers and joint ownership of the copyright. Registration is attained with the names of all the contributing authors of the work. Royalties are divided and paid according to any previous agreements by the performance rights organizations and corresponding music publishers.[27]

## Registration

If you plan to commercially exploit your songs, recordings, books, music videos, movie scripts, etc., you should register your copyright. *The United States Government recognizes the person or company who register a claim of copyright as the copyright owner.* Registration of a copyright customarily protects the copyright holder from unauthorized use or infringement of their creative work. Of course, there are some exceptions. The copyright office records the time of *your claim of copyright* for registration. If a registered song is actually an infringement of another song, it is not protected. However, the original copyright holder may have to take legal action to prove creative authorship. Enclose one copy for unpublished works (not distributed) and two for published works. The U.S. Copyright Office receives over *600,000 applications* for copyright annually.[28 & 29]

## Certificate of Registration

Copyright registration is effective on the date the Copyright Office receives your properly completed forms, deposit of a copy of the work, and application fee. Once it has processed the forms, copy(s), and application fee, the Copyright Office will determine whether the materials deposited constitute copyrightable subject matter. If so, the Registrar will issue to you a *certificate of registration.* If you have a question about the status of your application, the Copyright Office will furnish free information after 16 weeks. You will receive either a certificate of registration to indicate your song or creative works copyright has been registered or a letter or telephone call seeking additional information. If the application cannot be accepted, a letter explaining why it was rejected will be sent to you. If you need copyright confirmation quicker than the typical 16 weeks, you will be charged a fee and the *Certifications and Documents Section* of the Copyright Office will answer questions only *after* they receive your payment.[30]

## Copyright Registration Forms

- **TX:** For published and unpublished non-dramatic literary works.
- **SE:** For serials and works intended to be issued in successive parts including periodicals, newspapers, magazines, newsletters, annuals, journals, etc.
- **PA:** For published and unpublished works of performing artists (musical and dramatic works, pantomimes and choreographic works, motions pictures and other audiovisual works).
- **VA:** For published and unpublished works of visual arts including pictorial, graphic, and sculptural works.
- **SR:** For published and unpublished sound recordings.

## Corrections and Amplifications

- **CA:** For supplementary registration to correct or amplify information given in the Copyright Office record of an earlier registration.

## Other Forms

- **GR/CP:** An adjunct application to be used for registration of a group of contributions to periodicals in addition to an application Form TX, PA, or VA.
- **IS:** Request for issuance of an import statement under the manufacturing provisions of the Copyright Act.

## Deposit of Copies

Deposit copies of your materials with the form and a fee of $20.00.

- *For an unpublished work, send one complete copy or phonorecord.*

- *For a published work (meaning distributed), send two copies or phonorecords of the best edition.*

- *If the work is first published outside of the United States, send one complete copy or phonorecord as published.*

- *In the case of a contribution to a collective work, send one complete copy or phonorecord of the best edition of the collective work.*[31]

## Mailing Address

Include your return address with ZIP code and your daytime telephone number. Your copyright registration packet should contain:

*(1) proper form fully completed;*
*(2) non-refundable filing fee (currently $20.00); and*
*(3) copy(s) of your creative work (songs recorded on a cassette).*

Send the packet to:

***Register of Copyrights***
***Copyright Office***
***Library of Congress***
***Washington, D.C. 20559***

## Copyright Notice

The copyright law suggests that a *notice* be affixed to all copies "in a manner and location" that will provide "a reasonable notice of the claim of copyright."[32] The copyright notice consists of three elements:

*(1) The symbol ©, the word "Copyright", or the abbreviated "Copr.";*

*(2) The year of creation (unpublished) or the year of first publication (if distributed);*

*(3) The name(s) of the owner of the copyright in the work, an abbreviation by which the name(s) can be recognized, or a generally known alternative designation of the owner.*[33]

Phonorecords are defined by the copyright law as:

*. . . material objects in which sounds, other than those accompanying a motion picture or other audiovisual work, are fixed by any method now known or later developed, and from which the sounds can be perceived, reproduced, or otherwise communicated, either directly or with the aid of a machine or device.*[34]

Therefore, the term *Phonorecords* includes cassette tapes, CDs, LPs, 45 rpms, CD-ROMs, disks, and other recorded music platforms. Our old LP's (which are now gathering dust in some closet), cassettes, CD's, minidisks, and even music stored in semi-conductors are considered phonorecords. Copyright of a phonorecord protects the *performance derivatives* of the artists on the recording, the photographs and artwork of the cover, and the printed lyrics on the inserts.[35] *The copyright notice for albums, CD's, etc. is the letter (p) in a circle.* In addition, most labels register their logos and special artwork as *business trademarks.* They provide a *notice* of the registered trademark by placing an ® on the cover. Also included on the surface of the phonorecord is the year of first publication (distribution) of the recording and the name(s) or known abbreviation of the name of the copyright owner(s).

## Infringements

The copyright notice on a song or recording helps alert the public to the copyright owner's *right to be compensated* for their creative efforts. If someone violates any of the exclusive rights by copying, performing, displaying, distributing (selling copies) or by creating a derivative work from someone else's songs, works, etc. *without permission* and payment, they are in *violation* of the copyright law. The exceptions, of course, are fair use rights and compulsory licenses, where permission is automatically granted but payments are still often required. If there is an indication of a copyright infringement, the copyright owner is required to:

*1. Institute legal action by serving written notice (of the complaint) to the person(s) or company thought to be in violation, and by sending an additional copy of the notice to the Copyright Office.*

*2. Request civil court action to place an injunction to prevent or restrain additional infringement of the copyright.*

*3. Request civil court action to impound all copies or phonorecords claimed to have been made or used in violation of the copyright owner's exclusive rights (and all the presses, molds, matrices, masters, tapes, etc. used to make the copies in question).*

*4. As part of a final judgment or decree, the court may order the destruction or reasonable disposition of all copies or phonorecords and construction devices.*

*5. Request the court to make the infringer of the copyright liable for either:*

(a) *Actual damages and additional profits* are defined as the recovery of actual damages suffered by the copyright owner as a result of the infringement and any profits accrued by the infringer.

(b) *Statutory damages and profits.* However, at any time before the final judgment, instead of actual damages and profits, the copyright owner may elect to be awarded statutory damages of not less than $500.00 or more than $20,000 per creative work.

(c) If the infringement was committed willfully, the court, in its discretion, may increase the award of statutory damages to not more than $100,000.[36]

If there is an infringement law suit, a proper copyright notice and registration date provide valuable evidence of ownership. The law states:

*If a notice of copyright . . . appears on the published copy or copies to which a defendant in a copyright infringement suit had access, then no weight shall be given to such a defendant's interposition of a defense based on innocent infringement in mitigation of actual or statutory damages.*[37]

## International Copyrights & The Berne Convention

Not all countries have the same copyright laws. *The Berne Convention for the Protection of Literary and Creative Works* is recognized as the primary international copyright agreement. It ensures *international copyright protection* for American citizens' "creative works" in the 80-plus Berne member countries. In return, international members' "creative works" are protected in America. A song is considered a Berne Convention work if: (a) in the case of an unpublished work, one or more of the authors is a national of a nation adhering to the Berne Convention; or, if the work is published, one or more of the authors is a national of a nation adhering to the Berne Convention on the date of the first publication, or (b) if the work is first published in a nation adhering to the Berne convention.[38]

## Copyright Notice and The Berne Convention

The Copyright Law of 1976 was modified in order for the United States to become a member of the Berne Convention. Previously, a copyright notice had to be placed on all published "works." (Registration of the copyright with the *Library of Congress* in Washington D.C. was required before an infringement lawsuit could be filed.)[39] As of March 1, 1989, the copyright notice is no longer required. Currently, the Copyright Law simply states that:

*. . . a notice of copyright . . . **may be placed** on the publicly distributed copies.*[40]

Although the notice is no longer required, it is a good idea to place it on songs, recordings, music videos, printed sheet music, and other creative works. The notice and copyright registration still offer additional proof of ownership and willful infringement during legal actions.

## Sage Window

**Grant Smith, Entertainment Attorney**

*In order to win a copyright infringement action involving musical compositions, it is necessary to prove two things: (1) a "substantial similarity" between the two songs and (2) "reasonable access" to the original song by the alleged infringer. The substantial similarity can address both the music and the lyrics or a combination of the two. It can be in the melody, the timing, the chord structure and several other musical characteristics of a tune. Reasonable access simply addresses whether the alleged infringer had the opportunity to have heard or been told about the original song. This element is the most difficult to prove. You almost have to prove that the alleged infringer actually heard the song and then, perhaps, attempted to write around it.*

**Q. Is that why music publishers refuse to accept tapes mailed or handed to them?**

**A.** Precisely. Publishers know that if they accept a tape, someone may someday sue them for a copyright infringement, even if they've never heard the song or can't recall having heard it. I would assume that in the U.S. District Court in Nashville Tennessee, there are probably 15 cases a year. There are more in the Southern District of New York and the Central District Court of California.

**Q. How many cases have validity?**

**A.** Eighty percent or better. Before we file a case, we employ an expert to take the two pieces of material, analyze them, and write an opinion letter about the analysis. We do that before we file a complaint because we want to be certain that we are on solid legal ground. We have what is called Rule 11 under the Federal Rules of Civil Procedures, which prohibits lawyers from filing what could be termed a "frivolous lawsuit." We have to make due investigation and be as certain as possible that the facts our clients are alleging are true.

**Q. How would you prove intentional infringement?**

**A.** There is a lot of unintentional copyright infringement, and in our current case (Billy Ray Cyrus), we alleged that the infringement could be unintentional or intentional. We won't know which until we get a chance to determine what the defendants' access really was. The statutory remedies for the plaintiff are different if it's intentional as opposed to unintentional.

**Q. How are you paid?**

**A.** Most copyright infringement cases are taken on a contingency basis. But if you prove intentional infringement, as opposed to unintentional infringement, the court can award fees for the plaintiff's lawyer.

**Q. Why didn't he just settle this case?**

I have no idea. Perhaps he thinks he's right. I don't know. Registration of a copyright creates an almost irrebuttable presumption of who created the song. In this case, our client registered his song with the copyright office, published it through his own publishing company, recorded the song, and had several hundred units manufactured several year before the defendants' song was written.

**Q. So he had product on the market?**

**A.** Yes, but it didn't sell because of a lack of national radio play and distribution. It was played on stations in Georgia, and he performed it himself in venues in Georgia, Florida, Alabama, and Tennessee.

**Q. So, what we are really talking about is whether this was coincidental or not.**

**A.** Yes.

**Q. What are the odds of that happening?**

**A.** That's going to be up to the jury.[41]

*– Grant Smith, Entertainment Attorney, Nashville, TN*

## Musical Arrangements

The copyright law addresses musical arrangements, orchestrations, etc. as *a work-or-hire* when the work is commissioned by a business or musical enterprise. The arrangement of a previously public domain musical work is considered an *original work.*

## Sampling

*Sampling* is the process of using a portion of an already-existing recording in a new recording or performance. The recording artist, act, or author integrates previously-recorded material with original material. The use of a previously-recorded and, therefore, *copyrighted material* (records, etc.) in a new production is considered a copyright infringement. Permission is required from both the sampled song's music publisher and record label.[42]

*Sampling* is also the term used to describe the second stage of the analog to digital recording process.[43] In digital recording music is converted to electronic signals by microphones or other recording devices. Then, the electronic signals are *sampled* and converted into binary codes.

## Termination (Recapturing) of Assigned Copyrights

Termination (or recapturing) of an assigned copyright may be accomplished by the author(s), surviving spouse, surviving children or grandchildren:

*1. At any time during a five-year period beginning at the end of the 35th year from the date of assignment to the music publisher, etc., or (if published) at the end of the 35th year from the date of publication.*

*2. The notice must state the effective date of termination (which must fall within the five-year period), and it must be served to the music publisher, etc. not less than two or more than ten years before that date.*

*3. A copy of the notice must be filed and recorded with the Copyright Office before the date of termination.*

*4. On the date of termination, all rights assigned are reverted to the original copyright owner or their estate if not living.*

*5. The termination rights for pre-1978 copyrights was changed with the 1976 Act. When Congress extended copyright protection to 75 years (from 56 years), they also prolonged the right of termination an additional 19 years.*

## Street Realities

You've moved to Los Angeles and picked up a full-time job driving a taxi and another part-time gig flipping hamburgers. In your spare time, you've continued to write songs and meet with record producers, recording artists, and musicians. Are we having fun yet? Sure. One day, you turn on the radio and guess what you hear? <u>Your</u> song being sung by the top recording act in the country! Are we happy or what! You bet. You start thinking about all the money you're going to make. But wait. You never assigned your song to anybody in the "biz." You call the label and tell them your story. They say "Who are you?" "Get lost!" "We got the song from Midnight Music Publishing." (I'm making up this name to dramatize the story, and it has no reflection on a Midnight Publishing, if indeed, one exists). What are you going to do now if:

**(a)** You thought you had protected your song by sending a copy of it to yourself in an unopened letter?

> *If you're going to send yourself a copy of the song, make sure it is through certified mail and do not open it. Have you ever heard of steam opening a letter? Just register your copyright with the Copyright Office in Washington D.C. instead.*

**(b)** You did not register your copyright?

> *It is your word against theirs. The powerful publishing company*

*has the time, money, and a bank of attorneys for a court case. Even if you mailed the certified letter and have lots of creditable witnesses, you have a very slim chance of winning. If you have some of the "burden of proof" you need and you get a good attorney, you may be able to get a small settlement. It is rare for a publishing company or record company to pay a settlement. If they did, everyone and their uncle would be lining up to file copyright infringement lawsuits. A publishing or record company only pays when there is substantial proof, and they want to settle with the complainant in order to save legal fees.*

(c) You registered your copyright, sent a copy of the tape for deposit, and always placed a copyright notice on the tapes and lyric sheets you handed out?

*Now, you may very well have a chance. If your song is similar enough to the song on the radio, your attorney and their attorney will often hire an expert to analyze the song note by note. Your copyright was properly registered before the publishing company's, so now you have a solid case.*

## Key Definitions

Our current copyright law is legalese. However, by learning the following key definitions, you will be able to quickly grasp many of the law's concepts.[44]

• *An Anonymous work* is a work presented without an identified author.

• *Audiovisual works* consist of a series of related images (pictures, etc.) which are intrinsically intended to be shown by the use of machines or devices, such as projectors, viewers, or electronics equipment, together with accompanying sounds, such as films or tapes, in which the works are embodied.

• *A collective work* is a work, such as a periodical issue, anthology, or encyclopedia, in which a number of contributions (which are separate and independent by themselves) have been assembled into a collective new work.

• *A compilation* is a work formed by the collection and assembling of *pre-existing materials* or of data that are selected, coordinated, or arranged in such a way that the resulting work as a whole constitutes an original work of authorship. Compilations include collective works.

• *Best Edition* of a work is the edition published (distributed) in the United States at any time before the date of deposit, which the Library of Congress determines to be most suitable for its purposes.

• *Copies* are material objects other than phonorecords, in which a work is fixed by any method now known or later developed, and from which the work can be perceived, reproduced, or otherwise communicated, either directly or with the aid of a machine or device.

• *The copyright owner* is the person or company who created the original work or who purchased the work from the person who created the work as a work-made-for-hire. Ownership of a copyright may be transferred in whole or in part, including any or all of the exclusive rights.

• *The country of origin of a Berne Convention work,* for purposes of the United States Copyright Law, is any nation or nations adhering to the Berne Convention whose law grants a term of copyright protection that is the same as or longer than the term provided in the United States.

• *A work is created* when it is fixed in a copy or phonorecord for the first time; where a work is prepared over a period of time, the portion of it that has been fixed at any particular time constitutes the work as of that time, and where the work has been prepared in different versions, each version constitutes a separate work.

• *A derivative work* is a work based upon one or more pre-existing works, such as a translation, musical arrangement, dramatization, fictionalization, motion picture version, sound recording, art reproduction, abridgment, condensation, or any other form in which a work may be recast, transformed, or adapted. A work consisting of editorial revision, annotations, elaboration, or other modifications, which, as a whole, represent an original work of authorship is a derivative work.

• A *device, machine, or process* is one now known or later developed. As an example, the recording of music (a captured performance) into computer chips for later playback.

• *To display a work* means to show a copy of it either directly or by means of a film, slide, television image, or any other device or process or, in the case of motion picture or other audiovisual work, to show individual images non-sequentially.

• *A work is fixed* in a tangible medium of expression when its embodiment in a copy or phonorecord, by or under the authority of the author, is sufficiently permanent or stable to permit it to be perceived, reproduced, or otherwise communicated for a period of more than transitory duration. A work consisting of sounds, images, or both, that are being transmitted is fixed for purposes of this title if a fixation of the work is being made simultaneously with its transmission.

• *A **joint work*** (or collaboration) is a work prepared by two or more authors with the intention that their contributions be merged into inseparable or interdependent parts of a unitary whole. Duration of the copyright is 50 years after the death of the surviving author.

• ***Literary works*** are works, other than audiovisual works, expressed in words, numbers, or other verbal or numerical symbols or indicia, regardless of the nature of the material objects, such as books, periodicals, manuscripts, phonorecords, film, tapes, disks, or cards, in which they are embodied.

• ***To perform a work*** means to recite, render, play, dance, or act it, either directly or by means of any device or process or, in the case of a motion picture of other audiovisual work, to show its images in any sequence or to make the words accompanying it audible.

• *A **pseudonymous work*** is a work in which the author is identified under a fictitious name.

• ***Registration*** means to <u>register a claim</u> of copyright or to renew and extend the term of a copyright.

• ***Sound recordings*** are works that result from the fixations of a series of musical, spoken, or other sounds, but not including the sounds accompanying a motion picture or other audiovisual work, regardless of the nature of the material objects, such as disks, tapes, or other phonorecords, in which they are embodied.

• *A **transfer of copyright ownership*** is an assignment, mortgage, exclusive license, or any other legal conveyance, alienation, or hypothecation of a copyright or any of the exclusive rights comprised in a copyright, whether or not it is limited in time or place of effect, not including a non-exclusive license.

• ***To transmit a performance or display*** is to communicate a work by any device or process whereby images or sounds are received beyond the place from which they can be sent.

• *A **"work-for-hire"*** is a work prepared by an employee within the scope of his or her employment or work specially ordered or commissioned for use as a contribution to a collective work. The copyright holder of the "work-for-hire" is the employer of the songwriter (unless agreed upon in writing for shared ownership), not the person who created the work or song. The duration of a "work-for-hire" copyright is 75 years from first publication or 100 years from its creation, whichever expires first. The works of many music publisher staff writers are considered "works for hire."

## Summary

Copyright protection subsists in original works of authorship fixed in any tangible medium of expression, now known or later developed, from which the work can be perceived, reproduced, or otherwise communicated, either directly or with the aide of a machine or device.[45]

In the music and entertainment business, works of authorship include: (a) literary works, (b) musical works, including any accompanying words, (c) dramatic works, including any accompanying music, (d) pantomimes and choreographic works, (e) pictorial, graphic, and sculptural works, (f) motion pictures and other audiovisual works, and (g) sound recordings.

If you want to be a part of the music business, be happy, be thrilled and be grateful that the United States Congress and countries around the world provide protection to the creators of songs, music, books, music videos, and entertainment products. The copyright law provides the legal foundation for ownership and justifies the corresponding financial rewards. Songwriters initially own the songs they write, record companies own the albums they financially produce, and movie and music video scriptwriters own their scripts, films and television shows. Without strong American and international copyright laws, the ownership of creative products would be meaningless.

The music business, indeed the entire entertainment industry as we currently know it, would cease to exist without the copyright law. The men and women who invest so much of their time and effort into creating the songs, recordings and all the other entertainment products we enjoy and purchase would not be paid for their worthy endeavors. Music makes life so much more enjoyable. It is important that the individuals who create the music and entertainment products that enrich our lives be financially rewarded for their efforts.

## Ordering Your Own Copy of The Copyright Law

If you want to order a copy of the copyright law, all 142 pages, or if you need the proper forms (you will) to register your creative work, call the *Copyright Forms Hotline* at *1-(202)-707-9100*.[46] To save money and time, the Copyright Office permits the use of photocopies of the original forms on standard 8 1/2 x 11 inch white paper.[47] In the music business, the *PA form* is used to register a song (only the musical composition and lyrics and not the actual recorded sounds) accompanied by the deposit of lead sheets or sheet music. Use the *SR form* to register sound recordings. You can use the SR form to register both the songs and the recordings at the same time. However, the author of the songs and the producer of the tape must be the same person or organization that owns the copyrights to both "works."[48] The SR form secures the contribution of the performers who recorded the songs and the persons (producers and audio engineers) who are responsible for capturing and processing the sounds to make the final recording.[49]

## Registration Matrix[50]

| Type of Author(s) | Claim of Copyright | Form to Use | Nature of Authorship |
|---|---|---|---|
| Composer/Author | Claim copyright | PA | Music & words |
| Composer/Author | Claim copyright musical composition | PA | Music |
| Recording Artists & Musicians | Claim copyright of performance & sound recording | SR | Performance & sound recording |
| Composer/Author who creates music & performs it | Claim copyright of music & recording | SR | Music & performance or Music, words, & performance |
| Author who writes a poem & records it | Claim copyright of poem | TX | Text |
| Author who writes a play & records it | Claim copyright of play | PA | Script |
| Author who writes a poem & records it | Claim copyright of poem text & recorded performance | SR | Text & recording |
| Author who creates a musical composition & stores it on a computer disk | Claim copyright of musical composition | PA | Music or music and words |
| Author who creates a musical composition & stores it on a computer disk | Claim copyright of musical composition & performance | SR | Music performance or Music, words & performance |

## Chapter Footnotes

[1] Leaffer (1989).

[2] Ibid.

[3] Grossman (1977).

[4] Statute of Anne, 1710, as stated in Understanding Copyright Law (1989).

[5] The Constitutional Provision Respecting Copyright. The Copyright Law of the United States of America (1993).

[6] Called the "public domain."

[7] Leaffer (1989).

[8] There are currently attempts by songwriters and music publisher organizations to legislate the extension of the copyright ownership clause to life plus 70 years. If passed, it would provide 20 additional years for songwriters, their heirs and music publishers to receive song royalties.

[9] For additional information, see The Copyright Law of the United States of America, pp. 67-68.

[10] The cost of the juke box compulsory performance license is approximately $8.00 per machine.

[11] Summary from Music, Money and Success by Brabec and Brabec (1994), p. 356.

[12] Ibid.

[13] Any device that can be used to store and reproduce a creative work.

[14] Compulsory License must be requested by serving a **Notice of Intention** to the copyright owner 30 days after making and before distributing any phonorecords of the work, p. 36 The Copyright Law of the United States of America (1993).

[15] Passing on mechanical royalties to consumers also means that they are paying for the right to use and play the songs (on the recording) as often as they want.

[16] See Chapter Five: *Exploiting Copyrights*.

[17] The band playing your song in the night club doesn't owe you money, but the owner of the club who hired the band does.

[18] See Chapter Five: *Exploiting Copyrights*.

[19] An *assignee* is the person or company to which the copyright owner has assigned the exploitation of their exclusive rights.

[20] "Law Creeps Onto The Lawless Net" by Catherine Yang and "Copyright's New Digital Guardians" by Otis Port, Business Week (May 6, 1996).

[21] See The Copyright Law of the United States of America p. 13, and This Business of Music by Krasilovsky pp. 161-175.

[22] Jukeboxes are called "coin-operated phonorecord players" in the copyright law.

[23] As an example, Super Stations, such as Ted Turners' WTBS which is located in Atlanta but broadcasts on cable systems throughout the United States by the use of satellite retransmissions.

[24] The Copyright Law of the United States of America, pp. 35-58, (1993).

[25] The Copyright Law of the United States of American (1993).

[26] Songwriters should not pay a lyricist or composer to be a collaborator. Money paid *up-front* is considered unethical, as payment is usually collected through the success of the song and the amount of copyright ownership (shares) each participant retains.

[27] See Chapter 5 for co-author and co-publishing payment scheme.

[28] Untitled States Government Printing Office (SL-9).

[29] For more information on how to order a copy of the Copyright Law and how to register your copyright, please see Append. A.

[30] United States Government Printing Office Circular (SL-9).

[31] See The Copyright Law of the United States of America, p. 83 (1993).

[32] Ibid, p. 76.

[33] Ibid.

[34] Ibid, p.5.

[35] *Performance derivative* is the copyright protection afforded the musician's and vocalist's work (*performance*) on a recordings. It covers their performance, not the playing or *performance* of the recording in a business or public place.

[36] For additional information, see The Copyright Law of the United States of America, p. 92 (1993).

[37] Ibid, p. 76.

[38] Ibid, pp. 2-4.

[39] Leaffer, p. 7.

[40] For additional information, see The Copyright Law of the United States of America, p. 76 (1993).

[41] Interview with Grant Smith, Attorney, Nashville, TN (1994).

[42] Music, Money, Songwriting, and Music Publishing, Jeffrey and Todd Brabec (1994).

[43] See Multi-track tape recorders in Chapter 8.

[44] Condensed from The Copyright Law of the United States of America, (pp. 1-142 (1993).

[45] Ibid, p. 5.

[46] United States Government Printing Office Circular (SL-8).

[47] Ibid (SL-9).

[48] United States Government Printing Office Circular 50, p. 2.

[49] United States Government Printing Office Copyright Registration of Sound Recordings Circular, p. 2.

[50] Summary from matrix in The Copyright for Sound Recordings (1993) & The United States Government Printing Office Circular, p. 4.

# 3

# SONGWRITING

## Songwriting Tips
## Pitching Songs to Publishers

Music is considered *the art of arranging sounds in time so as to produce a continuous, unified, and evocative composition.*[1] The minimal unit of musical organization is the *tone* (a sound with a specific pitch and duration). Tones may be placed into different successive combinations (the *melody*), and two or more tones may be played or sung simultaneously (the *harmony*). All of the known styles of music may be placed and defined into three different strata:

*(a) "art" or "classical" music,* composed and performed by trained professionals originally under the patronage of courts and the religious establishments;

*(b) folk music, shared by the population at large (particularly its rural component) and transmitted orally; and,*

*(c) popular music, performed by professionals, disseminated through radio, television, records, film, and print and consumed by the mass public.*[2]

## Music and Emotions

Music is the emotional lifeblood of many Americans and citizens of the world. Why? There are many theories about how music affects us. Research appears to suggest that consumers *create for themselves* the following emotions when they hear various forms of music:[3]

| Sadness | Seriousness | Excitement | Happiness |
|---------|-------------|------------|-----------|
| Relaxation | Amusement | Sentiment | Longing |
| Patriotism | Devotion | Irritation | Wanting to Dance |

Music is an artistic complex form of communication. The artist's performance often amplifies the listener's constructed pathos. There is little doubt that the quality of a song's message, the performance of the vocalists, and the musicians must all come together to touch the emotions of various types of listeners. Music affects the pulse rate, respiration, and concentration. However, the emotion being created by the listener seems to last only as long as the music is being played or as long as we continue to replay the music in our minds.[4]

## Professional Songwriters

Music publishers profit on their ability to *find* and *sign potential hit songs*. Yet, they rarely have the extra time to listen to all of the unsolicited tapes sent from amateur songwriters. Publishers know that most profitable songs originate from established, professional staff and independent songwriters. However, professional songwriters were also once amateur songwriters. They had to learn to *thrive on rejection* and to perfect their ability to write commercial songs.

Most successful songwriters are "20-year, over-night" successes. It's a saying used in the industry to describe someone who has seemingly achieved success quickly but has actually been working for many years to be (or not to be, that is the question) good enough for success. Thousands of potential songwriters each year send cassette tapes (more than we want to count) to music publishers. Most of the tapes are rejected or returned with a *"not soliciting new material"* or *"not what we are looking for"* rejection letter. However, every so often, someone nobody's ever heard of will write a song, get it picked up by a publisher who will place the song with a major artist, who records it; and, before you know it, the recording becomes a smash hit. It's rare, but it still happens.

## Sage Window

**"***I think that people need to get the stars out of their eyes and realize that they're going into it as a business."*

**– Desmond Child, Songwriter**

## Commercial Songwriting

Songwriting is a *profession*. It customarily takes many years to achieve the competencies and industry contacts required to be successful.

**How can we become professional songwriters, composers or arrangers?**

*1. Have talent.* Some type of natural talent is cardinal to being a successful songwriter. The ability to observe social and personal situations and the ability to interpret the social consciousness is important. An ability to convey thoughts and observations emotionally through musical notations and lyrics is paramount. Being able to play an instrument in tune is one thing, being able to create and convey emotional messages is clearly another.

**2. Become an educated person.** A formal education in music, English, business, psychology, sociology, world history, etc. are enriching. Read as much as possible about whatever your passion is and become an informed, culturally-alive individual. Great songwriters often write their best songs about their own life experiences or passions; the things they care about the most. So, research the great philosophers, writers, political leaders of the present and past, whose works you admire. Find out what made them tick, what their thoughts are or were, and then expand on them by combining your own personality and creativity.

**3. Become a professional songwriter.** Join a professional songwriters' organization. There are many such organizations across the country where songwriters encourage each other, co-write, and get advice from the experts.

**4. Network, network, network.** Don't send your songs to a music publisher cold turkey. They want to know who you are! Build friendships and acquaintances through the local and national songwriter organizations and attend national seminars in New York, Los Angeles, and Nashville.

**5. Co-write with someone who is better than yourself.** Writing with others helps us "see a lyric" from a different perspective and improves our songwriting.

**6. Select the right publisher.** Select the type of publishers who have a successful track record in the musical genre you are using. As an example, if you're writing rock music, find a publisher who has been successful in rock music. Successful publishers know the right people, have the contacts, and can successfully "place" your songs with them.

## NSAI Song Evaluation Form

The *Nashville Songwriters Association International* (NSAI) offers the following checklist to evaluate the "commercial" content of songs:

> **Theme (underlying idea or concept)**
> 1. Is your idea one a lot of people can understand?
> 2. Is your approach to the idea unique or "fresh"?
> 3. Is your idea believable?
> 4. Do you have one clear theme?

**Lyrics (words)**
1. Do you have a memorable title or hook?
2. Do you have a strong opening line?
3. Are your words contemporary (i.e., not old-fashioned)?
4. Are your lyrics conversational?
5. Are your lines concise and do you make every word count?
6. Are your rhymes interesting (i.e., not predictable-moon/June, true/blue, rain/pain)?

**Melody (music)**
1. Do you have a strong marriage between melody and lyrics?
2. Have you established the appropriate mood through the rhythm and tempo?
3. Is your musical hook memorable?
4. Is there an interesting melodic change between verse and chorus and/or verse and bridge?
5. Does your melody build into the chorus?

**Overall Impact**
1. Does your song have a beginning, a middle and an end?
2. Are all the verses strong?
3. Is the message powerful?
4. Does the song generate emotion?
5. Is the storyline good?
6. Does the song resolve itself to the listener's satisfaction? [5]

The **NSAI Critique Checklist** is yet another way to evaluate your song. It divides the evaluation process into two groups: basic alerts and fine tuning.[6]

| BASIC ALERTS | FINE TUNING |
|---|---|
| **LYRIC** | |
| [] Tell one interesting story? | [] Universal theme? |
| [] Have an angle/hook? | [] Unique fresh approach? |
| [] Clear changes between parts? | [] Rhymes too predictable? |
| | [] Are words out-of-date? |
| | [] Beginning/strong opening line? |
| | [] Power and placement of the hook? |
| | [] Rhyme scheme change between verse and chorus? |
| | [] Familiar surprise? |
| | [] Believable plot/characters? |

[] Conversational writing/poetry?
[] Shift of viewpoint/voice?
[] Too repetitive?
[] Third person (he/she) for angry/sad/loser?
[] Consistent metaphors?

----

## Melody

[] Musical hook?
[] Music changes between parts
[] Tune fits lyrics?

[] Tempo fits the mood?
[] Memorable musical hook?
[] Placement of power notes?
[] Placement of musical hook?
[] Too repetitive?
[] Have two or three different musical parts (verse, lift, chorus, break, bridge, etc.)
[] Needs another part (bridge)?

----

## Demo Quality

[] Hear the lyric?
[] Tape hiss?
[] Production?

[] Too much production?
[] Production fits song?
[] Needs more production?
[] Needs another singer?
[] Intro/song/break/ too long, too short?

----

## Pitching Songs to Music Publishers

Assuming you've developed your songwriting as a craft, joined the professional songwriting organizations, learned the business, written some great songs, registered your copyrights, and networked in the business to the point where you know the right people (and better still, they know you), how can you pitch your songs to the right publisher?[7]

*1. Demo record three to four of your songs in an inexpensive yet "quality" recording studio.*

Don't waste money on a major recording studio production by overproducing the demo recording. In most cases, all you need is a couple of instruments (guitar, bass, etc.) and your vocal mixed louder than the instruments. Recording "strings," additional instruments, and vocal overdubs is a waste of your money.[8] Often a good home cassette recording is all you need. Try to capture the "feel" or "emotion" in the demo that best displays the essence of your songs.  The purpose of your demo is to secure a deal with a music publisher.  In many cases, the publisher will "doctor" your song and re-record it.  Record labels will do the same thing if they sign you as a recording artist.

*2.  Provide lyric sheets (typed lyrics of the songs) or printed lead sheets* *(lyrics and the musical notations of melody, chords, and rhythm).*

*3.  Call to make sure the publishers are accepting tapes.*

Make an appointment for a personal visit or let them know that you are submitting material (sending them a cassette with 3-4 songs).

*4.  Place a copyright notation on the tape, along with your name and address.*

Write a brief cover letter detailing your association with the publisher (how you know them or who referred them to you).

*5.  Keep a journal of where you have sent the tapes.*

Send publishers a "thank you" note for reviewing the material.  After a couple of weeks, call or write to ask about the status of the review process.  "Have you listened to my songs yet?"  Most likely, if the music publishers know who you are (which you established through your networking, professional song writing organization memberships, and contacts), they will often listen to your material.

*6.  If your songs are rejected, use the opportunity to build an honest friendship with the publisher by sending them a "thank you" note.*

Enclose a pre-paid envelope and request a couple of constructive comments about how you can improve the songs or your songwriting.  If they hear positive talent in your songs, music publishers will often help you improve your skills.  They know that once you get good enough, you will come to them first with your potential hits.  And that's why they are in business, to make a profit by exploiting a song's copyright.

*7.  Follow the golden rule in the music business.*

*Never say anything bad about anyone.  You never know who knows who, and it is always better to be seen as an honest and positive person.*  The type of person insiders like to have as friends, respect and want to work with in the future.

## What To Look For in a Music Publisher

Find a music publisher who is well-connected to the most successful people in the industry and who can *place* your songs with those individuals. They should be a progressive middleman between you (as a songwriter) and the record labels, producers, artist managers, and recording artists who are looking for your genre of songs. Find a publisher who will help you become a better songwriter by offering you constructive criticism and positive creative and financial support. Make sure they are honest business people who have a passion for your song and your success, as well as their own.

## Professional Songwriting Organizations

### *The National Academy of Songwriters*
6255 Sunset Blvd., Suite 1023, Hollywood, CA 90028
(213) 463-7178

The NSAI offers a *registration service* for songbooks by individual songwriters. The registration service establishes a "date of registration." The service should be considered a temporary procedure.

### *The Nashville Songwriters Association International*
15 Music Square West, Nashville, TN 37203
(615) 256-3354, FAX (615) 256-0034

The NSAI has approximately 4,500 members worldwide, and it sponsors regional *workshops* in various locations in the U.S. and Europe. The purpose of the workshops is to further the knowledge and craft of songwriting among participants through a series of specific songwriting lessons; to provide NSAI members who live outside of Nashville with a network of other songwriters, lyricists and composers; to keep members informed about issues and changes in the music industry; to establish unity among songwriters everywhere, which can help local writers perfect their craft and learn about the music and publishing business.[9] The NSAI also offers a *Song Evaluation Service* to its members. Songs submitted are evaluated for their commercial appeal based on the theme, lyrics, melody and overall impact.[10]

### *The Songwriter Guild of America*
6430 Sunset Blvd., # 1002, Hollywood, CA 90028
(213) 462-1108
1560 Broadway, # 1306, New York, NY 10036, FAX (212) 768-9048
1500 Harbor Blvd., Weehawken, N.J. 07087
FAX (201) 867-7535
1222 16th Ave. S., # 25, Nashville, TN 37212, FAX (615) 329-2623

The SGA was formed in 1931 by songwriters Billy Rose, George M. Meyer, and Edgar Leslie. As a voluntary songwriter association run by and for its members, it is devoted to providing songwriters the services and activities they need to be successful in the music business. SGA reviews members' contract offers and provides *The Popular Songwriters Contact* as an example of a publishing agreement from a songwriter's perspective.

## Key Definitions

• *"A" Player:* A top studio musician.

• *Accompaniment:* A vocal or instrumental part that supports another.

• *Arrangement:* To set (a composition) for other instruments for another style of performance.

• *Attack:* The beginning of a piece or passage of music.

• *Backbeat:* A steady, rhythmic beat characteristic of rock music.

• *Back-Up:* The background accompaniment for a performer.

• *Ballad:* Popular, slow tempo, romantic compositions.

• *Band:* A group of players who perform as an ensemble.

• *Blues:* Music that evolved from Southern Black American secular songs distinguished by slow tempo and flatted thirds, fifths, and sevenths.

• *Bridge:* Transitional passage connecting two musical movements.

• *Classical Music:* Eighteenth and 19th century European music, such as symphony and opera.

• *Color:* The quality or timbre of a musical tone.

• *Concert:* Performance given by singers or instrumentalists in any genre of music.

• *Conductor:* The director of an orchestra.

• *Counterpoint:* The technique of combining two or more melodic lines to establish a harmonic relationship.

- *Crescendo:* Increased volume, which increases intensity which can provide a dramatic/inspirational effect.

- *Ensemble:* A group of musicians or singers who perform together.

- *Falsetto:* Tones in an upper register beyond the full-voice range of a vocalist.

- *Genre:* A distinctive artistic style, form, or content of music or literature.

- *Harmonic:* A tone produced by a fundamental tone which can be natural or artificial.

- *Lyric:* Words of a song. Also, relating to or being a musical drama, especially opera.

- *Orchestra:* Classically trained musicians who play together (strings, woodwinds, brass and percussion instruments).

- *Passage:* Section of a composition.

- *Perfect pitch:* The ability to recognize and identify a specific pitch or pitches.

- *Synthesizer:* An electronic instrument that combines waveforms to create musical sounds and notations.

- *Symphony Orchestra:* A large orchestra composed of brass, string, wind, and percussion sections.

- *Symphony:* One of the extended compositional forms for full orchestra (in most cases, a sonata for orchestra).

- *Tune:* Proper musical pitch or slang for "a song."

- *Timbre:* The quality of a sound that distinguishes it from other sounds with the same pitch and volume.

- *Transpose:* To write or perform a composition in a different key than the original composition.[11&12]

## Summary

It's the partnership between songwriters and music publishers that provides structure, money, and methods of dissemination for songwriters to create, support, and distribute recordable songs to the music and entertainment industries. Realistically, the relationship between songwriters and publishers depends on the success of the songwriter's ability to *author great songs* and the music publisher's ability to *place the songs* with major recording acts. The bottom line is profits created by record sales, mass media broadcasting, public, and private use.

To become a successful songwriter, it is important to have the talent to write hit songs. Being an educated person appears to help songwriters express life experiences metaphorically through lyrics, notations, and chord progressions. Joining professional songwriting organizations and attending seminars provide aspiring writers with an opportunity to network and meet professional writers and publishers. Finally, it is important to record a demo of three or four songs and to pitch the tape to a music publisher. Make sure the publisher has agreed to listen to the songs before sending the tape. Then, follow up with a personal interview to gain insights and recommendations concerning individual songwriting skills and networking opportunities.

## Chapter Footnotes

[1] American Heritage Dictionary CD-ROM (1995).

[2] Encarta 95 CD-ROM The Microsoft Corp. (1995).

[3] Philosophy In A New Key by Susanne Langer (1951), and Charles Disserens The Influences of Music on Behavior (1926). Both Langer and Disserens are dated references, however, they are still considered benchmark research efforts that are often listed as suggested reading for music students.

[4] Philosophy In A New Key, Susanne Langer (1951). Langer suggests that "Music is known to affect pulse rate and respiration, to facilitate or disturb concentration, to excite or relax the organism, *while the stimulus lasts.* But beyond evoking impulses to sing, tap, adjust one's step to musical rhythm, perhaps to stare, hold one's breath or take a tense attitude, Langer feels that music does not ordinarily influence behavior."

[5] Reprinted by permission of the Nashville Songwriters Association International © 1996 NSAI, All Rights Reserved. NSAI is a not-for-profit organization devoted to the service of songwriters. Established in 1967 by professional songwriters in Nashville, NSAI now numbers more than 4,500 members worldwide. For information contact: NSAI, 15 Music Square West, Nashville, TN 37203, (615) 256-3354.

[6] The Critique, Rick Beresford & NSAI (1993).

[7] "Pitch" is the term used by industry insiders to describe songwriters', music publishers', and perspective recording artists' demo tapes and personal meetings set up by music publishers and record labels to audition new songs and recording artists.

[8] See Chapter 8: The Recording Studio Process. Publishers and record labels will re-record the demo in most cases.

[9] Source, Donna Beck Michael, Regional Workshop Director NSAI (1996).

[10] NSAI promotional material.

[11] Summary from The American Heritage Dictionary CD-ROM (1995).

[12] Suggested by Alan Remington, Orange Coast Community College (1996).

# 4

# MUSIC PUBLISHING

**Tin Pan Alley**
**Types of Publishers**
**Departments**
**Songwriter/Publishing Deals**

In the early days of our nation, songwriters made deals with book publishers to "print and sell" their latest songs. *Printed* copies of the lyrics or *sheet music* was the only method of mass distribution available to songwriters. Book publishers (knowing a good thing) hired salesmen to sell the sheet music wholesale to local five-and-dime stores, who, in turn, sold them to the public.[1] It didn't take long for the book publishers to see the potential profits in music publishing. In 1892, the song *"After The Ball"* sold over 1 million copies of sheet music.[2]

## Tin Pan Alley

Seeing the potential profits in music publishing, many of the book publishers became entrepreneurial *music publishers* and moved to New York City (usually from Chicago) where they could *place* their new songs with the most popular Broadway shows and Vaudeville acts. They hired songwriters to write the songs and songpluggers to place the songs with the shows and artists.[3]

*World War II* spread American music around the world. World markets were created as different forms of *recorded music* were broadcast on American armed forces radio stations. The broadcasts were enjoyed by many Europeans and Asians as well as by the allied soldiers. Music publishers viewed radio airplay, concerts, and night club performances as promotion. A typical promotion cycle involved bands, radio, and films. Popular bands were used in films. Their radio performances promoted the films, and the films promoted records and print sales.

Many veteran Vaudeville performers became radio stars and later moved to

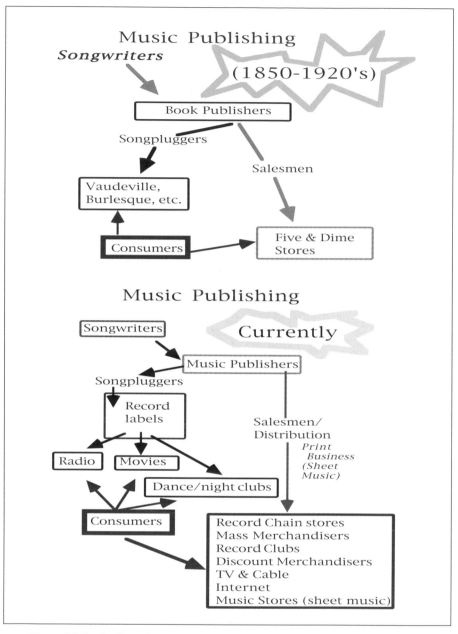

*Figure 4.1 Vaudeville and Burlesque shows created an opportunity for book publishers to promote sheet music to the public who could then purchase the sheet music at local stores. As sales increased, book publishers changed their form of business to music publishing. With media technology improvements, music publishers changed their sales "pitch" from Vaudeville to the movies with sound and to radio with live performances. The developing record labels used the movies and radio performances to promote the sale of sheet music and records in stores. Later, during the 1940-50's as the "live radio stars" moved to television, labels provided radio stations with recorded music (as an alternative entertainment product to air). Today, from a historical perspective, the book publishers have become the music publishers. Songpluggers still pitch songs to acts and to record labels. Furthermore, the modern mass media of radio, TV, and movies have replaced Vaudeville and Burlesque shows.*

television.[4] By the mid-1950's, *Rock & Roll* had evolved from the Beale Street Blues, slave minstrels, country folk music, and Chicago's electric blues to become the language of independence for many teenagers. American teenagers, with time and money, created a huge new industry-rock music.[5]

## Splits

Songwriters rarely have the time, money, and industry contacts to place "material" with major recording artists. Music publishers do. It's *"let's make a deal time."* In exchange for approximately 50% of all the potential revenues a song may generate, music publishers doctor songs (if they need to be improved), demo record them, place the songs with major recording artists, distribute the printed music and folios to retail outlets, administer the copyright, collect the royalties, and split the monies with the songwriter(s).

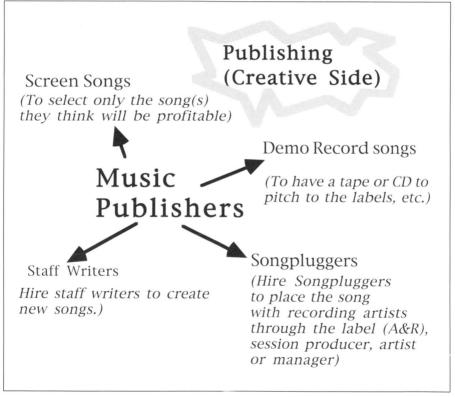

Figure 4.2 *Music Publishing is the link in the creative chain between songwriters and recording artists. Publishers screen the good songs from the poor ones. Staff writers create new songs or doctor songs that need some additional work. Publishers demo record songs they believe have potential. Songpluggers pitch the songs to record labels through the label's A&R department or directly to producers, artist managers, and recording artists.*

## What Publishers Look For in a Songwriter

Music publishers search for songwriters who see songwriting as *a passion* and as *a craft* they work at daily. Yet, what music publishers really want are the types of songwriters who *can consistently deliver potential hit songs*, which can be turned into financially-profitable hit recordings. Additional characteristics include:

*1. Songwriters who view the songwriter/music publisher relationship as a career partnership. Although in many cases, it is often adversarial, music publishers appreciate songwriters who understand the business aspects of publishing.*[6]

*2. Writers who are available to co-write and help new writers improve.*

*3. Writers with industry contacts who network and help place their own songs with industry insiders and major acts.*

*4. Writers who have and will offer their musical talents and vocal abilities to demo record their songs. Writers with great voices are seen as a bonus, as they may develop into recording artists.*[7]

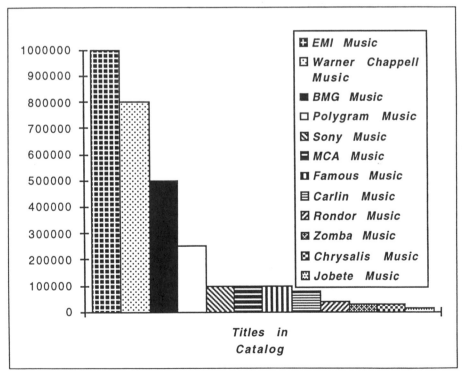

*Figure 4.3 Music publisher's size is determined by the number of titles in their catalog. Value is determined by the number of titles producing revenue.[8] The money created from a few good songs regularly establishes the "worth" of a publishing company.*

## Types of Music Publishers

There are many types of music publishers, including:

1. *Full-Line* music publishers (which may be songwriter-, producer-, or recording artist-owned publishing companies) provide songwriters, producers, and recording artists with increased revenues because they retain partial control of their copyrights and, therefore, a share of the revenues generated. *Full-Line publishers* have many departments and industry connections. Even the music publishers affiliated with major labels or mega entertainment organizations are considered full-line companies, as they are often independent, *stand-alone* organizations.

2. *Major publishers* are affiliated with labels and mega entertainment corporations. Most major music publishers are full-line.

3. *Independent publishers* are not affiliated with any one label; however, they frequently sign co-publishing deals with major entertainment corporations and artists' own publishing companies.

4. *Specialty Publishers* usually limit their catalogs to one or two genres of music. Profits are generated by record labels and the sale of sheet music to specific types of performance acts and venues. Examples include:

(a) *Concert or classical music arrangements for ballet, opera, and symphony performances,*

(b) *Gospel or Christian music for religious record labels and church performances,*

(c) *Children's music used by labels, concert performances, movie soundtracks and in toys, and*

(d) *Jazz, big band, and other types of specialty, niche music.*

5. *Foreign publishers* may or may not be affiliated with a mega organization. Most are full-line companies doing business in their perspective countries. Most have cooperative agreements with mega entertainment corporations and an American music publisher. Foreign royalties collected from an American's recordings are often split 50/50 with the foreign publishers, which means the American publishers and writers collect 50% of royalties from the respective foreign territories. American publishers collect royalties for the foreign releases in America and have a corresponding collection agreement with the foreign publishers.

6. *Vanity publishers* are owned by songwriters who can't secure a publishing deal with any other type of music publisher.[9] They are not connected to the powerful personalities in the industry who can place their songs with the right artists and labels, and, therefore, they rarely attain any significant music publishing royalties.

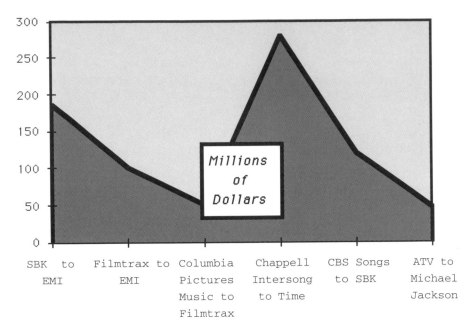

*Figure 4.4  Recent acquisitions of music publishing companies include: CBS Songs to SBK Songs in 1986 for $120 million and then SBK Songs to EMI Music in 1990 for $187 million; Columbia Pictures Music Group to Filmtrax in 1988 for $50 million and then Filmtrax to EMI Music in 1990 for $100 million.  Other acquisitions include Chappell Music to Time Warner in 1987 for 280 million, and ATV Music to Michael Jackson in 1985 for 47 million.*[10]

## Departments

Music publishers range in size from sole proprietorships (one-person operations) to partnerships (two or more owners) to fully-staffed, multi-departmental, international corporations.  Whatever the size, successful publishers have or contract out the following tasks:

**1. *Acquisitions*** analyze songs that have been submitted.  The creative department in smaller publishing companies may also screen songs.  They are often looking for a needle in a haystack as hundreds of songs are submitted to major music publishers.  For *legal purposes*, most unsolicited tapes are never listened to.  Unless the publisher knows who you are and has agreed to listen to your material, the tapes will be discarded or returned.

**2. *Legal* (*business affairs*)** may be part of acquisitions in smaller music publishing companies.  The legal department *secures the song's copyright* from the writer, *registers the transaction* with the Copyright Office in Washington DC, and files the returned *Certificate of Recordation*.[11]

**3. *Administration*** takes care of the business, including offering *licenses* to the users of the company's songs which includes record labels, the motion picture industry, and television networks.  They also register newly acquired songs with the songwriter's corresponding performance rights organizations[12] and notify their wing in foreign countries or foreign sub-publishers of the new acquisitions.[13]

**4.** *Creative* consists of staff writers who are paid an annual salary to write their quotas of acceptable songs; audio engineers, who demo record the songs; demo musicians and singers; and songpluggers, who use the demo recordings to place the songs with recording artists, labels, artist managers, and producers. Staff writers co-write with new and other professional industry writers.

*Songcasting*, or the songplugger's act of placing the right song with the right recording artists, provides music publishers with their long-term financial successes. Songcasting the right songs to the right recording artists is very important to the financial success of the music publisher, as well as the artist's career.

Recordings become *communicative messages* that have to emotionally connect with the public to achieve radio airplay and record sales. If the recording fails to "turn on" the consumer, then the songwriter, music publisher, record company, recording artist, and record producer have failed. *Hundreds of thousands of dollars and professional credentials are sometimes forfeited in the process of an ineffective recording.* Therefore, matching the right song to the right artist *before* the recording session and production/marketing money is spent is important.

**5.** *Marketing & Distribution*. Publishers print, distribute, and promote sheet music to retail outlets. Smaller independent publishers often hire sub-publishers to market and distribute their print (sheet music) to retail outlets and music stores.[14]

**6.** *Payroll or royalty* departments use computer programs to correlate the use and projected royalties due from various sources. Collected royalties are usually split 50-50 with the songwriter (or songwriters, if multiple writers were involved) after expenses have been recouped by the publisher.[15]

## Assignment of Exclusive Rights

The Copyright Law allows for the *transfer of ownership* of a copyright or any of *its corresponding exclusive rights*. The transfer must be in writing and signed by the owner(s) of the copyright or their authorized agent.[16] The transaction is registered in *the Copyright Office* as a *recordation* of an original copyright.[17] A new copyright *is not being registered,* just the names of the new copyright owners on the previously registered copyright. It is important for songwriters to realize that assigning a song's exclusive rights to a music publisher usually means the transferring of their copyright (ownership) to the music publisher.[18]

You've been offered a deal. In most cases, you will be exchanging your copyright and your corresponding exclusive rights for 50% of all the money (equity) the publisher can exploit from the song's recordings, sales, and performances. Publishers gain the right to *exploit your copyright* and corresponding exclusive rights by acquiring your copyright. What you are really doing is transferring your ownership of the song (the copyright) to a music publisher in exchange for whatever is negotiated.[19] Notice of the *transfer of the rights* must be in writing and signed by you (the original author of the song) and by a representative of the music publisher.[20] The length of the agreements are for the *duration of the copyright*, except for a statutory reversion option between the 35th and 40th years of publisher ownership.[21]

## Transferring Copyright Ownership

The Copyright Office serves as an *office of public record* for copyright ownership transfers between songwriters and music publishers. A *notarized document* (not in the form of a letter) will act as *prima facia* evidence of the copyright ownership transfer. The following are required:

*1. The **actual signatures** of the persons involved or a **photocopy** of the original signed document submitted. It must be accompanied by a sworn or official certification stating that the attached reproduction is a true copy of the original signed document. The **sworn certification** must be signed by a least one of the parties to the signed document or by an authorized representative of that person.*

*2. The **document must be complete** by including all the written agreements between the parties including schedules, appendixes, exhibits, addendum, etc.*

*3. The document must be **legible** and capable of being reproduced in microfilm copies.*

*4. Include the **copyright recordation fee** of $10.00 per title, plus 50 cents for every page over six.*

*5. Once the fees, transfer of ownership, or other documents have been received by the Copyright Office, the Register of Copyrights will review the paper work and return the original documents with a **Certificate of Recordation**.*[22]

## Types of Deals

There are seven basic types of publishing *deals* and hundreds of variations which can be negotiated. The seven include: the song shark deal, "work for hire", independent or single song contracts, staff writer deals, exclusive songwriter deals, co-publishing, and administrative or sub-publishing agreements.

**1. *Song Shark Deal:*** Whenever a publisher compliments your song and then asks you to put up some money to "share the expenses," you are probably being cheated. *You don't pay them, they pay you*! It is your song, your property, not theirs. Song Shark deals are considered a rip-off because they are in the business of making money off of the songwriter (who pays for a publishing deal) instead of the royalties they would receive from the record companies, radio stations, etc. who are using your song. The only money Song Shark publishers make is what you paid them to take your song. In most cases, they do not have the industry contacts to get your song "placed" with a major artist, producer, or record label, and correspondingly, you will probably never receive any royalties because your song was never used by the industry.

Another type of song shark deal is when a publishing company buys your song outright for a very small fee. The *one-time buyout* of a hundred dollars may appeal to you if you need the money. However, a major hit can often earn $400,000 or more for the writer and publisher. So, if you have given up all your ownership rights through a buyout offer, you will not be able to receive any future royalties. Think of your song as a valuable commodity and then find a music publisher who is willing to offer you the standard 50/50% industry split on whatever the song earns. Also, find a publisher you "click with" who has the industry insights and contacts to get your song placed. It's a more honest approach to the profession, and it will provide you with long-term income opportunities if your song is indeed successful.

**2. *"Work-For-Hire" Deal:*** A *work-for-hire* returns us to the days of Tin Pan Alley when songwriters were paid a salary up front for their songs. Examples of "work-for-hire" include specific "one-time jobs," such as writing jingles or commercials for radio or TV. The employer of the "work-for-hire" is considered the author and copyright holder of the music. However, you will gain valuable industry experience and contacts. The disadvantage is that everything you write is owned by your employer, and all future royalties are paid to the copyright holder, which, of course, is not you.

**3. *Staff Writers:*** Staff writers are persistently considered *exclusive writers* for a specific music publisher.[23] They are paid a yearly salary in exchange for a quota of acceptable songs and a percentage of the profits.[24] The music publisher is in effect "betting" the writer's annual salary that the writer will create the types of songs that will recoup the annual salary plus a profit.[25] Novice staff writers are often surprised to learn that the songs they write are owned by the music publisher and not by the writer who created the song. However, the writer *retains authorship of the song.* Staff positions are desirable because they provide songwriters an opportunity to improve their songwriting skills, make industry contacts, network with other writers, co-write, and make a reasonable living at the same time.

**4. *Single Song Contracts:*** Single song agreements are offered to both staff and independent songwriters. Publishers require writers to complete and sign a *single song contract* for each song submitted and accepted. A *power of attor-*

*ney clause* in a music publisher/staff songwriter agreement authorizes the music publisher to complete the agreement, even if the songwriter refuses. Independent songwriters may use a one-time *single song agreement* to develop a working relationship with a publisher. The publisher may also add a *right of first refusal clause* stipulating that the publisher has the right to offer the writer a single song contract before any other publisher is allowed to hear the song.

**5. *Exclusive Writers Agreement*:** Very successful songwriters are sometimes offered *exclusive agreements.* These writers are the "stars" of the music industry, receiving better front money and bigger royalty splits from their exclusive publishers. Exclusive writer deals may include the *right of first refusal clause* similar to the one in the single song contract.

**6. *Co-publishing Agreements*:** Songwriters, producers, recording artists (with their own publishing companies) and smaller independent music publishers often make *co-publishing deals* with larger, better "connected" publishers. What is important to remember about the co-publishing agreement is the *share of the copyright ownership and, therefore, the share of the song's equity.* Industry terminology and the practice of *converting percentages to shares* tend to make co-publishing agreements complex. The maximum percent of any "whole" is 100%. Yet, the music business splits the 100% of a song's revenue into 50% songwriter and 50% publisher and then reconverts each 50% into a 100% share for the writers and publishers. It is the language used in the industry. Here is an example of what is really happening. The typical deal has a 50/50 split of all royalties except printed sheet music and folios.[26]

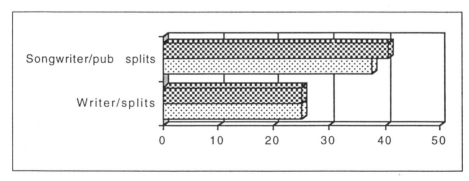

*Figure 4.5 Typical co-writer splits are 25% each of the 50% writers share. By having their own publishing companies, both writers can increase their percent (or share) of the song's equity.*

With the co-publishing deal, we have to look at it from a different perspective. Let's say you co-wrote a number one hit with another writer. That is easy to figure out. Each receives 25% of the 50% songwriters' "share" and the publisher receives the other 50%. However, co-publishing deals between songwriters/publishers (songwriters who own their own publishing companies) and industry music publishers can be quite complicated because the songwriter/publisher receives both the writing and publishing shares.[27]

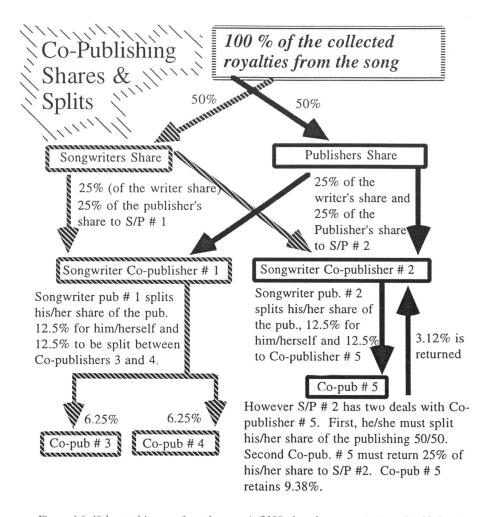

**Co-Publishing Shares & Splits**

**100 % of the collected royalties from the song**

50%        50%

Songwriters Share

Publishers Share

25% (of the writer share)
25% of the publisher's
share to S/P # 1

25% of the
writer's share and
25% of the
Publisher's share
to S/P # 2

Songwriter Co-publisher # 1

Songwriter Co-publisher # 2

Songwriter pub # 1 splits
his/her share of the pub.
12.5% for him/herself and
12.5% to be split between
Co-publishers 3 and 4.

Songwriter pub. # 2
splits his/her share of
the pub., 12.5% for
him/herself and 12.5%
to Co-publisher # 5

3.12% is
returned

Co-pub # 5

6.25%        6.25%

Co-pub # 3    Co-pub # 4

However S/P # 2 has two deals with Co-publisher # 5. First, he/she must split his/her share of the publishing 50/50. Second Co-pub. # 5 must return 25% of his/her share to S/P #2. Co-pub # 5 retains 9.38%.

*Figure 4.6  If the total income from the song is $100, then the songwriter's and publisher's splits are $50 and $50. However, because there were two songwriters, they split the writers share 50/50 for $25 dollars each. Both songwriters are also their own publishers. They split the publishers share 50/50 for $25 dollars each. To "place" the song with a major artist, songwriter/publisher #1 made a "deal" with co-publishers 3 and 4. He/she agreed to split his/her 25% of the 50% "publisher share" with the two co-publishers or $12.50 and $12.50. The two co-publishers (#3 & #4) agreed to split their 12.5% 50/50 for 6.25% each. Songwriter/publisher #2 made a deal with his/her co-publisher (co-publisher #5) to split his/her share of the publishing 50/50 or $12.50 each. However, songwriter/publisher #2 had a co-publishing agreement with co-publisher #5 that he/she would receive back 25% of his/her co-publishers "share" or $3.12 leaving co-publisher #5 with $9.38.*

| DEAL PARTICIPANTS | WRITER/PUBLISHER | SHARE | PUBLISHING SHARE | TOTAL |
|---|---|---|---|---|
| Songwriter/Pub. | # 1 | $25.00 | $12.50 | $37.50 |
| Songwriter/Pub. | # 2 | 25.00 | 15.62 | 40.62 |
| Co-Publisher | # 3 | none | 6.25 | 6.25 |
| Co-Publisher | # 4 | none | 6.25 | 6.25 |
| Co-Publisher | # 5 | none | 9.38 | 9.38 |
| **Totals** | | $50.00 | $50.00 | $100.00 |

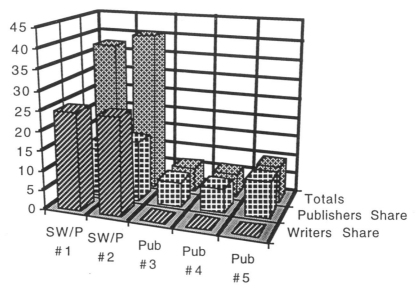

*Figure 4.7 Songwriters are able to "capture" more of their song's equity by having their own publishing companies and by co-writing and co-publishing with other writers and music publishers. In our example, songwriter #1 increased his/her share of the song's equity from 25% to 37.50% and songwriter # 2 increased his/her share to 40.62%.*

Co-publishing often works to the advantage of both the songwriter/publisher and established industry music publishers. The songwriter/publisher needs the major connections, distribution, and "industry power" of the major publisher. In exchange, the co-publishers want the great songs of the well-established and highly successful songwriter/publishers. The music publisher receives a share of the equity (copyright ownership) which can quickly increase the "value" of their catalog.

**7. *Administration & Sub-Publishing:*** Successful songwriters use major music publishers or an *exclusive music publishing agent*[28] to administer their song's copyrights. Songwriters keep most of their publishing (85-90%) with this type of arrangement. The publishers (who keep 10-15%) issue mechanical licenses, register songs with the corresponding performance rights organizations, and collect the revenues.[29]  *Administrative agreements* are advantageous to songwriters who demo record their own songs and have the networking contacts to get them placed with major recording artists.  Contracts are often two to five years with additional one-year options.[30]

## The Difference Between Co- and Sub-Publishing

*Co-publishing* ordinarily occurs *during the acquisition of a song* when more than one publisher is involved.  Major publishers have offices around the world and in the entertainment centers of the United States, Asia, South America, and Europe.  Songwriter-, music producer-, and recording artist-owned publishing companies need *co-publishing* or *administration deals* with the major publishers for distribution.

*Sub-publishing* transpires frequently between two or more publishers *after the acquisition of a song* by one publisher who then licenses sub-publishers to administer and exploit the song's potential equity.  Publishers seek *sub-publisher* deals to handle various aspects of the business including the paper business (printing of sheet music and sales), legal, documentation, and demo recording.  Sub-publishers are often paid 10-15% of net sales.[31]  *Foreign subpublishers* are used to exploit an American publishing company's songs and to collect the foreign mechanicals, performance, and print royalties (where applicable).  They usually split 50/50 the monies collected in their host country or region of the world.[32]

## Reassignment of Rights

Sometimes the marriage between the songwriter and music publisher fails.  The quality of their agreement means very little unless both profit.  Written contractual goals that are not fulfilled often lead to either side terminating the contract.  However, legal action is often required to prove non-performance of a contractual agreement.  A music publisher's default may be caused by many reasons, including:

*1. failure to provide licenses to music users;*

*2. failure to pay royalties in a timely manner;*

*3. failure to place the song with a major recording artist or an artist signed with a  record label.  Placement is defined as the use of the song in an actual master recording that will be released for sale to the public.  An artist (or producer) placing a "hold" on a song (for a recording to be made in the future) is not usually considered compliance of the publisher's obligation to get a song recorded;*

*4. failure to provide sheet music (of the song) to music stores and other retail outlets;*

*5. failure to "place" the song in radio and TV commercials, advertisements, and movie sound tracks; or*

*6. failure to protect the copyright against infringement. Permission to use a copyright (a song) is usually granted through the issuing of a license. Compensation for the use of the song is paid as the licensing fee. Both song-writers and music publishers must continually monitor infringement actions.*

## Rolling the Dice

The songwriter(s) often feel the publisher may have failed to place the song with the right artist, advertising agency and so on. However, it is important to remember that the publisher is only paid from the royalties they generate. Publishers take a financial risk when they sign a song. They must complete a demo recording, print sheet music, file for a Certificate of Recordation, and pay the salaries of the administrative staff and songplugger. Publishers can only be pro-active concerning:

1. Whether an artist will record a song, and

2. Whether the song can be placed with movie companies, advertisement agencies and other music users.

Therefore, contracts often state that music publishers have satisfied their contractual obligations when they have **"to the best of their ability"** attempted to place the song with music users. It is often very difficult for a songwriter (or their attorney) to define and prove that a music publisher did not work "to the best of their ability" in an attempt to place the song with various music users. In addition, publishers can usually provide a stack of invoices and paid state-ments as "proof" of their attempt to place the song with record labels, record-ing artists and other types of music users.

Copyrights can sometimes be reassigned by:

1. Writing a *letter of termination* to the publishing company requesting release from the contract. If the publisher has not been able to place the song, then they may agree to terminate the contract. It must be a mutual agreement. Publishers may negotiate some payment to help cover expenses. Termination of the contract should also state that *all future rights* will be assigned to anoth-er publisher, or

2. Writing a **Notice of Breach** to the publisher which states and defines a specific area of the contract that is not being satisfied. Publishers are usually given a 60-day notice to cure the situation. If the notice is ignored, legal action may be required to terminate the contract.[33]

## Artist Line

It is very difficult to accurately estimate a song's potential earnings. However, music publishers have computerized the average previous earnings of their songs recorded by major artists. When a song is placed with a specific artist, the music publisher can glance at the average previous earnings to determine the song's potential income from performance and mechanical licenses. Artists are ranked as:

   • *"A-line" artists are considered superstars with platinum recordings of 1 million sales or more.*

   • *"B-line" artists have gold record sales of 500,000 units or more.*

   • *"C-line" artists are signed to a major label and have not sold gold or platinum.*

Newly signed artists are considered a "risk" as their recordings have not yet been released to the public for sale, the results of which, determine if they are an "A", "B", or "C-line" artists.

## Music Publishing Contracts and Publishing Terms

   • *Accounting Statement.* Music publishers will provide a semi-annual accounting statement that lists the money the publisher paid the songwriter in advance, plus chargeable expenses against the money credited or due to the songwriter from the royalties received.[34]

   • *Advances*. Are monies paid to the writer from the music publisher for the right to exploit their song(s). Advances are not considered a salary. They include a one-time payment for a song, the cost of the demo recording, hiring of an independent promoter, legal cost, and even travel expenses including per diems. Advances are repaid to the publisher by the user (label) from a song's earnings.

   • *Administrative Rights.* Whoever controls the administrative rights of a copyright controls the potential revenue-generating assets of a song. Administrative rights include the right to assign or transfer the copyright at any time, the right to control licensing, and the right to collect royalties for the use of the song.

   • *Authorship*. The legal relationship between the songwriter and a publisher will determine "who" is the author of a "work." If the songwriter is an employee, then the publisher is usually considered the "author" of a song. If the songwriter is an independent contractor, the songwriter is usually considered the author of a song.

   • *Bonuses.* Negotiated non-recoupable monies paid to songwriters (and often recording artists and producers) for albums that reach various sales levels, usually gold (500,000), platinum (1,000,000), or multi-platinum (2,000,000 plus).

• **_Collaboration._** When two or more people work together to create a song, recording, etc.  It is suggested that all the specific items of the agreement be in writing, including exceptions of the traditional royalty splits, permission to change each other's lyrics, and a listing of who will pay demo recording, legal, and promotion expenses.  However, once the working arrangement is decided, a written agreement concerning the actual copyright is not required.  The Copyright Law calls the songs written by more than one individual a "joint work."  Ownership is shared by all of the contributors.[35]

• **_Cross Collateralization._** In songwriter deals, if a claim is made against a writer's song, then the publisher may _hold payment of all royalties_ from all the songwriter's "works" held by that publisher.  In a recording contract, the cross-collateralization clause usually refers to the withholding of royalties from the sale of one or more different albums to cover the labels financial losses from the artist's other albums.

• **_Demo Recordings._** It is often the music publisher's obligation to demo record a song so that it can be presented to a major recording artist, the A & R Department at record labels, record producers, and artist managers.  Expenses are often recouped by the music publisher out of the songwriter's future royalties.  The quality of the recording (number of musicians, tracks, etc.), ownership of the master tape, and a share of the expenses are sometimes negotiable, depending on the level of status of the songwriter.  Co-publishers often share demo recording costs.

• **_Exclusivity._** A songwriter will only write for the music publisher they are signed with and all material (including songs used in recordings, commercials, movies, CD-ROM programs, music videos, etc.) created during the contractual agreement will be represented by that specific music publisher.  There are exceptions that may be negotiated as a separate agreement, including specific genres of music that the publisher or co-publisher does not represent on specific songs.

• **_Float._** A delay in the payment by a music publisher of a songwriter's performance royalties.  If a writer assigns performance royalties to be paid through a music publisher (performance royalties are usually paid directly to the songwriter by the Performance Rights Organization), the publisher will often "float" the payment in order to earn interest off of the monies. This is a practice that is not supported by songwriter organizations, and they encourage songwriters to eliminate this clause from a songwriter/publisher contract.[36]

• *Free Goods.* For songwriters and music publishers, free goods are the songs on the CDs, DCCs, minidisks, cassettes, etc. that labels provide to retail outlets and record clubs to stimulate sales and club memberships. Free copies supplied to radio stations and other media for promotion and publicity are considered promotional "free goods." Mechanical royalties are generally not paid on commercial and promotional "free goods." However, labels are regularly restricted to the number of free goods and promotional copies they can provide by contractual agreements negotiated with the music publishers and recording artists. An audit of the record label may be required to determine the actual number of free goods and promotional copies distributed.[37] Nevertheless, it should be remembered that the labels also have an economic interest in free goods and promotional copies as they have paid for the recordings, pressings, shipping and "in reality" are giving away the recordings in hope of sparking additional sales and profits.

• *Holds.* Recording artists often ask a music publisher to place a song "on hold" while they are considering it for their next album project. A hold means that the publisher has agreed that the artist can have the song before someone else has the opportunity to record it.

• *Independent Contractor.* If a writer uses their own musical instruments, doesn't have to meet a publisher song quota, has their own demo recording studio or pays for their own recordings, and if they are not receiving a salary or employment benefits, then they are considered an independent contractor.[38]

• *Moral Rights.* The changes in a song that someone may want to make, when recording a cover version are called moral rights. You can *somewhat* control others' negative creativity legally by contractually obligating the publisher to seek the writers' approval for any changes in the music, lyrics, title, or when a song is to be used in movies (synchronization license) or commercials (transcription licenses). If the movies or commercials are about something the writers do not support (examples may include smoking ads), then the writers will have the right to reject or control the song's use.[39]

• *Originality.* In a song contract, the writer has to state that a "creative work" is original and not plagiarized from another person's creative efforts. This statement provides legal "proof" the publisher can use to protect itself (sometimes against the writer) if sued by somebody else who legally proves the song is really theirs.

• **Recoupment.** The royalties collected from a song's use in recordings, broadcasting, etc. are used to recoup or repay the music publisher's advances to the songwriter. Royalty payments are also used in many other facets of the music and entertainment industry to recoup the "front" money or advances contracted to recording artists for album projects and concert tour support. Recoupment is accomplished through the collection of mechanicals, performance royalties, sync licenses, foreign royalties, print, transcription, and DART royalties (blank cassette and digital tape recorder royalties collected to compensate for digital home recordings).

• **Royalties.** Monies received from the user of a song, including mechanical royalties, performance royalties, sync., foreign royalties, print, transcription, and DART royalties.

• **Song Quotas.** The number of songs songwriters are required to author for the publisher. Solo songwriters are credited with one song, and co-writers usually with 1/2 a song each, however, it can vary, i.e., 60/40, etc.[40]

• **Term.** The length of a songwriter/music publisher "deal" may be for a single song, a group of songs, or a period of time, from 1 year, plus another 1-year option, to a multi-year contract.

• **The Pipeline.** A term used to describe the location of royalties that have not yet been paid. There are often delays of 6 to 18 months for the collection of domestic royalties, 2 years for foreign royalties.

## Summary

Music publishing is a gamble. Nobody knows which songs are going to become hit recordings. When publishers listen to a song and say "that's a hit," what they are really saying is that, from their personal experience, they think the song *has the potential* to be a hit. A successful song has equity that is divided into writer and publisher "shares." There are several types of deals including the non-deal offered by song sharks, specific employment "work-for-hire" arrangements, staff writer pacts, single song contracts, co-publishing, administrative, and sub-publishing agreements.

Music publishers either have their own departments to handle specific tasks or they sub-out the following tasks to sub-publisher. *Acquisitions* are always searching for new songs and writers to sign. Attorneys or legal assistants work in *Business Affairs* negotiating writers and single song contracts. Then, they file for a Certificate of Recordation with The Copyright Office in The Library of Congress. The *Creative Department* consists of staff writers who are paid a salary to write a quota of acceptable songs. Songpluggers use their knowledge of the streets and music business contacts to pitch songs to the producers, artists, labels (A & R) and managers who have new album projects in the works. *Marketing* helps promote new recordings (and, therefore, the songs) to other media, including film projects. Finally, *Administration* or *Payroll* issue checks to songwriters from the royalties collected.

## Chapter Footnotes

[1] Music Publishing: A Songwriters Guide, Randy Poe (1990).

[2] The Music Business Handbook & Career Guide, Baskerville (1990), p.1.

[3] The Music Business Handbook & Career Guide, Baskerville (1978).

[4] Television was invented in the late 1930's, but its development was delayed until the late 1940's by World War II and economics.

[5] The History of Rock & Roll (Part One) Cinamax Productions (video tape).

[6] Determining the "value" of a song is very difficult. If a song does not perform as well as expected, the writer may blame the publisher and the publisher may blame the writer. The equity of a song and cumulative value of songs and writers are better judged over a period of 3 to 5 years. It often takes years for all money to be collected "in the pipeline."

[7] Suggested by Robert Mulloy, Associate Dean of Music Business, Belmont University, Nashville, TN.

[8] "The Rich Set Sights on Famous," Steve Redmond (Editor) MBI (1994).

[9] "Non-active" is defined as songwriters who publish their own material but rarely have it picked up by a major label or recording artists.

[10] Ibid.

[11] See Appendix A, Transferring Copyright Ownership.

[12] ASCAP, BMI, or SESAC.

[13] Foreign publishers are alerted of acquisition so they can place songs with foreign artists, labels, film and television production companies, and collect the proportional royalties.

[14] Called "The paper business."

[15] Staff writer advances are customarily deducted from royalties ("recouped"). There are many types of "deals" negotiated. Some repayment schedules call for immediate recoupment, others begin after the first year, and still others after the second or third year.

[16] This Business of Music, Shemel and Krasilovsky (1990), p. 145.

[17] For additional information, see Chapter Three, section "Transferring Copyright Ownership."

[18] There are, of course, exceptions depending on the success of the songwriter and, therefore, negotiating power. In addition, many successful songwriters are also publishers who simply negotiate co-publishing deals with major music publishers.

[19] There have been many examples of songs sold to music publishers (mostly in the 1950's and early 1960's) for a set fee ($100.00 or less). Many of the songs became hits, yet the writers did not receive any additional revenues because they had sold all of their interest in the song.

[20] See Transferring Copyright Ownership.

[21] Songwriters have a five-year period between the 35th and 40th years of a copyright/publishing control to *recapture* their original copyright. Music publishers often want a long-term contract in order have time to recoup the publishing expenses of demo recording, printing, and plugging a song. However, you can also negotiate publisher performance clauses into a contract. Examples include demo recording, placement of a song with a major recording artist, etc.

[22] Summary of the Copyright Office, Library of Congress form Recordation of Transfers and Other Documents. U.S. Government Printing Office, April, 1988, 202135/60,045.

[23] "Exclusive" means that the songwriter can only work for that particular music publisher. Some writers put a "right of first refusal" option in their contracts which allows them to "pitch" their songs to other publishers if the song is rejected by their contracted publisher.

[24] Yearly salaries for beginning staff writers are estimated to be $18,000 to $25,000. Source: The Musician's Business & Legal Guide, edited by Holloran (1991), pp. 312-313. Successful writers earn into the hundreds of thousands per year salary range.

[25] Staff writers are often paid a yearly salary, which the music publisher recoups from royalties. Once the song's "royalties" have repaid the writer's salary or advances, the first year's additional royalties are often split between the writer and publisher. Some publishers return all additional first-year royalties (after the writer's salary has been recouped) and then split or retain future royalties. The more successful the writer, the more the payment schedule favors the writer. A more powerful publisher may have a contract that is skewed favorably toward the company.

[26] Songwriters are paid as much as 10% of the suggested average retail price of sheet music. Folios are printed combinations of many songs, and the writers often "split" the combined writers share.

[27] Interview, Casey Kelly, September 11, 1994, Nashville, TN.

[28] The Essential Songwriter's Contract Handbook by NSAI (The Nashville Songwriters Association International (1994), p. 26.

[29] See ASCAP, BMI, or SESAC.

[30] The Essential Songwriter's Contract Handbook, NSAI (The Nashville Songwriters Association International (1994), p. 28.

[31] Music Business Handbook & Career Guide, Baskerville, Sherwood Publishing (1990).

[32] The Music Publishers' Forum (which represents independent publishers) recommends that foreign sub-publishers be restricted to performance, mechanical and print royalties. They suggest that American publishers should continue to control the licensing of lyric and video rights, jingle and grand rights. Music Business Handbook and Career Guide, Baskerville, Sherwood Publishing (1990).

[33] The Musician's Business & Legal Guide, Holloran, (ed.) Printice Hall (1991), p. 335.

[34] The Essential Songwriter's Contract Handbook, NSAI (The Nashville Songwriters Association International (1994), p. 66.

[35] See Chapter Two: Copyrights.

[36] The Essential Songwriter's Contract Handbook, NSAI (The Nashville Songwriters Association International (1994), p. 35.

[37] Ibid, p. 51.

[38] Ibid.

[39] Passman, All You Need To Know About the Music Business (1993), pp. 270-271.

[40] Source, Bob Mulloy, Associate Dean, Music Business, Belmont University (1995).

# 5

# EXPLOITING COPYRIGHTS

**Performance Rights Organizations
Performance Licenses
Mechanicals
Synchronization Licenses
Foreign Revenues**

Publishers or their authorized agents provide various types of licenses to music users to collect money (royalties) for the use of their music. *Performance Rights Organizations* represent both music publishers and writers individually and issue *blanket licenses* to collect royalties from music users. In addition, publishers offer *direct* or *source licenses* for specific uses of the music. As you can see, there are many types of licenses, each with its own specific purpose.

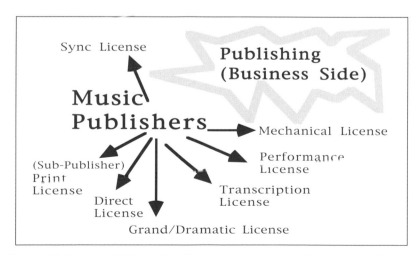

*Figure 5.1 Music Publishers offer licenses to music users for the use of their songs (called material). The publishers control the copyright and, therefore, must be paid by the music users for the use of the songs.*

## Mechanicals

Publishers *license the use of their songs* to record labels in exchange for a *mechanical license* fee. The royalty rate, called the *statutory mechanical rate,* is currently 6.95 cents for each song or 1.3 cents per minute for songs over 5 minutes in length.[1] Until 1994, the *Copyright Royalty Tribunal*[2] reviewed and set the mechanical statutory rate. The rates are now set by the *Copyright Office of the Library of Congress.*

| SONG | #LENGTH | RATE | MECHANICALS |
|------|---------|------|-------------|
| Song A | 3:31 | Statutory Rate | 6.95 cents |
| Song B | 5:01 | 1.3 per minute | 7.80 cents |
| Song C | 9:46 | 1.3 per minute | 13.00 cents |

*Figure 5.2  Mechanical rates for songs over 5 minutes are 1.3 cent per minute. Time is rounded up to the next full minute. Therefore, a song 5:01 is paid at the 1.3 cents per minute rate for 6 minutes.*

## Mechanical Collection Agencies

Mechanicals are paid directly (a direct license) to music publishers or through a mechanical license collection agency, such as *The Harry Fox Agency* in New York, *Copyright Management, Inc.* in Nashville, or *The Canadian Mechanical Rights Reproduction Agency* (CMRRA) for Canadian music publishers. The mechanical license agencies collect most of the mechanical royalties owed to music publishers. After agency commissions are deducted (usually 3 to 5%), the remaining royalties are sent to the corresponding music publisher. The Harry Fox Agency's commissions for collecting mechanicals, sync royalties and issuing licenses are:

| | |
|---|---|
| Mechanical Licensing | *4.5%-2.75% of royalties collected*[3] |
| Sync. Licensing | *10% of royalties collected $250 maximum for each composition* |
| Other, broadcast & cable TV, commercials | *4% of royalties collected $2,000 maximum per composition* |
| Transcription Licensing, background music, syndicated radio, inflight, etc. | *5% of royalties collected $2,000 maximum per composition* |
| Import Licensing | *4 1/2% of royalties collected*[4] |

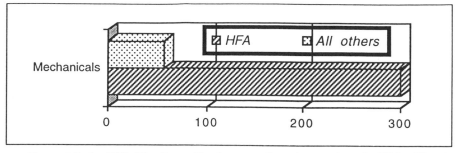

*Figure 5.3  In 1992, The Harry Fox Agency collected approximately $300 million in mechanicals, 84% of all American mechanical royalties.*[5]

*Copyright Management, Incorporated* (CMI) is one the of The Harry Fox Agency's main competitors.  In addition to the collection of mechanical royalties, CMI collects sync, print, grand, literature, and multi-media royalties from music uses.

### Royalty "Splits"

Publishers typically *split* the collected mechanical royalties 50/50 with the signed songwriters who wrote the songs.  However, in reality, most music publishers have the policy of first recouping (deducting) any advances paid to the staff writer out of the writer share of the royalties.  Therefore, negotiated percentages of profits are paid to the songwriter *after* recoups are satisfied.[6]

### Reserves

Mechanicals are paid quarterly by record labels, yet as much as 50% of the fees are *held in reserve* until the products are sold.  No mechanicals are paid on *promotional copies* and *free goods*, which are promotional albums sent to radio stations, other mass media outlets, and retail stores to increase sales.  Mechanicals are paid at 50% of the statutory rate for records sold through *record clubs*.

### Controlled Composition Clause

Labels use the *controlled composition clause* in the copyright law to negotiate a mechanical royalty of 75% of the statutory rate.  To be considered a controlled composition, the *recording artist* must be a co-writer or granted part ownership or control of the copyright.  As an example, if the statutory rate of 6.95 cents is used on an album of ten songs (all under 5 minutes in length), the record label owes the publishers 69.5 cents per album sold.

| *Statutory Mechanical Rate* |
| --- |
| **6.95 cents x 10 songs = 69.5 cents per album** |

Record labels save money by requiring their recording artists and producers to record *controlled composition songs*. Music publishers and songwriters who do not accept the controlled composition royalty rate may find their songs *dropped* from an album project. However, everything is fair in love and war, and if one label requires the song to be a controlled composition, another may not. Labels often pay statutory rates for great songs they think may help one of their artists increase record sales.

| *Controlled Composition Rate* |
|---|
| **6.95 cents x .75 = 5.21 Cents x 10 songs = 52.1 cents per album** |

Have you ever wondered "why" some of your albums have only 8 or 9 songs on them? If the record label determines that it will only pay the controlled composition clause *rate per album* of 52.1 cents and the artists or producer want a song(s) licensed at the statutory rate of 6.95 cents, fewer songs are placed on the album.

The *controlled composition clause* does make a difference in the "bottom line." It saves the record labels 25% of their mechanical licenses fees. As an example, labels can save approximately $87,000 on a gold album of ten songs, $174,000 on a platinum album, and $348,000 on an album with two million units sold.

**Per Album Difference between Mechanicals at the Statutory Rate and the Controlled Composition Rate**

| # OF UNIT SALES | STATUTORY | CONTROLLED | DIFFERENCE |
|---|---|---|---|
| 500,000 x 69.5 ¢ = | $347,500 | 52.1 cents = $260,500 | $ 87,000 |
| 1,000,000 x 69.5 ¢ = | $695,000 | 52.1 cents = $521,000 | $174,000 |
| 2,000,000 x 69.5 ¢ = | $1,390,000 | 52.1 cents = $1,042,000 | $348,000 |

## Foreign Mechanical Royalties

Unlike the American practice of individual song mechanical licenses, most foreign countries require one mechanical license for all songs on an album. Registration is *mandatory*. Mechanicals are collected by government-owned agencies and turned over to the foreign music publishers. A percentage of the retail price is collected for the mechanicals which is split among all the songs on the album and between the foreign and American publishers. Therefore, there is not a set foreign mechanical rate, and the amount of money collected varies from country to country and album to album. Totals collected also depend on the number of songs on the album and how many albums were sold. *Foreign sub-publishers* often collect the mechanicals from the government agencies and split the royalties with

American publishers by making payments directly or through an American collection agency, such as The Harry Fox Agency.[7]

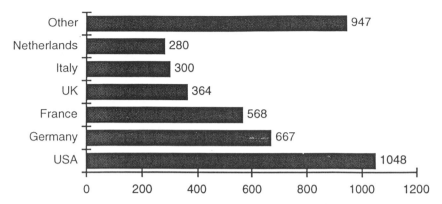

*Figure 5.4 Global music publishing royalties for 1992 totaled $4.71 billion. The United States royalties topped $1.05 billion dollars or 23% of all revenues collected. Germany collected $667 million (14%); France, $568 million (12%); Japan, $544 million (11%); UK, $364 million (8%); Italy, $300 million (6%); The Netherlands, $280 million (6%); and all others, $947 million dollars or 20%. It can take up to five years to collect foreign royalties.[8]*

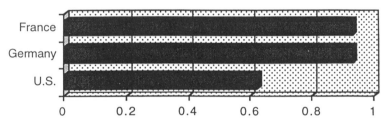

*Figure 5.5 Foreign mechanical rates (8.5%-10.5%) are expressed as an average percentage of the retail selling price (RSP) or the average published price to dealers (PPD).[9] American mechanicals per 10 song album averaged 62 cents 1992. However, in Germany and France, the average amount of money collected on mechanicals was 93 cents per album.[10]*

## Right of "First License"

Music publishers have the right to determine which recording artist will *first record* their songs. The more famous the artist, the more albums the label is likely to sell. Which, in turn, will increase mechanical royalties and often radio station performance royalties collected and sent to the music publisher.[11] However, once the song has been released for distribution or sale to the public, anybody can then record a *cover version* of the song. Mechanicals must still be paid.

## Cover Tune Mechanicals

To obtain a mechanical license for an already-released song you want to "cover" (re-record), The Harry Fox Agency suggests that you send a check for the mechanicals and the following information:

- *The name and address of the company or person to whom the license is to be issued*
- *The title and writers of the composition and the publisher(s) if known*
- *The record number and configuration*
- *The name of the performing artist*
- *The album (product) title*
- *The playing time of the compositions(s) in minutes and seconds*
- *The release date of the record (month and year)*

## Music Publishers' Mechanical Organizations

There are three major music publishing mechanical rights organizations including, the American Mechanical Rights Association (AMRA), Copyright Management, Inc. (CMI), and the National Music Publishers Association (NMPA), of which The Harry Fox Agency is a constituent.

> ### *American Mechanical Rights Association*
> 333 South Tamiami Trail, Suite 295, Venice, FL 34285
> (212) 877-4077

AMRA represents American and foreign mechanical rights organizations. It charges a 4.5% commission fee on foreign mechanicals, slightly higher than The Harry Fox Agency. The phone number is a New York number, however, it often is redirected to the Florida address.

> ### *Copyright Management, Inc.*
> 1102 17th Ave. South, Nashville, TN 37213
> (615) 327-1517

*CMI* is a full-line service agency for *independent music publishers*. It has offices in Nashville and Los Angeles and affiliates in 37 foreign territories. It licenses mechanicals, plus the print, sync, grand, lyric, and multi-media users of music. CMI has developed a quality control computer database system to check the levels of projected royalties, based on reported performances and chart listings, to the actual royalties collected. It has working agreements with BMI and ASCAP to receive all its publishing members' shares of performance royalties. Writer statements are then prepared for the publishing companies which send the payments to their writers.

> ### *The National Music Publishers Association*
> ### *The Harry Fox Agency, Inc.*
> 711 3rd. Ave., New York, NY 10017
> (212) 370-5330

The NMPA was formed in 1917 to maintain high standards of commercial honor and integrity among its members, to promote equitable principles of trade and business, and to foster and encourage the art of music and songwriting. The NMPA formed The Harry Fox Agency in 1927 to provide a clearinghouse and monitoring service for licensing musical copyrights. It has approximately 10,000 music publisher members.[12]

## Performance Royalties

*Performance royalties* are owed to music publishers and songwriters by the users of a song in a *public performance or business*. When we buy an album, CD, DCC, minidisk, cassette, etc., we own the product. We can play the music as often as we want - that is private use of the music in a non-public performance. However, if a song is used by a business (including radio stations, television, cable TV, night clubs, concerts, football stadiums, restaurants, airlines, etc.), then the owners of the business are required to pay for the use of the song. It is only fair that the businesses that use music to make money (or use ambient music to set a mood to help them make money) pay a very small fraction of their profits for the use of that music.

## Performance Rights Organizations

In 1967, the United States Supreme Court approved a lower court ruling that upheld the rights of songwriters and music publishers to authorize an agency to represent them in the collection of performance royalties.[13] *Performance rights organizations* collect performance royalties from the users of music for their affiliated writers and publishers. *The American Society of Composers, Authors, and Publishers* (ASCAP), *Broadcast Music Incorporated* (BMI), and SESAC are the American performance rights organizations.[14] SESAC is now the registered name for *The Society of European Stage Authors and Composers*, which is not used anymore. After *business fees* are deducted, the remaining royalties are split 50/50 and sent to the songwriters and music publishers by means of separate checks.[15] *The 50% sent to the writer is considered a 100% writer's performance share (royalty), and the 50% sent to the music publisher is considered 100% of the publisher's performance share (royalty).* Examples of non-American performance rights organizations include: *SOCAN* (Canada), *PRS* (U K), *SACEM* (France), *GEMA* (Germany), *SIAE* (Italy), *JASRAC* (Japan), *SADAIC* (Argentina), *APRA* (Australia), *AKM* (Austria), *SABAM* (Brazil), *ACUM* (Israel), *CASH* (Hong Kong), *SACM* (Mexico), and *RAO* (Russia).[16] Worldwide, there are approximately *forty-eight performance rights organizations* representing various countries and territories.

## Historical Perspectives

ASCAP was formed in 1914 to help music publishers and songwriters collect their performance royalties. It is a non-profit organization owned and operated by its songwriter and music publisher members. In the late 1930's, ASCAP raised its fees for performance royalties. In retaliation, many broadcasters formed their own performance rights organization, BMI, in 1940. These stations refused to play any ASCAP songs.

After law suits, the justice department filed a civil lawsuit alleging antitrust violations on the parts of ASCAP, BMI, NBC and CBS. The performance rights organizations settled, and the radio stations returned to broadcasting music licensed by all the performance rights organizations.[17] BMI is still owned by the 675 original radio stations who formed the organization, and it is still a *not-for-profit* organization.

SESAC is a different story. Much smaller than ASCAP and BMI, it is privately owned and a for-profit business. It was formed by Paul Heinecke in 1930 to represent European publishers and religious works. In 1992, the company was purchased by Freddie Gershon, Ira Smith, Stephen Swid, and the merchant banking house of Allen & Company.[18]

## Affiliation

Writers are often called ASCAP, BMI or SESAC writers, while music publishers are ASCAP, BMI, or SESAC publishers. In reality, most music publishers form three separate music publishing companies, all with different names and different songs in their catalogs, and affiliate each company with a different performance rights organization. *Songwriters and publishing companies may only be affiliated with one performance rights organization at a time.* However, co-writers may have different affiliations, in which case, their respective PRO pays them their royalty share.

## Performance Rights Membership

*Membership* in a performance rights organization is open to both publishers and composers who have at least one song *commercially* recorded, published, publicly performed or distributed. BMI and SESAC writers and publishers are designated as *affiliates*, ASCAP as *members*. ASCAP participation requires slightly different professional writing standards of at least one song commercially published, recorded, or *likely to be performed*. Music publishers must also have the ability and finances to exploit a song's potential equity. ASCAP has approximately 65,000 members, BMI about 160,000 affiliates, and SESAC about 3,500 affiliates. ASCAP and BMI retain commissions of about 20% + for the expense of collecting royalties. SESAC retains approximately 50%, yet pays its writers competitively.[19]

## Blanket License

Public music users (businesses) are offered *blanket licenses* by the songwriter's affiliated PRO (Performance Rights Organization) to pay for the use of the song (recordings and performances). *License fees* are negotiated between the performance rights organizations representing their members (songwriters and music publishers) and the users of the music. ASCAP, BMI and SESAC license radio, television, cable TV stations and networks. All three license hotels, motels, restaurants, nightclubs, concert halls, specific concert performances, airlines, trade shows, amusement parks, malls, and almost any other source of music performances they can find. Their job is to find the public (business) users of music and to collect *licensing fees* for their use of the music.

Fees for blanket licenses are determined by "weighing" various factors, including the *type of media* (radio, TV, etc.), the *size of the prospective broadcast audience* (national, local, etc.), and *the type of performance* (music in a movies, TV show, theme music, etc.). *None of the performance rights organizations sample hotels and concerts for violations.* However, many small business owners are not aware of the copyright law and their obligation to pay for the "music they use" in the daily operation of their business. Many become frustrated when confronted with a bill for the music they thought was free. However, once the law is explained, most understand why the copyright owner should be paid.

License fees are estimated and issued on the size of the facility's potential occupancy rate and the use of the music (CD's being played, live band, etc.).[20] *Trade organizations* (hotels, restaurants, etc.) license the music to the users they represent. Additional audits are often conducted in non-licensed facilities (night clubs, restaurants, etc.) to encourage compliance with the copyright law.[21]

*Figure 5.6 Performance rights royalties are split by ASCAP, BMI, and SESAC and sent separately to the writers and publishers. Fifty percent is equal to 100% of the writers share and the other 50% is equal to 100% of the publishers share. As stated earlier, mechanical fees are paid to the publisher who splits the royalties (less collection fees and commissions) with the writer. Sync fees (for music use in the production of movies, TV shows, music videos, etc.) are often collected by The Harry Fox Agency and paid to the songwriter through the music publisher. The exception is SESAC who collects sync fees and pays the writers and publishers each directly.*

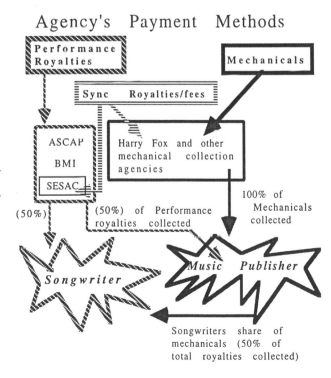

Agency's Payment Methods

## Collection Procedures

Both ASCAP and BMI use *random sampling and statistical analysis* to determine the number of performances and, therefore, payments to their writers and publishers.

| PRO | OWNERSHIP | TYPE OF BUSINESS | COLLECTION METHOD RADIO | TELEVISION |
|---|---|---|---|---|
| ASCAP | *Members* | Non-Profit | *Statistical Sample* | Cue Sheets |
| BMI | *Broadcasters* | No-for-Profit | *Statistical Sample* | Cue Sheets |
| SESAC | *Private* | For-Profit | *Trade Mag/Charts* | Cue Sheets |

ASCAP records a random sample of local radio and television broadcasts and generalizes the results to national performance figures. It also samples the TV networks, PBS, and cable channels.[22] BMI requires a random sampling of radio stations to log (keep a list of each song's performance) once a year. BMI uses producer's cue sheets to determine music performances for national and cable TV performances. All three use *TV Guide* to calculate TV local performances. SESAC uses field monitors to check for music usage and *Broadcast Data Systems* (BDS) to calculate performances for its SESAC Latina division. The BDS system monitors and "hears" a recording by comparing the radio stations' airplayed songs to the *digital fingerprint* of the recording it has stored in its data bank. If there is a correlation, the monitor tallies an airplay performance. Using BDS to monitor actual airplay performances is the wave of the future for performance rights organizations. The system is already being used by *The Billboard Monitor* to determine *the airplay charts*.[23] Stations and publishers are provided a listing of the songs aired, along with the date, time, and the number of times each song was played each week. In the future, radio and TV stations may pay only for the songs they use instead of the current blanket license system.[24]

## In The Pipeline

For publishers who do not have sub-publishing agreements in foreign territories, ASCAP, BMI, and SESAC will collect performance rights monies and pay their respective songwriter and publisher members. SESAC also negotiates sync licenses. However, foreign royalty payments can take up to 2-5 years for collection and payments to songwriters and publishers. This "time period" or delay in foreign payments compared to domestic payments is called "in the pipeline," as royalties have been earned and will be paid eventually.

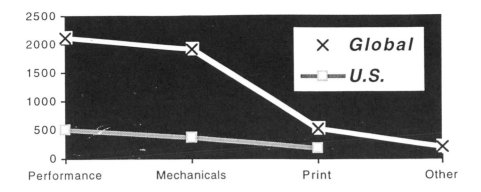

Figure 5.7 World music publishing royalties collected for 1992 totaled $4.71 billion dollars. Performance royalties equaled $2.1 billion, or 45%; mechanicals, $1.9 billion, 40%; print, $519 million, 11%; and sync. and other royalties, $200 million, or 4%.[25]

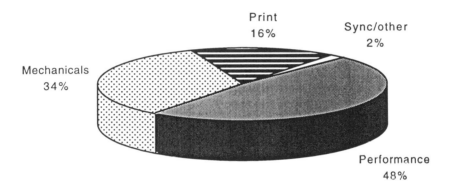

Figure 5.8 American 1992 music publishing royalties totaled $1.05 billion. Performance royalties collected equaled $501.94 million, or 48% of the American total; mechanicals were $356 million, or 34%; print $172 million, or 16%; and sync and other licenses royalties totaled $20 million, or 2%.[26]

## Payment Methodology

ASCAP's collection formula includes *the station weight* (based on the license fees paid to ASCAP and the depth of sampling), *the use weight* (based on the kind of performance: feature, background, theme, etc.), *feature multiplier* (additional credits calculated for featured performance representing performances in areas not surveyed, such as hotels, bars, skating rinks, etc.), *strata multiplier* (to bring licensee's *total credits* in line with the *share of income* from all surveyed media), and *radio feature premium* (three-tiered premium payment structure that allows ASCAP to make larger payments to hit songs on radio).[27]   ASCAP claims to have collected at least $100 million more than any other Performance Rights Organization in 1995. That makes it the largest PRO from a revenue generating perspective.[28]

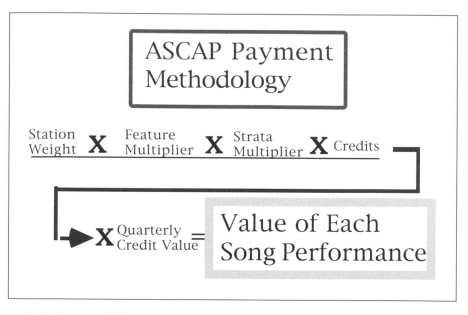

ASCAP Payment Methodology

Station Weight **X** Feature Multiplier **X** Strata Multiplier **X** Credits **X** Quarterly Credit Value **=** Value of Each Song Performance

BMI uses a different computation method. Songs played on the top 25% of radio stations (as ranked by their BMI license fee) are paid at approximately 14 cents per performance. All songs played on other radio stations are paid approximately 7 cents per play. Songs with the highest cumulative history (current quarter's performances constitute 10% of the current quarter's radio and local television performances of all songs) are paid a *Super Bonus Payment* of 4 times the base rate. *Upper-Level Bonus* payments are paid for songs in the 15% listing of the current quarter's radio and local television performances. *Mid-Level Bonus* payments are issued to songs in the 25% bracket, and *Entry-Level Bonus* of twice the base rate is issued to all songs with 25,000 or more performances.

### Payment Rates and Schedules

ASCAP and BMI pay competitively but not equally for the same chart placement. Different levels of payment are offered for different genres of music. To make it even more confusing, ASCAP and BMI do not pay the same amount of money for songs within the same genre. In other words, due to the way the charts are compiled, the time of the year, the PRO's payment scheme methodology, and the competition from other records and recording artists, some number one records receive more airplay (performances and, therefore, money) than other number one records. Since ASCAP and BMI pay performance royalties based on the number of performances, plus bonuses, all of the records charted do not receive equal payments. SESAC is unique in that it pays performance royalties based on trade magazine chart placement. SESAC bases its *Chart Payment Schedule* on a record's placement on the weekly *Billboard Magazine*, *Radio & Records*, and *The Gavin*

*Report* charts. Because SESAC's payment schedule is competitive with the other performance rights organizations, we can attain an estimate of a song's performance equity by genre.

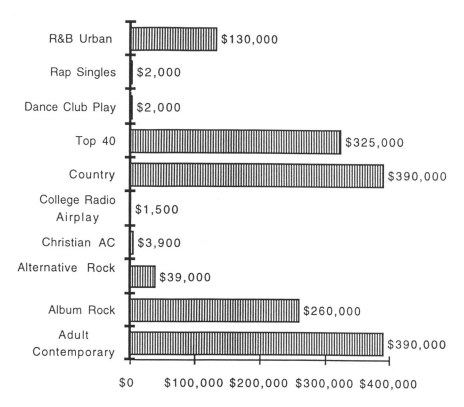

*Figure 5.9 SESAC's 1996 payment schedule gives us an indication of the amount of money a # 1 song can earn in Performance Royalties.*[29]

The major performance rights organizations include ASCAP, BMI, SESAC, and all the European PRO's which are represented by *The Congress of International Societies of Author and Composers* located in France.

**ASCAP-American Society of Composers,**
**Authors and Publishers**
52 Haymarket, Suites 10 & 11, London SWIY4RP
011-44-71-973-0069
7920 Sunset Blvd., Suite 300, Los Angeles, CA 90046
(213) 883-1000
Two Music Square West, Nashville, TN 37203 (615) 742-5000
One Lincoln Plaza, New York, NY 10023 (212) 621-6000

**BMI-Broadcast Music, Incorporated**
320 West 57th Street, New York, NY 10019 (212) 586-2000
8730 Sunset Boulevard (3 Third Floor), Los Angeles, CA 90069
(213) 659-9109
10 Music Square East, Nashville, TN 37203 (615) 259-3625

**SESAC**
55 Music Square East, Nashville, TN 37203 (615) 320-0055
421 West 54th Street, New York, NY 10019 (212) 586-3450

**The Congress of International Societies
of Authors and Composers**
CISAC 11, Rue Keppler, 75116 Paris, France

## Additional Information About PRO's

Although Performance Rights Organizations are often considered clearinghouses for songwriters, their duties are limited to:

• *supporting songwriter's professionalism and the nurturing of the craft through workshops and seminars;*

• *collection of performance song revenues;*

• *legally and politically supporting songwriters' rights to performance royalties; and*

• *celebrating songwriters' and publishers' success through company award shows and print publications.*

## PRO's Do Not:

• *Place songs with music publishers, however, they are very well-connected with the top publishers in the world and can refer a writer to individuals at various companies if the writer is established or very promising.*

• *Collect grand or dramatic rights performance royalties even if music is being used in the live performance. Permission to perform "plays, etc." are granted directly from the copyright holder.*

## Synchronization, Print, Direct, and Other Licenses

Sync, grand, transmission, and commercial licenses fees are negotiated.

Sync license for music videos are often granted free to the record label in exchange for the label's production of a promotional music video. The cost for the music used in the production of motion pictures, TV shows, etc. is ordinarily based on the size of the production budget and the talents of the negotiators. Commercial licenses are commonly paid as a one-time lump sum. It is not unusual for a writer and publisher to receive a million or more dollars for the use of their song in a national major food or soft drink commercial. Transmission fees are determined by the number of outlets "wired" or people who will normally hear the music.

Print or sheet music is often handled by a specialized sub-publisher. They print the sheet music, catalogs, and folios and distribute them to retail outlets. Royalties are often split 50/50 between the music publisher and sub-publisher. Straight royalties to the music publishers (if splits are not involved) are between 10-15% of retail list prices.

## DART Act & Royalties

| *Songwriter/Publisher Share* | |
| --- | --- |
| • Songwriters | 16.66% |
| • Music Publishers | 16.66% |
| *Recording Portion* | |
| • Record Companies | 38.41% |
| • Recording (Royalty) Artists | 25.60% |
| • AF of M (Studio Musicians) | 1.75%[30] |
| • AFTRA (Studio/Harmony Singers) | 0.92%[31] |

The *1992 Audio Home Recording Act* (commonly known as the *Digital Audio Recorders and Tape Act* or *DART Act*) provides royalties to songwriters, publishers, producers, recording artists, and record companies to compensate for their loss of royalties due to consumer copying or dubbing of their CD's and other media. Digital recorders are a concern to the industry because there isn't any loss in sound quality when making copies. *A 3% tax is imposed by the federal government on the wholesale price of blank audio tapes, and a 2% tax is imposed on the wholesale price of digital tape recorders.*[32]

The recording industry portions of the DART royalties are determined by dividing the total number of records distributed by the various number of recording artists and record labels who have released a product. For example, if you are a recording artist and your label pressed and distributed 100,000 copies of your latest album on CD's, DCC's, mini disks, or cassettes, you can divide the 100,000 by the total number of albums nationally distributed, over the same period of time, to determine the percent of *DART recording artists royalties* you will receive. Then simply multiply the total amount of DART recording artists royalties collected by the government by your percent of total albums distributed.

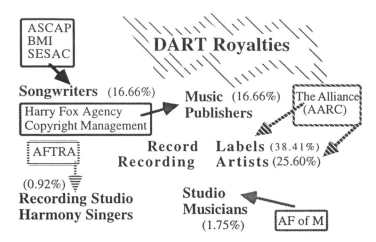

*Figure 5.10 It is hard to figure DART songwriter and music publisher royalties because they are based on the distribution of records or radio station performances, whichever is greatest. DART songwriter royalties are usually best determined by performance rights organizations. Music publishers' DART royalties are currently being collected by The Harry Fox Agency, Copyright Management, Inc., and other collection organizations.[33] Recording artists' and record labels' DART royalties are currently being collected by the RIAA and supervised by AARC (an alliance of artists and label representatives). AFTRA collects recording studio harmony singers' (background singers') DART royalties.[34]*

## SCMS on Digital Tape Recorders

Digital recorders sold in the United States are required to have the *Serial Copyright Management System* (SCMS), which allows the owner to make only one digital copy at a time. Digital copies cannot be made from digital copies.[35]

### Top American Music Publishers

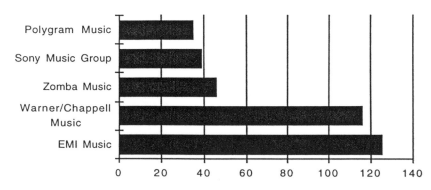

*Figure 5.11 Leading music publishers for 1995, based on the number of charted singles in <u>Billboard Magazine</u>, includes: EMI Music with 125; Warner/Chappell Music, 116; Zomba Music, 46; Sony Music Group, 39; and Polygram Music, 35.[36]*

## Key Terms

• **Background Music:** Music used in movies or "made-for-TV movies," music played as part of games shows, and music used on news shows.[37]

• **Clearance Forms, Title Registration Forms and Indexing:** BMI, ASCAP and SESAC require their affiliated writers and publishers to complete forms that will notify them of the existence of a song being distributed to the public for sale and/or public performance.

• **ISCI Number:** A standard coding number used in the industry (consisting of four letters and four numbers) to track the song's use by mass media performances and record sales.

• **Initiation Fees:** None of the PRO's require an initiation fee for writers at the time they join the organization. BMI requires a one-time $100 *administration fee* to publishers when they join.

• **Local:** A song performance payment based on a local, instead of national, usage.

• **Membership Dues:** ASCAP requires an annual membership fee *(dues)* of $10 for writers and $50 for publishers.

• **Superthemes:** A term used by BMI to describe music used as theme music on 30-minute or longer network TV shows for more than 13 weeks; if the theme is the only theme music used, is played 40 seconds or more and is used as the opening and/or closing theme.[38]

## Summary

There are several "sources" of revenue for songwriters and music publishers in the music business. They include *Mechanical Licenses,* which are offered directly by music publishers or through a mechanical rights collection agency (such as The Harry Fox Agency) who represents the publishers. They collect royalties from record labels, etc. for the use of songs on albums, CDs, cassettes, etc. Royalties are paid to the publishers who recoup any advances given to songwriters. The remaining 50% share is paid by the publishers to the songwriters. *Performance Licenses* are issued by performance rights organizations (ASCAP, BMI, and SESAC) who represent the song publishers and songwriters individually. They collect royalties from businesses that use public performances of live or recorded music in their daily operation. Royalties are split and paid (after commissions) separately to the songwriters and music publishers.

Other revenue sources for music publishers and songwriters include *printed sheet music license* used for printing and selling sheet music in retail outlets; *Sync License* for music used in the production of mass media TV, motion pictures, and video productions; *Commercial License* for music used in radio and TV commercials; *Transcription License* for music used in hotels, restaurants, etc.; *Grand License* for the music used in theater productions; *Import License* for music (on CDs, cassettes, etc.) shipped into the United States; and *DART Royalties*, which provide monies to cover the revenues lost due to home copying of digital music products.

| Music User | Type of License | Collection Agency |
|---|---|---|
| *Movie/TV/Video Production* | Sync License | H. Fox SESAC |
| *Radio/TV Stations Cable Systems* | Performance License | Performance Rights ASCAP, BMI, SESAC |
| *Resturants, Night Clubs, Hotels, Sports Areas, and Concert Venues* | Performance License | Performance Rights ASCAP, BMI, SESAC |
| *Jukebox Owners* | Performance License | Performance Rights ASCAP, BMI, SESAC |
| *Record Labels* | Mechanical License | Mechanical Rights Org., CMI, and The Harry Fox Agency |
| *Muzak* (for production of music) | Transcription License | H. Fox SESAC |
| *Muzak* (for airing of music in business) | Block License | ASCAP BMI SESAC |
| *Sub-Publisher* (for sheet music to be sold in music stores) | Print License | Music Publisher |
| *Interactive Networks Merchandising Commercials* | Direct License | Music Publisher |
| *Theater/Plays* (producer) | Dramatic/ Grand Rights License | Music Publisher |
| *Symphony Orchestra Owner/Producer* (musical arrangement of public domain classical music) | Direct License | Music Publisher |
| *Sub-Publisher* (foreign record sales) (foreign media broadcasts) | Foreign License | Foreign Publishers to The Harry Fox Agency or CMI, etc. Broadcasting from foreign PRO's to American PRO's. |

# Chapter Footnotes

[1] The "Statutory Rate" is scheduled to increase January 1, 1998.

[2] The Tribunal was composed of Commissioners appointed by the President and approved by the United States Senate. The term of office was 7 years. For more information, see The Copyright Law of the United States of America (1993), pp. 112-118.

[3] The NMPA lowered its commission rates on mechanicals in 1994 from 4.5% to 3.5% because of a 17% increase in gross revenues collection. It also lowered the sync rates from 5% to 4% for the last two quarters of the year, Billboard Magazine (9-9-1994).

[4] The National Music Publishers' Association, Inc. and The Harry Fox Agency, Inc. 75th Anniversary publication (1992), p. 13.

[5] NMPA/Billboard Magazine (1994).

[6] As stated earlier, many different types of deals can be structured. However, the publishing company will usually attempt to recoup advances as soon as possible.

[7] Foreign Sub-Publisher splits range from 10% to 25% for collecting American product and up to a 50/50 split for foreign-recorded "cover tunes." Passman, All You Need To Know About the Music Business (1993), pp. 242-243, & The Essential Songwriter's Contract Handbook by NSAI (The Nashville Songwriters Association International) (1994), p. 50.

[8] Survey of 43 countries sponsored by NMPA Billboard Magazine (1994).

[9] Music, Money and Success by Brabec and Brabec, Schirmer Books (1994), p. 325.

[10] "Global Pub Royalties Hit $4.71 Bill in 1992," Billboard Magazine (1994).

[11] However, once a song has been recorded and distributed to the public for sale, anyone can record the song. You still have to obtain and pay "mechanicals," but you do not have to request permission to record the song.

[12] The National Music Publishers' Association, Inc. and The Harry Fox Agency, Inc. 75th Anniversary publication (1992), pp. 4-15.

[13] The ruling states:"... a central licensing agency, such as ASCAP, is the only practical way that copyright proprietors may enjoy their rights under federal copyright laws and that broadcasters and others may conveniently obtain licenses for the performance of copyrighted music." The Music Business Handbook & Career Guide, Baskerville (1990).

[14] SESAC is now the registered name of the Society of European Stage Authors and Composers.

[15] Performance royalties are collected for the "performance" of a song, not for the recording artist who sings it. In some European countries, a fee is collected and paid to the recording artist for the number of times their recordings are played on radio stations. There have been several attempts in the United States to change the law to allow recording artists to be paid a "performance" or "play fee." The movement has gained very little support among lawmakers.

[16] ASCAP (1996).

[17] Music Publishing, A Songwriter Guide, Poe (1990).

[18] SESAC Promotional package (1994).

[19] Industry Sources and PRO's Writer Packets.

[20] ASCAP does send investigators to night clubs. In New Jersey, lawmakers are considering a law that would require the performance rights investigators to identify themselves when they enter a New Jersey business looking for a violation. "ASCAP to Sam: Play It Again, but Pay for it," by Stephanie N. Mehta, The Wall Street Journal (9/27/1994).

[21] According to a BMI representative, "BMI's policy is to first illustrate the benefits BMI's music brings to a business. We then explain the legal responsibility that accompanies the use of copyrighted music and ask the owner to sign a license agreement. When a business repeatedly refuses our requests to comply with the law, we are forced to exercise our rights under the Copyright Law." "BMI files suit against lounge for not having jukebox license," Beverly Keel, The Nashville Banner (Oct. 19, 1993).

[22] ASCAP records approximately 60,000 hours of local radio airplay, 30,000 hours of local TV, and all performances of network TV.

[23] See Chapter 10: Marketing Music.

[24] Radio and TV stations may play any songs in a performance rights catalog. However, license fees are set by many variables instead of paying for each song aired.

[25] "Global Pub Royalties Hit $4.71 Bill in 1992," Billboard Magazine (1994).

[26] NMPA/Billboard Magazine (1994).

[27] ASCAP promotions material (1994).

[28] ASCAP and BMI Writers Packet (1996).

[29] ASCAP and BMI have separate payment schedules that include bonuses and points which do not allow us to make a factual comparison with the SESAC payment schedule. However, because all three are competitive, we can infer that SESAC's payment schedule is similar to BMI's and ASCAP's.

[30] The AF of M (The American Federation of Musicians) is the musicians' union that represents studio musicians for label recording sessions. See Chapter 5 for additional information.

[31] AFTRA (The American Federation of Television Radio Artists) is the union for background and harmony singers. See Chapter 5 for additional information.

[32] The AARC is an alliance of recording artists and record label representatives formed to oversee the collection of DART royalties.

[33] ASCAP, BMI, SESAC.

[34] The AARC is currently administered by the RIAA (Recording Industry Association of America) which tabulates record distribution and sales.

[35] The DART tax does not apply to professional digital tape recorders or tape. All You Need To Know About the Music Business, Passman (1994) 2 edition, pp. 248-249.

[36] "1995-The Year in Music", Billboard Magazine, pages YE-6 through YE-84 (December 23, 1995).

[37] BMI Writers Pack Information (1996).

[38] Ibid.

# 6

# MEGA ENTERTAINMENT CORPORATIONS

**BMG**
**Thorn EMI**
**MCA**
**Polygram**
**Sony**
**Time Warner**

## Historical Perspectives

The music industry is rarely defined as *entrepreneurial* in nature. However, it is rich in historical processes that appear to be opportunistic, risk-taking, and proactive, which are key entrepreneurial traits. In 1899, Fred Gaisberg, an American producer living in England, recorded the singing barmaid from the Rules Restaurant located next door to his studio. The company eventually became *Thorn/EMI* with 1993 gross revenues of approximately $7.5 billion.[1]

Thomas Edison had already invented the phonograph when Chichester Bell and Charles Tainter (both English) invented the Dictaphone in 1887. The Columbia Phonograph Company (named after the District of Columbia) used wax cylinders to record the U.S. Marine Band directed by John Philip Sousa. That early company evolved into Columbia Broadcasting Systems (CBS) and a conglomerate of entertainment-media-driven operations. In 1991, and several mergers, CBS Records and CBS Films were sold (two separate deals) to the Sony Corporation of Japan for approximately $8 billion.[2]

In 1924, Dr. Julies Stein, a Chicago eye specialist who played the violin and saxophone for dance bands, created his own booking agency called the Music Corporation of America, now better known as MCA. Japan's Konosuke Matsushita founded his electronics company by inventing the two-way light socket in 1918.  In 1990, the two merged when Matsushita purchased MCA for $6.1 billion.

## Mega-Entertainment Corporations

Over the years, many of the small entrepreneurial recording ventures have grown and merged into six diversified world entertainment corporations.[3] Today, the *megas* are the only companies with the money, business structure, and distribution systems that can create, produce, market, promote, publicize, distribute, and deliver music, movies, computer games, and other entertainment products consistently to the global markets.  During 1994-95, the six mega entertainment corporation's record sales accounted for approximately 88% of the total 25 billion dollar world market.[4]

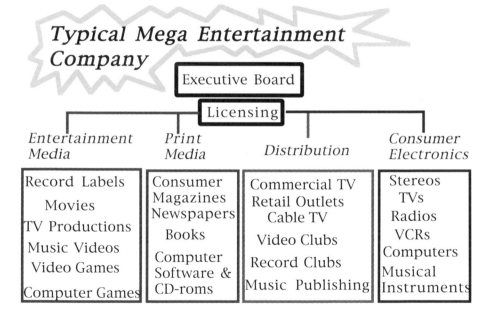

Figure 6.1  A typical mega entertainment corporation has several divisions, including: Entertainment Media, which provides the creative production of music, movies, videos, TV shows, and computer games; Print Media, which includes the writing and printing of books, magazines, and newspapers (sometimes on CD-ROMs) often used to promote and publicize the entertainment media stars and products; Distribution, which includes the methods and lines of supplying print and electronic media products through commercial broadcast, cable TV, retail outlets, music publishers, records, and video clubs; and Consumer Electronics, which manufactures the radios, TVs, VCRs, and computers consumers rent or purchase to play their video games, CDs, minidisks, DCCs, and video tapes.

## BMG

*Bertelsmann AG* was started by Carl Bertelsmann in 1835 as a lithographic printing company. Today, it is Europe's leading media company and is #2 in the world after Time Warner. One of Bertelsmann's first books, a hymnal, helped the company to grow, despite the poverty and low literacy rate in the 1830's. The company was shut down by the Nazis during W.W.II.[5] Its major growth was in the 1950's when it developed a "book club" concept which accumulated huge profits from the sale of print media distributed directly to consumer homes. *Bertelsmann's Music Group* (BMG) was formed when RCA Records joined forces with Bertelsmann's Ariola Records and Arista Records in 1987. Divisions include *BMG Classics*, which contains the RCA Victor and RCA Victor Red Seal labels who record symphonic, operatic and chamber music. *Bertelsmann's book clubs* have over 25 million members in 15 countries, and BMG *Direct* has over four million American record club members. Bertelsmann acquired the *Gruner+Jahr* magazine publishers in the 1970's and currently owns Bantam, Brown, Doubleday and Dell publishers. *BMG Video,* founded in 1991, produces music videos, children's programming, and family documentaries.

Major and affiliated record labels and entertainment companies include Arista, Career Records, Reunion, RCA, Zoo Entertainment, BMG Classics, BMG Kidz, BMG U.S./Latin, Fox, Imago, Jive, Private Music, Windham Hill, BDD Audio Publishing, and BMG Video.[6] Products are shipped to stores throughout the United States and 35 other countries.

BMG currently operates music publishing companies in 22 countries. Catalogs embrace all types of music including contemporary hits in country music, gospel, Latin, pop, rock and rhythm and blues (better known as "R&B"). The parent company also owns radio and TV stations and newspapers in Germany. BMG recording artists include Al Green, Clint Black, Crash Test Dummies, Alan Jackson, and ZZ Top.[7]

BMG (which is just a division of Bertelsmann AG) is primarily a privately-owned company. Shareholders include the Bertelsmann foundation, The Mohn Family members, Reinhart Mohn, and Dr. G. Bucerius.[8]

### BMG EQUITY OWNERSHIP

| | |
|---|---|
| Bertelsmann Foundation | 68.8% |
| Mohn Family | 17.9% |
| Reinhard Mohn | 2.6% |
| Dr. G. Bucerius | 10.7%[9] |

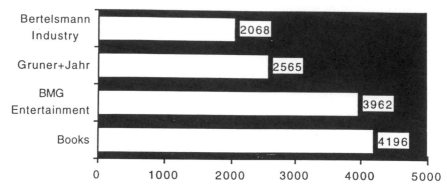

**Bertelsmann Revenues by Division**

| Division | Revenue |
|---|---|
| Bertelsmann Industry | 2068 |
| Gruner+Jahr | 2565 |
| BMG Entertainment | 3962 |
| Books | 4196 |

*Figure 6.2 Bertelsmann's four major divisions earned roughly $12 billion in 1994. BMG Entertainment earned approximately 31% of the total revenues.*[10]

## Thorn EMI

*Thorn Electric and Musical Industries* (Thorn EMI) of England has five divisions including *Thorn EMI Music,* its assemblage of worldwide music business groups; *Thorn EMI Rental,* 1,200 RAC and Remco consumer electronic and home appliance rental stores in the U.S. and other storefronts worldwide; *HMV Group,* a chain of 160 music stores; *Thorn Lighting,* a supplier of lighting fixtures in 22 countries with over 100 markets; and *Security and Electronics,* a top global security company. The company was started in 1928 by Jules Thorn as an electrical lamp service company[11] Thorn EMI sold its interest in Thames Television in 1993. Thorn EMI employs over 47,000 people in 38 countries, with 8,270 in the music division, 21,803 in the rental business, and approximately 17,500 in all the other EMI corporations. Approximately 27,000 are employed in the UK, 8,000 in the rest of Europe, 11,300 in North America, 2,500 in Asia, and the remaining 700 in other countries.[12]

EMI's music world headquarters are in New York City. Over the years, it has acquired many labels: Capitol Records, United Artists Records, The Sparrow Corporation, and Charisma Records. It bought Richard Branson's Virgin Music Group in 1992 for $834 million dollars.[13] It co-owns Chrysalis Records, SBK Records, and Hungary's Quint Records. Other EMI music divisions are EMI Publishing and its classical label, EMI Classics.

EMI recently formed a new international label, the *HEMISHPHERE Initiative.* Each year, twelve theme albums feature EMI artists from around the world. The label's mission is to sell local EMI recording artists' previously recorded yet unreleased material worldwide.[14] In 1962, EMI made history with The Beatles. In 1992, EMI did it again with Liberty Records (Capitol-Nashville) and recording artist Garth Brooks. Other EMI and affiliated label artists are Arrested Development, Beastie Boys, Blur, Janet Jackson, Megadeth, Frank Sinatra, Jon Secada, Smashing Pumpkins, Roxette, Traffic, UB40, and Wilson Phillips.[15]

# EMI

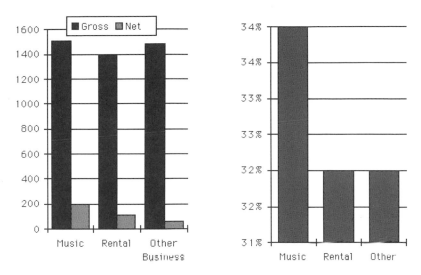

*Figure 6.3 In 1993, EMI's balance sheet showed a net profit of approximately 379.3 million English £ (approximately $605 million) and gross revenues of 4.5 billion £ (approximately $7.2 billion). Gross income for the music division for 1993 was 1.507 billion £ (approximately $2.41 billion). The rental division gross turnover was 1.338 billion £ ($2.14 billion) and all other EMI businesses grossed 1.486 billion £ (approximately $2.38 billion). Profits are estimated at 12%, approximately 197 million £ ($315 million) in the music division, 115 million £ ($185 million) in rental, and 65 million £ ($105 million) in all other EMI businesses.[16]*

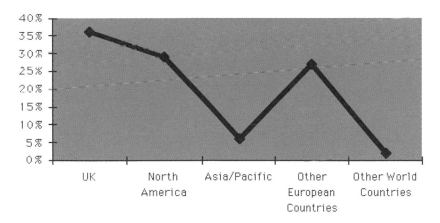

*Figure 6.4 Thorn EMI's 1994 gross income of £4,292 million (approximately $6.5 billion dollars) was acquired from sales of products from various parts of the world. UK sales accounted for 36%; North American, 29%; Asia/Pacific, 6%; other European countries, 27% and all other countries, 2%.[17]*

## MCA

As mentioned, *Music Corporation of American* (MCA) was purchased by *Matsushita Electrical Industrial* of Japan in 1990 for $6.1 billion. Endaka (the rising exchange rate of the yen to the dollar) has made it more difficult to achieve overseas profits for Japanese companies. Matsushita recently restructured its divisions into *entrepreneurial entities* in an attempt to counter the narrowing profits. Each Matsushita division is responsible for its own productivity and profitability.[18] Consequently, Matsushita sold 80% of MCA in 1995 to The Seagrams Company of Montreal Canada for $5.7 billion. Seagrams is one of the world's leading distributors of spirits (scotch and cognac), wine, wine coolers, fruit juices, and soft drinks. It sold its 24.4% of DuPont in 1995 to buy MCA.[19]

Seagrams was started by Sam Bronfman in 1916 as the Bonaventure Liquor Store Company. It sold liquor through the mail, which was the only legal way to sell it during the Canadian prohibition. In the 1920's, the company engaged in bootlegging to smuggle whisky into the United States during prohibition. In 1928, the company went public and changed its name to Distillers Corporation-Seagrams Limited.[20]

In the 1920's, MCA created the novel concept of *packaging* two or more bands for concerts, which increased profits for the bands and venues.[21] Packaging is still used to secure employment for bands, as well as TV and movie personalities in most of the entertainment industry. MCA has purchased or been affiliated with ABC Records, Brunswick, Decca, Dot, Dunhill, GRP, Paramount, and Geffen Records.[22] Boston, Elton John, Jodeci, Guns N' Roses, Meat Loaf, Trisha Yearwood, and Vince Gill are some of MCA's better known recording acts.

**Seagrams/MCA Revenues**

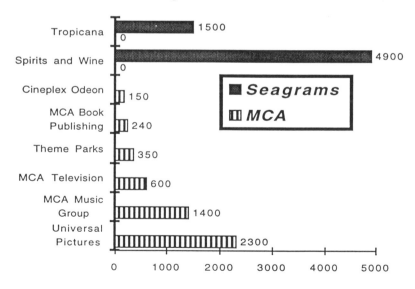

*Figure 6.5 MCA's estimated 1994 revenues include $2.3 billion for the Universal Pictures division; $1.4 billion for MCA's Music Group; $600 million from the television division; $350 million from theme parks; $240 million book publishing and $150 million generated by the 2,800 screen Cineplex theater operation. Seagram's revenues for 1994 are $4.9 billion from spirits and wine and $1.5 billion from sales of Tropicana fruit drinks.[23]*

## Polygram

*Polygram* is 75%-owned by the world's third largest electronics company, Philips Electronics of Holland. Philips is aggressively into research and development. It manufactured x-ray and radio tubes in the early 1900's and invented today's compact disc and the digital compact cassette.[24] Polygram is a mega entertainment corporation. Ancillary labels under Polygram include: A&M, Fontana, Island, Mercury, Motown, Phonogram, Polydor, Sonet, Nippon Phonogram, and Sir Andrew Lloyd Webbers' Really Useful Holdings. Polygram Films is also affiliated with Gramercy Pictures, Interscope, and Jodie Foster's Egg Pictures.[25]

Polygram expanded into the former Soviet Union with a 51% investment in Boris Zosimov's *Moscow's Biz Enterprises* in 1994. The label, Alien Records, distributes Polygram's products in Russia, which is plagued with a poor economy and high levels of record piracy. However, the Russian population of 180 million may develop into a huge entertainment market once the economy improves and copyright laws are tightened.[26]

Polygram and its affiliated label recording artists include Bryan Adams, Chris de Burgh, Billy Ray Cyrus, Sheryl Crow, Def Leppard, Marcella Detroit, John Mellencamp, Aaron Neville, Sting, and artists from the original London cast of <u>Phantom of The Opera</u>.

## Polygram Leads Global Recorded Music Sales

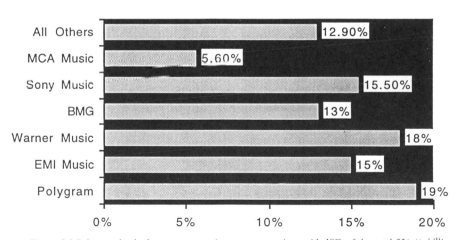

*Figure 6.6 Polygram leads the mega entertainment corporations with 19% of the total $25.15 billion 1994-5 recorded music global market. The other five mega's sales included Warner Music with 18%; Sony Music, 15.50%; EMI Music, 15%; BMG,13%; MCA, 5.6%; and all other non-affiliated independent record labels with 12.9%.[27]*

## Sony

*Sony Music Entertainment* is a wholly-owned subsidiary of the *Sony Corporation*, a $36 billion a year electronic software and hardware producer and manufacturer.[28] Sony bought CBS Records in 1988 for $3.5 billion and the film division (Columbia and TriStar Pictures) in 1989 for $4.5 billion. Affiliates are CHAOS Records, Epic, Epic Associated, Epic Soundtrax, Sony 550 Music, Sony Wonder, TriStar Music Group, Sony Tree Music Publishing, Sony Pictures Entertainment, the TriStar movie studios, Columbia Records, and Robert de Niro's Tribeca movie and film production company.[29]

The Sony Corporation has consolidated its entertainment acquisitions under the Sony Music Entertainment, Inc., Sony Pictures and Sony Electronic Publishing divisions. Sony Music Entertainment, Inc. is composed of three basic parts, which are then sub-divided into a complex network of interlinking companies. The three divisions are:

1. **Sony *Music***, headquartered in New York, which employs over 11,000 worldwide. It manufactures audio and video cassettes, CDs, minidisks and laserdiscs for Sony's affiliated record label products. *Sony Music Distribution* ships all the music products. *Sony Publishing* acquires and administers Sony's music publishing catalogues. *Sony Music Special Products* produces songs and music for special markets. *Sony Wonder* produces children's and family music, film and video productions. Sony Music also has a joint venture partnership with the other megas to sell its products through *The Columbia House* direct marketing operation.

2. **Sony *Music International***, headquartered in New York, employs over 6,000 worldwide. It has 35 subsidiaries, 4 joint ventures and 21 licensees worldwide. Labels include Copacabana, Raw, Rebenstein, Savannah, and Soho Square Records.

3. **Sony *Classical*** is the classical music division with headquarters in Hamburg, Germany. Labels include Masterworks, Sony Broadway, and Vivarte Records. Sony Classical Film and Video produces and distributes classical music, films, and documentaries.[30]

### Electronics Division

Sony's *electronics division* collects 75% of its revenues and about 50% of its operating income. It developed the Sony Walkman tape player, beta cam (8 mm) and video recorders. It recently developed the consumer recordable minidisk player.[31] Sony assembles its American consumer electronic products at manufacturing plants in San Diego. It shows many of its movies at its own *Loews* movie theaters throughout the United States. Sony makes both *Sega* and *Nintendo* video games and owns *Merv Griffen's Enterprises*, which produces the Jeopardy and Wheel of Fortune TV shows.[32] Sony Music and its affiliated labels' recording artists include: Basia, Michael Bolton, the Budapest String Quartet, Mariah Carey, Harry Connick Jr., Julio Iglesias, Michael Jackson, Isaac Stern, Barbra Streisand, The Spin Doctors, Yo-Yo Ma, and John Williams.

## 1994 Sony Corporation Sales

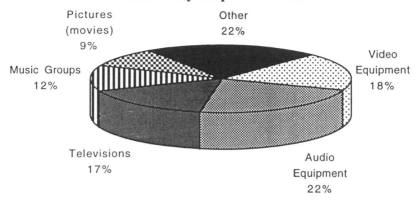

*Figure 6.7 Sony Corporation sales for 1994 reflected video equipment, 669 billion yen; audio sales, 841 billion yen; televisions, 618 billion yen; music group sales, 462 billion yen; Sony Pictures, 328 billion yen; and other, which included the sales of semiconductors, electronic components, information-related floppy disk systems, etc., 817 billion yen (the exchange rate is approximately 100 yen to one U.S. dollar).[33]*

## Time Warner

In 1989, Time Publications and Warner Communications International exchanged stock and money to merge into *Time Warner, Inc.*[34] Time, Inc. was started in 1922 by Briton Hadden and Henry Luce. In addition to Time Magazine, it published Life and other social and business periodicals. *Warner Bros.* was founded by Harry, Jack and Sam Warner in the late 1920's. Classic movies produced included "Casablanca" and "Rebel Without a Cause."[35] In the 1989 merger, Time Publications received 17.3 million shares of Warner Communication International stock. Time also purchased another 100 million shares. Warner Communication received 7 million shares of Time stock. The total cost of the merger was $14.3 billion of which $8.3 billion were loans. In 1991, Time Warner sold 6.5% of the company to *Toshiba* of Japan (1991 gross sales of over $30 billion) and another 6.5% to *C. Itoh* of Japan (the world's largest trading company with 1991 annual sales of over $151 billion).[36]

## Time Warner's Owners

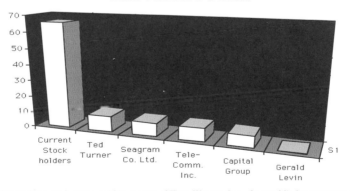

*Figure 6.8 Ted Turner became a 10% owner of Time Warner, Inc., the world's largest music entertainment company by selling his Turner Broadcasting, Inc. to Time Warner for $8 billion in September of 1995. Gerald Levin owns less than 1 percent which is represented in the above graph as 0%.[37]*

Time Warner is betting on advanced technology, which combines computers, telephones, and cable TV systems to deliver music and entertainment programming through interactive shopping directly to consumers' homes. It has developed an interactive cable system and a wireless telephone system as new market opportunities.[38] Thus, Time Warner will be able to digitally deliver its music, TV shows, and films directly to the consumers. *Warner Music Group,* which owns 50% of the Columbia House Record Club, expects its direct sales to increase by 30% within five years. Warner Music also provides satellite music into homes through established cable TV systems.

## Warner Music Sales

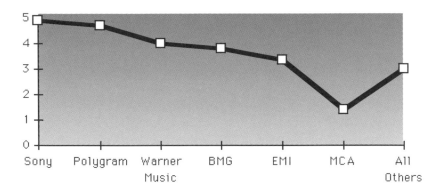

*Figure 6.9 Warner Music ranks third in 1994-95 world recorded music sales with $4 billion. Other megas estimated sales include Sony Music, $4.9 billion; Polygram, $4.7 billion; BMG, $3.8 billion; EMI, $3.35 billion; MCA Music, $1.4 billion; and all other record labels, $3 billion.[39]*

## Overseas Product Sales

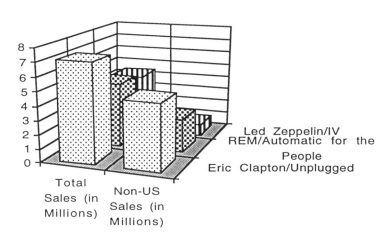

*Figure 6.10 Fifty-five percent of Warner Music's 1993 record sales were from overseas sources. Two examples include: Eric Claptons' "Unplugged" which sold a total of 7.1 million units, of which 4.77 million units were sold overseas. REM's "Automatic For The People" moved 4.64 million units, 2.43 million foreign sales. However, Led Zeppelin's album "IV" sold 4.3 million units in the U.S. and less than a million overseas.[40]*

Time Warner owns the *Six Flags* theme parks, has a joint venture with Polygram, Sony, and EMI for the *VIVA Music Video network* in Germany, and may merge with Rupert Murdoch's Star TV to gain Asian cable and broadcast TV access.[41] Time Warner also owns *Warner Bros. Films* and *Cartoons, Home Box Office (HBO),* and *Time Warner Cable systems.*

## Time Warner Revenues

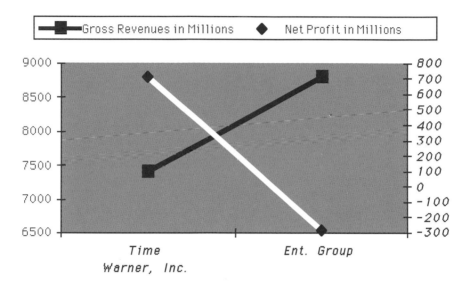

*Figure 6.11 In 1994-5, Warner Music's net revenues were $713 million on gross revenues of $7.3 billion. The film, cable and programming side of the company (Time Warner Entertainment Group-green line) had a net loss of (-287) million on an income of $8.7 billion. Warner Music's profits were almost 9 times greater than the Entertainment Group's losses and were used to cover the expenditures.* [42]

Time Warner has made an $8 billion bid for Ted Turner's news and entertainment companies. When completed, Turner Broadcasting Systems, Inc. will add approximately $2.8 billion in gross revenues and $22 million in profits to the annual Time Warner profit and loss statement. Turner's holdings include the TBS Superstation, TNT cable network, The Cartoon Network, New Line and Castle Rock movie production studios, Hanna-Barbera Cartoons, Headline News, CNN, and CNN International, plus the Atlanta Braves baseball franchise.

Warner Music has approximately 40 owned or affiliate labels, some of which are: A*Vision Entertainment, Atco, Asylum, Atlantic, Chameleon, Eastwest Records America, Elektra Entertainment and Electra Nonesuch, Paisley Park Records, The Medicine Label, Rhino, Sire, Third Stone, Warner Bros. Records, Warner Bros. Nashville International, Warner New Media, Warner Special Products, WEA Corp., and WEA Manufacturing. It has over 170 worldwide offices and divisions distributing products.[43]

*Warner/Chappell Music* is one of the world's largest music publishers.

*Warner Direct* serves non-retail customers and its 50% of the Columbia House Record and Video Club.[44]   Warner Music and its affiliated labels' recording artists include: Phil Collins, Huey Lewis and The News, Little Texas, Metallica, The Eagles, Joan Jett, Rod Stewart, Rush, and Dwight Yoakam.[45]

## DreamWorks/Disney ABC

A seventh mega entertainment organization may develop from the latest business venture of Jeffrey Katzenberg, David Geffen and Steven Spielberg. The three entertainment "movers and shakers" have formed a new digital interactive company that will combine creative artists with the money and power of Bill Gate's Microsoft computer software company.  The company has tentatively been titled *DreamWorks* and will include the production and distribution of movies, music, television shows, computer and interactive CD-ROM entertainment programming.  DreamWorks has signed to work with ABC Television. The merger of Disney and ABC Television (Capital Cities) with the efforts of DreamWorks may make the new Disney/ABC company the world's seventh mega entertainment corporation.  The new company has estimated 1995 revenues of $19.3 billion, with a cash flow of $4.6 billion.  The merger combines *Walt Disney Pictures* and *Touchstone Pictures* with *ABC Production.*  Disney's record label will be combined with ABC, ESPN, Lifetime, A&E, and The Disney cable TV channels, plus newspapers in 13 states, book and magazine publishers Fairchild and Chilton Publications, 11 TV stations, 228 affiliate TV stations, and 21 radio stations.[46]

## Summary

There are currently six mega entertainment corporations that control approximately 88% of the western and free world's contemporary entertainment industry.  They are BMG of Germany, MCA owned by Seagrams of Canada, Sony of Japan, Polygram based in the Netherlands, Thorn EMI of England, and the sole American entity of Time Warner.  Most superstars and famous recording artists are signed with major or affiliated record labels that are either owned or subordinate to one of the six mega entertainment corporations.   Spielberg, Katzenberg, and Geffen's new venture enterprise *DreamWorks* combined with Disney/ABC Television and the leading computer software company Microsoft Corporation may develop into a seventh mega.

Mega entertainment corporations are regularly divided into divisions that horizontally and vertically connect major and affiliate companies.  The megas do not all have the same business structures, however, most have interlinking companies that produce, publicize, promote, market, and distribute entertainment products.  As an example, a typical mega corporation will have an *entertainment division* to house the movie, TV, film companies, record labels and computer game businesses.  The *print media division* offers consumer magazines, newspapers, and trade papers to promote and publicize artists, movies, TV shows, and musical recordings.  The *distribution division* supplies the products to consumer retail and mass media outlets.  Finally, the *consumer electronic division* makes radios, TV, VCRs computers and musical instruments.

## Chapter Footnotes

[1] 1994 EMI Annual Report (1994).

[2] The Music Business World Report (1993).

[3] Due to their global structuring and dominance in the entertainment industry, industry insiders are starting to refer to the six largest entertainment companies as "mega entertainment corporations."

[4] Business Week (March 6,1995) and Company Reports (1995).

[5] Company Reports and Hoover Company Profiles (1996).

[6] Major labels are defined as components of a mega entertainment corporation.  Their sole purpose is to create profits from the creation, manufacturing, distribution, promotion, publicity, and marketing of recorded musical products.

[7] Bertelsmann, A World of Expression (1994) Summary from brochure distributed by Bertelsmann AG: Corporate Communications and Public Affairs Carl-Bertelsmann-StraBe 270 D-3311 Gutersloh.

[8] Making the World Go Round: (1994) Bertelsmann brochure distributed by Bertelsmann AG: Corporate Communications and Public Affairs Carl-Bertelsmann-StraBe 270 D-3311 Gutersloh.

[9] Ibid.

[10] Company Reports and Hoover Company Profiles (1996).

[11] Hoover Company Profile Database, and The Reference Press, Inc. (1996).

[12] Thorn EMI 93 Annual Report Thorn EMI London (1994).

[13] "In Focus: Virgin Group," Steve Redmond (Editor) MBI (1994).

[14] "Local Acts Go Global," Steve Redmond (Editor) MBI (1994).

[15] Affiliated record labels are often co-owned or financed by a mega or major record label.  They offer the megas and major labels alternative artists and niche markets.

[16] Ibid.

[17] Hoover Company Profile Database, and The Reference Press, Inc. (1996).

[18] "Tradition be damned, Matsushita's radical restructuring has it well on the way to a turnaround," Robert Neff, Business Week (1994).

[19] "The Mogul, Just How Risky is Edgar Bronfman Jr's Hollywood Gamble?" Michael O'Neal, Ronald Grover and William C. Symonds, Business Week (April 24, 1995).

[20] Hoover's Handbook of World Business (1993).

[21] Venues are usually halls or auditoriums used by music promoters to hold concerts, presentations, dances, etc.  Sizes range from major league sports auditoriums to small dance halls and bars.

[22] The Music Business World Report (1993 & 1994).

[23] "The Mogul, Just How Risky is Edgar Bronfman Jr's Hollywood Gamble?" Michael O'Neal, Ronald Grover and William C. Symonds, Business Week (April 24, 1995).

[24] Hoover's Company Profiles and The Reference Press, Inc., Austin, TX (1996).

[25] The Music Business World Report (1993 & 1994).

[26] "Charting New Ground in Russia," Steve Redmond (Editor) MBI (1994).

[27] Information gathered from company Annual Reports, Soundscan and Business Week.  Business Week, Paula Dwyer, Margaret Dawson and Dexter Roberts (January 15, 1996).

[28] News from Sony Music Entertainment, Inc. Corporate Communications release (1994).

[29] The Music Business World Report (1993) and News from Sony Music Entertainment, Inc. Corporate Communications release (1994).

[30] News from Sony Music Entertainment, Inc. Corporate Communications release (1994).

[31] The Music Business World Report (1993 & 1994) and "C. Itoh, Toshiba to pump $1 billion into Time-Warner," Bob Deans, The Nashville Tenneasean (Oct. 30, 1991).

[32] "Creating a Seamless Company," Seth Lubove and Neil Weinberg, Forbes Magazine (1993).

[33] Sony Annual Report (1994).

[34] The Music Business World Report (1993).

[35] Company Annual Report and Hoovers Company Profiles (1996).

[36] "C. Itoh, Toshiba to pump $1 billion into Time-Warner," Bob Deans The Nashville Tenneasean (Oct. 30, 1991).

[37] "Dream deal still faces many hurdles," Skip Wollenberg Associated Press as reported in The Tennessean, "Business" page 1E, (September 23, 1995).

[38] "Now Time Warner is a Phone Company," Mark Landler, Mark Lewyn and Kathy Rebello, <u>Business Week</u> (1994).

[39] Information gathered from company Annual Reports, Soundscan and <u>Business Week</u> Magazine. <u>Business Week</u>, Paula Dwyer, Margaret Dawson and Dexter Roberts (January 15, 1996).

[40] "Warner Prepares for the Future," Steve Redmond (Editor) <u>MBI</u> (1994).

[41] "Warner Prepares for the Future," Steve Redmond (Editor) <u>MBI</u> (1994).

[42] Corporate Reports and <u>Hoover Company Profiles</u> (1996).

[43] <u>Warner Music International Directory</u> (1993).

[44] <u>The Music Business World Report</u> (1994).

[45] "The Billboard 200," Mega label record artists as listed by <u>Billboard Magazine</u> (1994).

[46] "Disney's Kingdom: As seismic shifts shake the media biz, Eisner lands on top-for now," Michael O'Neal, Stephen Baker, and Ronald Grover; <u>Business Week</u> (August 14, 1995).

# 7

# RECORD LABELS

**Operating Structures
Major Labels
Affiliated Labels
Independent Labels
Artists Deals**

Major labels use the megas' money to finance their operations and album projects, the megas' mass media and print media to promote and publicize their artists, and the megas' distribution systems to sell their albums worldwide to consumers through direct, retail and rental outlets.

| BMG | EMI | MCA | Polygram | Sony | Time Warner |
|---|---|---|---|---|---|
| Ariola | Capitol | MCA | Polydor | CBS | Warner Bros. |
| Arista | | Geffen | Mercury | Epic | Asylum |
| RCA | | | | Sony | Elektra |
| | | | | | Atlantic |
| | | | | | Reprise |

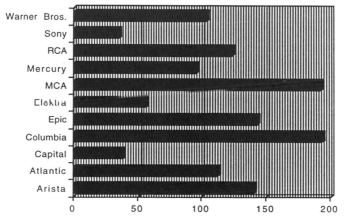

*Figure 7.1 Examples of 1994 top major record labels include Arista with 141 charted singles and albums; Capital, 38; Epic, 143; MCA, 192; RCA, 123; and Warner Bros. Records, 103.*[1]

## Major Labels

Major record labels are divided into functional departments which have their own autonomy, yet interlinking responsibilities. They must accomplish their individual missions, yet work together with the other label departments to accomplish the strategic mission of the label, which is, of course, to create and sell recorded music.

*Figure 7.2 Major record labels combine the creative and business sides of the industry into lean, entrepreneurial organizations. Labels, which are integral components of mega entertainment corporations, are usually led by a Chairperson of the Board or a Chief Executive Officer. The President oversees the daily operations of the label, department Vice Presidents supervise their individual areas. The Legal Department offers an official communication link between the creative and business components of the label. Other lines of communication transpire through memos and weekly sales, promotional and administrative meetings. Notice that music publishing is both creative (songwriting, demo recording, etc.) and business (collection of royalties including mechanicals, etc.).*

## Departments

A typical major record label might have the following departments or duties combined into one or two departments.

(1) ***Artists and Repertoire:*** A&R is the communicative link between the

label's creative and business sub-systems. They have one foot in the creative side and one foot in the business side. Their decisions about which acts and songs to sign are often based on research, past experiences, and consumer reaction. The profitability and survival of the label often depends on the decisions made by A&R.

A&R brings the acts to the label and administers the paperwork of an album project. Accordingly, A&R is often divided into two sections, creative and administrative. Creative A&R is the "ears" of the label, always searching for a new act or song that will help make the label (and themselves) more profitable. It is not an easy job. Between a half million to one million dollars are spent on "breaking" a new recording artist.[2] However, having musical and vocal talent does not guarantee a "hit recording." Consequently, A&R directors seek the types of acts who not only have talent, but who can also sell records. There is a difference, and record labels make and lose millions of dollars each year on which acts they sign and *connect* with the music-buying public.

Recordings are actually "packages" consisting of a great song that fits the image and persona of the artists, and an excellent vocal and musical performance by the artists and musicians, supervised by the session producer and "captured" on tape or computer by an audio engineer. Recordings may or may not fit or connect with the public, leaving the record company responsible for the session, marketing, and distribution expenses.

Accordingly, A&R employees often risk their careers on the acts and songs they sign. Successful acts establish the credibility of the A&R person who signed them. Failures can cost them their jobs. Successful signings provide additional record producing opportunities. Album productions enhance the A&R person's status as a record producer within the company and industry. Multiple successful signings and session productions (with the corresponding gold and platinum records) make the A&R/producer a powerful, very rich individual, often famous within the industry.

To avoid being a casualty of a poor decision, many labels make their "final" signing decision by committee consensus. The committee consists of the label's vice presidents of each department, the A&R person presenting the act, and the label's president or chairman of the board. Committee decisions made as a team effort offer the label an opportunity to use the *total quality management* (TQM) method to develop their strategic management plan for the act and label.[3] The purpose is to involve everyone (all the label employees) *as a team* to campaign for the success of the artists and their respective recordings.

## A&R Process

Record labels' A&R departments are the funnel between the creative and business sub-systems of the music business. Songwriters create songs, musicians and vocalists record demos, and then the writers pitch the tapes to music publishers. They select only the best songs to re-record and pitch to the record labels, producers, and artists managers, often through the A&R departments. Songs selected by A&R are evaluated for album projects and pitched to the recording production team, consisting of the producer, artists, and artists' managers. Labels budget and pay for the recording expenses, which they hope to recoup from record sales (see chapters 8 through 14). Accepted master tapes are pressed into consumer products (CDs, cassettes, minidisks) and distributed, marketed, and promoted through the mass media to generate sales.

## Sage Window

" *When I was signing Guns N' Roses, they stood out from everybody else. Now, there are hundreds of Guns N' Roses clones. If a band is trying to design their look after Guns N' Roses, I wouldn't look upon that favorably.*"[4]

**– Tom Zutaut, Director of A&R, Geffen Records**

**(2)** *Music Publishing:* Major labels use their own music publishing companies to promote and place their songs with their own artists. Most songs selected for album projects are funneled through the label's A&R department. Mechanical royalties are paid from the mega's major record labels to the same mega's music publishing companies. Performance royalties are collected by ASCAP, BMI, SESAC, foreign performance rights organizations and split internally between the mega's patriarchal labels and music publishing companies.[5] Sync rights are often reduced or paid between the TV and movie production companies within the same mega entertainment corporation. Of course, non-mega, published songs are often accepted. Songs are first considered on their "hit potential qualities," not on who owns the copyright. However, most record labels apply "pressure" to the non-major label or non-mega-affiliated publishing company to accept the controlled composition clause on any songs selected for recording.

## Sage Window

" *I was happy to have any deal. No other label would sign us. So it wasn't like we had a lot of choices.*"[6]

**– Arrested Development**

**(3)** *The Legal Department***:** The Legal Department is responsible for writing, negotiating, and (a) signing songwriters or their songs, (b) signing co-publishing deals, (c) signing new and returning recording artists, (d) signing label employees' government forms, (e) negotiating mechanical, performance, sync. and other licenses with domestic and foreign agencies, and (f) representing the label in legal actions. Accordingly, attorneys negotiate the "terms of agreement" between the creative and business sub-system players of this creative music and business village. Most labels have one or more attorneys on the staff full-time. Others have attorneys on retainer, which is a monthly stipend for their part-time employment.

**(4)** *Creative Development:* Creative Development is often divided into artist

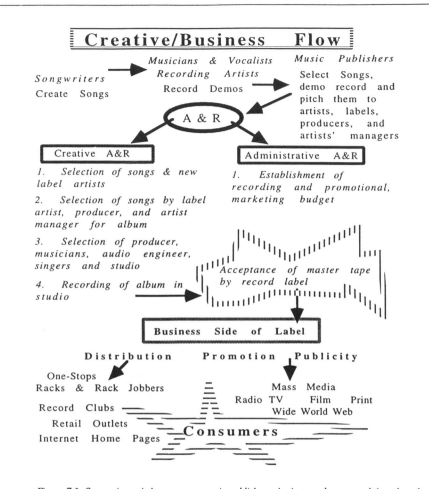

**Creative/Business Flow**

*Songwriters Create Songs*

*Musicians & Vocalists Recording Artists Record Demos*

*Music Publishers* Select Songs, demo record and pitch them to artists, labels, producers, and artists' managers

A & R

**Creative A&R**

*1. Selection of songs & new label artists*

*2. Selection of songs by label artist, producer, and artist manager for album*

*3. Selection of producer, musicians, audio engineer, singers and studio*

*4. Recording of album in studio*

**Administrative A&R**

*1. Establishment of recording and promotional, marketing budget*

*Acceptance of master tape by record label*

**Business Side of Label**

**Distribution**

One-Stops
Racks & Rack Jobbers
Record Clubs
Retail Outlets
Internet Home Pages

**Promotion**

**Publicity**

Mass Media
Radio TV Film Print
Wide World Web

**Consumers**

*Figure 7.3 Songwriters pitch songs to a music publisher, who in turn demo record the selected songs and pitch them to the labels through A&R. Songs selected are pitched to label artists for album projects. Once the master tape is accepted, the business side of the label presses and distributes the CDs, cassettes, etc. to retail and promotes and publicizes the artist and record through the mass media.*

and product development. Creative Development supervises both and combines their individual efforts into the label's marketing plan for the artists. Creative Development also acts as *Video Commission* for the label by assigning music video projects to video production companies. They supervise the script treatments, budgets, production, and provide the finished videos to the marketing department for promotion.

**(5)** *Artist Development:* Specialists are often hired to improve the artist's image, appearance, demeanor, and public personality. Trainers are hired to help the artist to control a weight problem, dentists to improve the smile, beauticians to suggest various types of cosmetics for television appearances, image consultants to suggest methods to help the act appear comfortable and confident with the news media.

**(6) *Product Development/Management:*** Product Development supervises and coordinates the development of the label's actual album projects. They coordinate the label's efforts to assure a successful launch of the *product* on radio and in retail markets. Product development coordinates the label's promotion efforts with the artist-manager-approved tour dates. Product Development makes sure that records are in the stores, point-of-purchase promotions are available, and that the marketing and promotion departments are filling the local papers and magazines with stories about the label's artists.

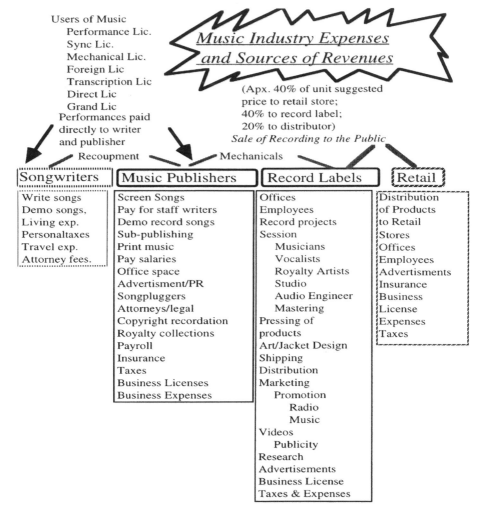

Figure 7.4 Publishers and labels put up a lot of money to create recordings they can sell to the public. The sale of the recordings by the labels and the issuing of licenses by the music publishers generate the revenues required to pay salaries, royalties, and the daily business operations and expenses.

The administrative supervision of the actual physical manufacturing of the CDs, minidisks, DCCs, cassettes, and videos at pressing plants is often considered the responsibility of *Product Management*. Video manufacturing is usually subbed out to a high-speed duplicating company. CDs, minidisks, DCCs, and cassettes are produced at pressing plants in the U.S., Asia, and Europe for distribution to retail and direct outlets.

(7) *Administration:*  The label CEO, President, and Vice Presidents work together, after the initial signing of an act, to suggest a producer, establish a budget, and develop a marketing plan for the act. A *strategic allegiance* is usually established with the artist's manager. It is notable that the manager must be careful not to let his or her association with the label executives become a conflict of interest with the recording artists they represent.[7] They must make pro-active decisions first in support of their artist and also the label. A sellable product (a recording) has to be created, and the artist's image frequently has to be enhanced. In pre-production, the recording artist, producer, artist's manager, and A&R representative determine which songs, musicians, and recording studio to use.[8] After the master tape is recorded and accepted by the label, a marketing plan that coordinates publicity, promotion, distribution, and sales is activated.

Upper level administrators are responsible for the development and implementation of a strategic management plan. This includes the development of a vision and mission statement, short- and long-term personal and financial goals, the organization's internal policies and objectives, and the responsibility of a continuous internal and external analysis.[9]

Administrators review the sales projections and accomplishments of each of the label's recording artists and personnel. Artists failing to achieve profitable unit sales are customarily dropped from the label after a couple of record releases. The label will fulfill their contractual obligations and simply not pick up their option to resign the artist. Artists who are not satisfied with a label may often "buyout" of their contract by mutual agreement, one lump sum payment, or future artist royalties generated from another label's agreement. However, successful artists often find it very difficult to terminate a current agreement. Court action is often required and rarely approved. Obviously, major labels have spent millions to make an artist successful, and they do not appreciate an artist who wants to jump to another label after the hard work of the label's employees and money has been spent to make the artist famous.

Label employees who fail to sign or generate profitable products or sales are encouraged to improve. After continued declines in profits, both productive and non-productive employees are commonly dismissed. It is not uncommon for the entire staff of a major label to be replaced if the label is not producing profitable acts and recordings.

(8) *Distribution*:  Once the master tapes have been accepted and pressed into consumer products, the mega's own distribution division ships the CDs, minidisks, etc. to wholesalers, including rack jobbers, one-stops, mass merchandis-

ers, chain stores, and TV packagers. Label distribution provides products directly to record clubs. Mega distributors include *BMG Distribution,* which ships, as an example, Arista and RCA Records; *CEMA* distributes EMI products; *MCA (UNI)* distributes its own MCA and Geffen Records; *Polygram Distribution (PGD)* ships Polygram, A&M Records and others; *Sony Music Distribution* ships CBS, Columbia, and Epic Records; and *WEA* distributes Atlantic, Elektra, and Warner Bros. Records.[10]

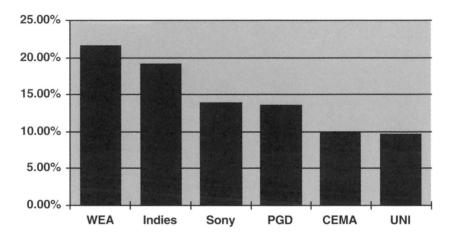

*Figure 7.5 The mega entertainment corporations have their own distribution systems. Total U.S. market share for 1995 by distribution includes WEA, 21.6%; Independent distributors, 19.2%; Sony, 13.9%; PDG, 13.5%; BMG, 12.4%; CEMA, 9.8%; and UNI, 9.7%.[11]*

**(9) *Marketing/Sales:*** Marketing and Sales often scrutinize the distribution of the label's products into direct and retail outlets. The process includes: (a) the transportation, warehousing, ordering and inventory of the label's products; (b) the implementation of consumer research data to ensure that the right products are available to the right types of customers (consumer preference research); (c) the development of industry standards for the CDs, minidisks, cassettes, and videos the labels are selling; and (d) assistance in the development of a marketing plan that will ensure the proper amount of marketing mix of products, pricing, and products available to various channels of distribution.[12]

**(10) *Promotion & Publicity:*** Record promotion is handled as a campaign with most of the label's efforts being focused on breaking a new release to radio stations. In addition, the labels often hire *independent promoters* to motivate local radio station airplay and retail sales. *Publicity,* which helps drive promotion, includes artists' appearances on TV talk shows (i.e., Jay Leno, David Letterman, Good Morning America, Crook & Chase, etc.) and the stories, pictures, and articles publicists plant in local newspapers, national trade and consumer magazines. Publicity is often thought of as free promotion because the artists do not have to pay for the stories, pictures, and articles used in the mass media. Nevertheless, most stories are really *supplied* to the mass media by a professional publicist who is paid by the label or artist through the artist's manager.[13]

**(11)** *International Divisions*: International coordinates the label's releases with foreign-affiliated labels, performance rights organizations, mechanical collection agencies, and the mega's other foreign entertainment divisions.

**(12)** *The Personnel/Payroll Department:* The Personnel/Payroll Department pays the bills and royalties, accepts sales payments, and reviews artist's recoupments. Most expenses are billed to the artist's accounts and are recouped through album sales. Accountants add the recording costs and label expenses (artists development, photography, tour support, and most of the marketing, promotion, etc.) to the recording artist's ledger. Artist royalties are paid only after the negotiated label expenses for the recording, marketing of the album, and all additional expenses (tour support, etc.) have been repaid from unit sales. Artists are regularly supplied quarterly or semi-annual *profit and loss statements* through their manager.

## Affiliate Labels

The megas offer financing, promotion and marketing of *affiliate label* products through the mega's distribution systems, print media, and film offerings. In exchange, the affiliate labels offer the mega entertainment corporations distribution of the mega's recording artists, videos, and albums in various niche or foreign territories. Most affiliate labels were originally started as independent labels by entrepreneur producers or recording artists. Examples include: Herb Alpert and Jerry Moss of A & M Records, David Geffen of Elektra and Geffen Records, Berry Gordy of Motown Records, recording artists Prince and his

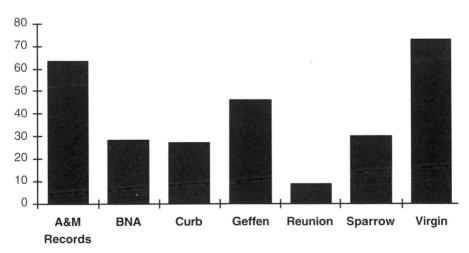

*Figure 7.6 Top affiliate labels include A&M Records with 63 charted singles and albums in 1994; BNA, 28; Curb Records, 27; Geffen Records, 46; Reunion Records, 9; Sparrow Records, 30; and Virgin Records with 73.*[14]

Paisley Park Records, Billy Ray Hearn's Sparrow Records, Blanton and Harrell's Reunion Records, Mike Curb of Curb Records, and Richard Branson's Virgin Records.

## Independent Labels

Even the best independent recordings of excellent quality rarely muster sales of more than a few thousand units through independent distribution. However, independent releases that "catch on" with the public through word-of-mouth, local radio station airplay, publicity, and sales may be "picked up" (signed) by an affiliate, major record label, or a major distribution company. Some recordings of classical, Christian, folk, rap, jazz, new wave, and alternative music are perceived as vanity record label products. Songwriters, music publishers, producers, movie studios and recording studio owners often form *independent record labels* to distribute their own otherwise unsigned recordings. The *indies* offer niche music formats perceived as too small for mass distribution and high front-end expenses of the major and affiliate labels. Sam Phillips, who owned Sun Records in Memphis, sold his interest in Elvis Presley to RCA Records for $30,000. He used the money for development of other acts (Johnny Cash, Carl Perkins and many others) and for business investments.[15]

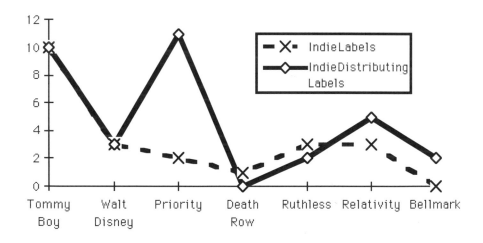

*Figure 7.7 Top independent labels include Tommy Boy with 10 charted albums; Walt Disney, 3; Priority, 2; Death Row, 1; and Ruthless, 3. Top independent distributing labels (labels who distribute their own products and some additional indie labels) include Priority with 11 charted albums; Tommy Boy, 10; Walt Disney, 3; Relativity, 5; and Bellmark, 2.[16]*

Repeat success with several artists will grab the attention of a mega entertainment organization. They may strike a deal with the indie to make it an affiliate label by monetarily supporting and interfacing its releases with the mega's distribution and publicity networks. Eventually, a mega may outright purchase a successful independent label to acquire its boilerplate name, its artists, and the master recordings.

The difference between an independent label and an affiliated label is often blurred. Some of the independents may be financed by a major label, yet be distributed by themselves or an independent distributor.[17] Others may finance themselves, yet have a distribution deal with a major label or an mega entertainment organization. Others release soundtracks from their films through their video distribution systems.[18]

## Top Charted Labels

According to *The Year in Music* by <u>Billboard Magazine</u>, the following are examples of the top record labels as ranked by the number of charted singles and album releases in 1995.

**Distinguished Record Labels**

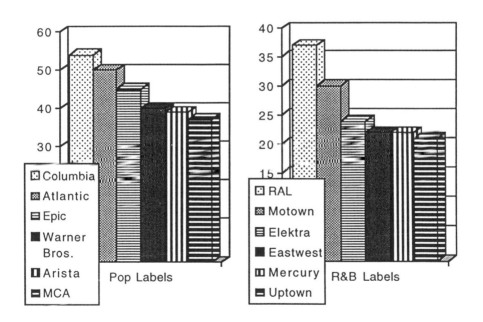

*Figure 7.8 Columbia Records leads the pop labels with 54 singles and albums charted. Other 1995 leading pop labels include Atlantic Records, 50; Epic 45; Warner Bros., 40; Arista, 39; and MCA, 37. Top R&B labels include RAL, 37, Motown, 30; Elektra, 24; Eastwest, 22; Mercury, 22; and Uptown, 21.[19]*

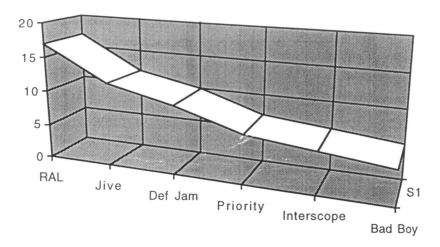

*Figure 7.9 RAL lead the 1995 Rap labels with 17 charted singles and albums. Others include Jive, 12; Def Jam, 10; Priority, 7; Interscope, 6; and Bad Boy, 5.*[20]

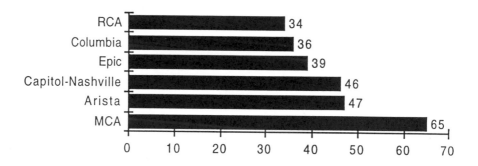

*Figure 7.10 MCA leads the country labels with 65 singles and albums charted in 1995. Others include: Arista, 47; Capitol-Nashville, 46; Epic, 39; Columbia, 36; and RCA with 34.*[21]

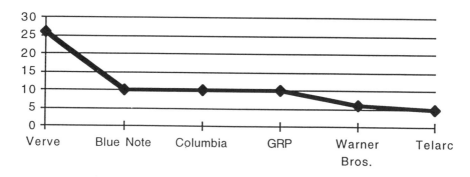

*Figure 7.11 Top 1995 Jazz labels based on charted albums includes: Verve, 26; Blue Note, 10; Columbia, 10; GRP, 10; Warner Bros., 6; and Telarc, 5.*[22]

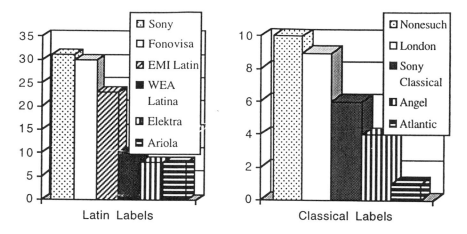

*Figure 7.12 Top Latin labels, based on the number of charted albums, include Sony with 31; Fonovisa, 30; EMI Latin, 23; WEA Latina, 10; and Elektra and Ariola, both with 8. Top classical labels based on charted albums in 1995 include Nonesuch, 10; London, 9; Sony Classical, 6; Angel, 4; and Atlantic, 1.*[23]

## Types of Deals

There are several types of recording agreements perspective artists can negotiate with the industry. They include music publishing demo recording, development, independent and major record label contracts, and even vanity "self-promotional" pacts.

**(1)** *Music Publishing Demo Recording Deals:* Music publishers offer promising vocalists with songwriting abilities opportunities to record their songs and develop their image. The publishers pitch the demo tapes to record labels in exchange for a percentage of artist profits if and when they are signed by an independent or major label. Publishers feel that since they spent the money to develop and record an artist, once the artist secures a record deal, they are entitled to a percentage of the artist's profits. Sometimes, a label will "buy out" the publisher's interest in an artist with a one-time lump sum of money. The publisher (or managers, producers, etc. who discovered and helped develop the act) relinquishes all future rights to the artists and their image in exchange for the negotiated amount of money. Self-proclaimed *talent agents* work the same way. They find and develop talent and then are "bought out" by the label. However, talent agents who pressure artists to invest their own money are not often considered legitimate by the industry.

**(2)** *Development Deals:* Record labels offer development deals to talented vocalists, groups, and bands they perceive as having the potential to develop into a major recording act. It's a chance for the artists to professionally develop their talent at the label's expense. The label pays for extra musicians, studio time, audio engineer, tapes, and producer. If the final *master tape* is accepted, the act is offered a recording contract. The cost of the recording is recouped through record sales.  If it is rejected, the recording is often used as a tax write-off.

(3) *Independent Label Deals*: Indie record labels, who have some form of retail distribution, offer novice recording artists and musicians the opportunity to be recorded and distributed.  *Amateur recording artists, musicians,* and *producers* often work together (and share the expenses) to record albums that can be used to promote a band, generate a local buzz, and sell off the bandstand at a live performance.  *Former major label artists* usually retain the names and addresses of their fan club members and then use the lists to sell their self-produced tapes and CDs.  *Alternative* music formats are often self-produced on computers and sold at conventions, festivals, church services, and concerts.  *Regional* and *genre* independent record labels sign recording artists who may only have a niche client base in a specific region of the country or genre of music.  Examples include Jerry Jeff Walker of Texas, artists on the formerly independent Windham Hill label, and bands specializing in *Latino music* or *Carolina Beach music*.  Major labels offer successful regional and genre labels affiliate status or often buy out the labels to gain the successful recording artists' contracts.  This happened with GRP Records, Jive Records, Reunion, Rhino, Sparrow, and Windham Hill Records.

(4) *Major Record Label Deals:*  There are no standard recording agreements offered by major labels.  Recording deals are negotiated by attorneys who represent the artists and label.  Each agreement is unique and tailored to the specific requirements of the label and artists.  Terms may vary from a single, one-time release to a multiple album, several-year obligation for both parties.

(5) *Vanity Label Deals:*  Recording artists and musicians who want to record albums, yet cannot acquire an independent, demo, development or major record label deal create their own "self" deals.  They pay for all expenses or find an investor who will pay for the studio musicians, studio rental, audio engineer, producer, mastering, marketing, promotion, and pressing of the CDs and cassettes.  Most vanity recordings lose money because they fail to receive radio station airplay and cannot generate enough sales to cover the production costs.  Successful vanity labels often become independent labels once they have established distribution alliances with record chain stores.

(6) **The Shark Deal** (similar to the song shark deal): Both are considered rip-offs.  Recording artists should never pay money for a recording contract.  It's the record label who pays the bills, takes the risks, and provides tour support money.  A legitimate label will cover the cost of recording, pressing of the CDs, etc. and market, promote, and advertise the artists and recordings.  Distribution is important for the success of an album.  If a label isn't affiliated or connected with a mega entertainment corporation or a major record label, it will have a very hard time placing recordings into retail outlets.  And, the only way legitimate record companies make money is by selling their recordings to the public, not from any money the artists paid to be signed to the label.

## Key Recording Contract Jargon

Exclusive recording agreements between artists and record labels are often complex, lengthy and confusing. It's not unusual for an agreement to be 75 to 100 pages. Here are some important issues every contract should address:

### • *Advances:*

*Recording artists are obligated for all the expenses incurred in the production and manufacturing of the master tapes.*[24] Fees include union scale for the royalty artist (paid for the actual recording), vocalists, arrangers, conductors, orchestrators, contractors, copyists, and studio musicians, plus salaries for the producers and audio engineers, and the cost of the studio rental, rehearsal hall, cartage, tapes, and per diem expenses. The record label will agree to pay to the recording artist, upon the acceptance of the master tapes, all the monies required (within negotiated limits) to pay for the cost of the recordings of the master tapes. If the master tapes are deemed unacceptable, the artist is still responsible for the initial cost of the recordings. Record project funds also include marketing, promotion, and publicity enhancement of the album and artist's career. Other funds are budgeted for concert tour support, equipment, and staging. However, *most advances are deemed recoupable from the artist's royalties from record sales.* Therefore, it is important to note, *that until the label's monetary advances are repaid, the artist will not receive any royalties.* In addition, if the artist spends more than the negotiated limits on the recording project, the additional expenses are often considered to be the artist's debt, not the label's. Labels usually pay for the mastering or converting of the digital tape to a matrix for CDs and split the cost of the music videos with the artist.[25]

### • *Audits:*

Record labels usually grant the recording artist (and the representing accountant) the *right to audit* the label's "books." It requires a 30- to 60-day notice, and the accountant will often be paid 10% of any additional royalties or "funds" collected.

### • *Controlled Compositions:*

Record labels habitually want to save money on album projects. One method is to pay only 75% of the statutory mechanical rate for any songs used on a signed royalty artist's recording. While the clause allows the record labels to pay 25% less for the songs on a recording, it provides the artist(s) with another source of income.[26] *Under the controlled composition clause, any royalty artist(s) who owns, controls, writes or co-wrote a song, used on their album, will receive a portion of the mechanical royalties.* In addition, the artist's label will automatically qualify to pay the reduced controlled composition mechanical rate or 75% of the statutory rate. In effect, the original writer(s) and publisher(s) forfeit 25% of their potential mechanical royalties while the artist(s) is paid part of the 75% of the mechanical royalties on songs they didn't create. The labels pay 25% less for the songs in the form of reduced mechanical fees, which are converted into profits.  This process may seem unfair to the original songwriter(s) and music publisher(s), however, it's important to remember that labels commonly risk one-half to one million dollars on albums and artists.  The controlled composition clause is a way for the label, writers, and publishers to share in the fundamental financial risks of doing business in this industry.  The artist is also risking their fame and long-term career by the selection of songs they decide to record and place on their albums.  Successful unit sales delivers shared profits to all the players, while failure forecasts shortened artistic careers.

### • Copyright Owner:

The recording artists, musicians, producers, audio engineers, guest artists, and musicians are required to agree that the record label (who is paying for the project) will retain the master tapes and *album copyright*.  Recording artists are commonly hired as "work for hires" during the actual recording of their album (see "work for hires" in this section).  *Therefore, they are classified as employees hired for a specific purpose (to create an album) and the copyright (for the album) remains with the employer (the record label).  Music publishers (who hold the copyright) are paid mechanical license fees for the use of the song in the pressings of the recording.*  The total amount of the fee is based on the number of units pressed, the statutory rate, and controlled composition clause.[27]

### • Cross Collateralization:

Labels use *cross collateralization* to apply the profits from the current recordings to pay for the continuing debt of previous albums.  Most artists do not want cross-collateralization clauses in their contracts, however, most labels will demand them.

### • Exclusivity:

Artists are required to agree to record and be represented by one specific label.  Artists may not record for any other label or project *without the written permission of their own label* (called a "sideman" clause in the contract).  In addition, artists are regularly restricted from re-recording any of their old hits for another label (usually negotiated to a minimum of 5 years after the affiliation with the present label is terminated).

### • Employment Term:

As stated previously, record labels often hire their artists as *work-for-hires* while they are actually recording their albums.[28]  Contract terms often include an initial year or 150 days of employment after the acceptance of the master tapes by the label.  Recording artists often agree to extend their contract with two to six additional *one-year options* with the same terms as the original agreement.  The initial one-year contract gives the label the time it needs to market and deliver the recordings to the marketplace.  If the recording moves a lot of units (sells well), the label will *exercise its option* to extend the contract for another year.  For new *successful artists,* the one-year options may be a disadvantage.  They are stuck with lower royalties than they could negotiate on a competing label.

However, most attorneys are aware of this situation and will negotiate increased royalty plateaus based on various levels of record sales. For a *developing artist,* one-year options are an advantage, as the label may have to wait until the third or fourth album before the artist develops a profitable fan base.

## • Label Rights:

Labels gain the right to manufacture, exploit and sell the artist's recordings. Artists grant the label the right to have their recordings performed in public, on radio stations, on TV shows, and in the movies. The right to use the song in a movie or TV production is negotiated by the music publisher, and the use of the actual recording, by the label.[29] Some labels have an *overcall option* which requires "hot artists" to record additional albums. In addition, most contracts allow the label to take action against any person or musical act who is using the artist's name or likeness without the permission of the label.[30]

## • Music Videos:

Music videos have become a valuable promotional tool for the industry. Labels supply the videos to channels, such as MTV, VH-1, BET, and CMT, to *break* a new act or recording. In addition, video broadcasts appear to drive approximately 20% of all record sales.[31] Labels and artists normally "split" the cost of producing the music videos. Artists are required to *agree to perform* in the videos and the label will agree to use the videos to sell the artist's image and recordings. Some major artists pay all production expenses in order to obtain sole copyright ownership. Later they *package* the videos as a video album. Traditionally, videos fail to sell more than a few thousand copies; 50,000 units is considered a "gold" video release.

## • Product:

Record labels regularly define in the recording agreement the "type of employment" and "musical recordings" acceptable to them. Artists are required to provide their personal services (as a vocalist and performer) in the production of master tapes. *The final master tapes must be of satisfactory technical and creative quality and be acceptable to the label's president or designated authority.* The master tapes are required to be delivered in accordance with a *pre-arranged delivery schedule,* and *any tapes deemed offensive, immoral or legally infringing on the rights of others may be rejected.* The minimum "product commitment" is usually one full album of eight to ten sides (songs) depending on the use of the controlled composition clause.[32] The final master tapes are usually required to be a fully-mixed and edited to a *two-track analog, a digital tape or DAT* format. *Union affiliation agreements, recording team bills, insert jacket information, and mechanical licenses* are required when the master tapes are presented to the label.

## • Promotion and Publicity:

Artists are frequently required to assist in the promotion of their albums and images by appearing for pictures, art work, and interviews arranged by the label or the artist's manager. Artists are required to make *personal appearances* on radio, television, and talk shows through live and telephone interviews to promote and publicize themselves and their latest recordings.

### • Royalty Rates and Terms:

In exchange for the right to use the recording artist's name and image and for the right to exclusively represent the artist recordings, *labels pay the recording artist a percentage of the suggested retail price of each unit (recording) sold.*[33] The amount of the royalty rates are usually set by the number of units sold. The more units sold and the more famous the artist, the higher the royalty rate the label is willing to pay. In addition, artist and producer royalty rates are commonly linked to escalating unit sales plateaus. *Foreign royalties are often computed in foreign currency and split with a local affiliated label.* Royalties are split on *compilation albums* with more than one royalty artist.

### • Service:

Artists will be required to agree *to perform to the best of their ability* in preparing and recording their albums. They may be required to *hire a producer* who will supervise the recording sessions and record budget. Labels rarely allow unknown artists to produce themselves. Artists need a *successful track record* of record sales before labels are willing to gamble millions on artist egos to produce their own albums.

### • Unions:

Record labels have *labor agreements* (called a signatory) with the unions (examples include AF of M and AFTRA) and are required to pay union scale (set levels of payments, taxes, health and welfare, and pension fees). New artists are required to join the appropriate unions when signing a recording contract.[34] Artists are also required to secure from all performers and musicians that are signed with another label, a *written release* which permits them to perform on the artist's master recordings. In exchange, the artist's *host label* will place a *courtesy appearance notice* on the albums.

### • Work-for-Hire:

As we already know, labels contract the royalty artists, studio musicians, producer, and audio engineers as "work-for-hires." They are employed to create specific recordings of a master tape which the labels will then use to generate funds to pay the recording expenses and to make a profit. The *employer* of "work-for-hires" is considered the copyright owner of the album or "art" the artists were hired to create.

## Summary

There are six global mega entertainment corporations that control the vast majority of the world's major and affiliated recording labels. These mega entertainment corporations have *entertainment media divisions* that house major record labels, TV production companies, and movie studios to create and produce recordings, movies, computer games, and TV shows. Affiliate labels look to the megas for financing, distribution, and promotion. Independent labels who record niche, genre, and vanity projects often use their established links with the major labels to distribute their recordings through the mega entertainment corporation's distribution systems or through independent distributors to the public.

Different types of record labels offer several kinds of recording deals to prospective recording artists. Legitimate deals include music publishing, demo recordings, development deals, regional and genre agreements made and paid for by affiliate and independent labels. Shark deals are based on ego and sometimes cost the artists and producers their life savings. Vanity deals are, in effect, self-record deals, as artists pay for their own recordings and then press CDs and cassettes on their own label.

Major label agreements are complex and always require an attorney to complete. Labels customarily "front" the money required to complete the actual recording, pressings, promotion and marketing of the album. Labels negotiate "points" or a percentage of the suggested retail price of cassettes and CDs and pay the artist accordingly after the label has recouped its original expenses.

## Chapter Footnotes

[1] "1994 end of the year spotlight," Billboard Magazine (December 24, 1994).

[2] Actual cost of "breaking" a new act generally depends on the type of artist, the genre of music, and the type and size of the target audience.

[3] TQM is the term often used to describe Total Quality Management, which is a method of business management policies and procedures developed by Dr. W. Edward Demming. See Dr. Demming: The American Who Taught the Japanese about Quality, Rafael Aguayo (1991) and The Demming Management Method, Mary Walton (1986).

[4] The Recording Industry Career Handbook, The NARAS Foundation (1995).

[5] See Chapters Two and Three.

[6] Ibid.

[7] An important point as suggested by Dr. Alan Remington (1995).

[8] See Chapter 5.

[9] Strategic Management, James M. Higgins, and Julian W. Vicnze (1989).

[10] All you Need To Know about the Music Business, Donald S. Passman (1994).

[11] Soundscan as reported in Billboard Magazine (Dec. 23, 1995).

[12] Summarized from Marketing: Creating Value for Customers by Gilbert A. Churchill, Jr. and J. Paul Peter (1994).

[13] See Chapter 10: Marketing Music.

[14] "1994 end of the year spotlight," Billboard Magazine (December 24, 1994).

[15] Source, industry insiders.

[16] Ibid.

[17] Tommy Boy Records, "Is You Is Or Is You Ain't An Indie?" Billboard Magazine (March 26, 1994).

[18] Walt Disney's soundtrack for the film "Aladdin," "Is You Is Or Is You Ain't An Indie?" from Billboard Magazine (March 26, 1994).

[19] "1995-The Year in Music" published by Billboard Magazine, pages YE-6 through YE-84; (December 23, 1995).

[20] Ibid.

[21] Ibid.

[22] Ibid.

[23] Ibid.

[24] The exception is the cost of "mastering" the master tape from a two-track analog or DAT to CD, cassette, etc. See Chapter 8.

[25] The 1630 process described in Chapter 10.

[26] See the Controlled Composition Clause in Chapter 5.

[27] Mechanical license fees are currently 6.95 cents per song per record sold (statutory rate) or 75% of the statutory rate (5.21 cents) if the recording artist owns, controls or wrote part of the song. See Chapter 3 and 4.

[28] For the legal definition and use of the term "phonorecords" see Chapter 2.

[29] A sync license is required. See Chapter 5 for additional information.

[30] Elvis impersonators do not claim to be the real Elvis. In addition, the real Elvis Presley is not alive, and, therefore, his income is not being affected. However, there are some reports that he has been spotted at a Burger King, somewhere in middle America . . . just kidding.

[31] "Life, Love and Music Video Hell: This Business of Making Music Videos," Music Video Conference sponsored by NARAS and Nations Bank, Nashville TN, (December 7, 1994).

[32] A "side" is the recording of one song.

[33] Points are a percentage of the average suggested retail unit price.

[34] The Phonograph Record Labor Agreement between the labels and the American Federation of Musicians (AF of M) and The Code of Fair Practice for Phonograph Recordings between the labels and the American Federation of Television and Radio Artists (AFTRA).

# 8

# THE RECORDING PROCESS

**Stages of a Recording Session**
**Signal Flow**
**Session Procedures**

No matter what kind of job you end up having in the music business, *everyone should know what goes on in the recording studio.* Studios are an integral part of the music business; the place where dreams are made and sometimes broken. When the musicians play their instruments and the recording artists sing their songs, a *universal language called music* is being produced and captured for us all. Magical sounds that give us "emotional goose bumps" are generated there. Hundreds of thousands of dollars are spent there, sometimes on a single session. This chapter examines the studio and the vital career professionals who create the types of recordings the music industry can turn into *units* or products (CDs, cassettes, DCCs, minidisks, etc.) which can then be sold to consumers.

## Rooms

Recording studios are divided into *performance rooms* (often called the studio) where the recording artist and musicians perform; a *control room*, where the producer and audio engineer supervise and record the artists' and musicians' performances; an *equipment room,* which isolates the noise of the tape machines from the control and performance studios; and a *storage area* for microphones, music stands, headsets, cords, direct boxes and other recording equipment.

## Acoustics

All the talents of the recording artist, studio musicians, audio engineer and producer are only as good as the studio's acoustics. Poor acoustics can destroy the best creative efforts of world-class musicians. Floating walls, ceilings and floors are used to isolate sound from room to room in a performance studio and control room. Grooves are cut in the floors, walls are mounted on rubber tubes, and ceilings are often spring-loaded. Windows between the performance studios and control room are made of thick, double-pane glass with 5-1/2 inches of air space between each panel. Soundproof doors complete the package.

## Aesthetics

While the musicians and vocalists create the music in the performance studio, the audio engineer and producer enhance the quality of the sound in the control room. Just as colors of paint on the walls and lights are used to help create an emotion, the studio's acoustics are used to emphasize and match the *feel* of the song to the image and vocal characteristics of the recording artist. Placement of the performers and their microphones add the final acoustics for the recording.

## Microphones

Microphones convert soundwaves into electronic signals. Knowing which one to select, where to place it in the performance studio and in what proximity to the talent is extremely important. Proper selection and usage is the difference between a "great" sounding session and something less.

• **Dynamic mics** have a coil of wire in the element (or top) of the mic. Soundwaves vibrate a plastic diaphragm, which moves the coil in and out of a permanent magnetic field. This movement converts the soundwaves into an electronic signal.

• **Ribbon mics** operate on the same principle as dynamic mics, except they have flexible, metallic-ribbons soundwaves vibrate in and out of the permanent, magnetic force field. Because the ribbon is flexible, the quality of sound generated is often considered "warmer" and "smoother."

• **Condenser mics** have two plates which hold a static electronic charge; one is a permanent plate, the other, a moveable plate. Soundwaves vibrate the moveable plate, changing the distance between the two plates, which generates the electrical output of the mic. Condenser mics need batteries or phantom power supplied from the console.

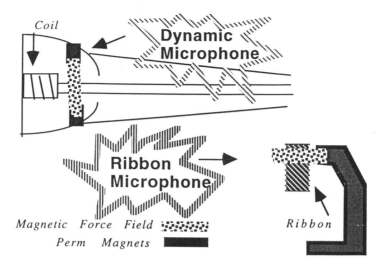

Figure 8.1 *Soundwaves move the coil of wire or metal ribbon in and out of the magnetic force field, transducing the acoustic soundwaves into electronic signals.*

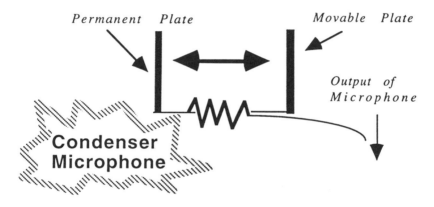

Figure 8.2 *The soundwaves vibrate the moveable plate changing the distance between the two plates. The movement creates an imbalance in the electronic charge on the two plates, generating the output of the microphone.*

## Microphone Pickup Patterns

Microphones have different *pickup patterns* or areas where they are most sensitive to sound.

• **Omni-directional** pickup patterns allow soundwaves to enter from all directions into the mic at approximately the same loudness level.

• **Cardioid** pickup patterns cancel the sound from the sides and rear of the mics. They sense soundwaves which are only directly in front of the mic. Most mics in the recording studio use cardioid pickup patterns to avoid instruments leaking into other instruments' mics.

• **Bi-directional** pickup patterns receive soundwaves from the front and back of the mic and cancel out soundwaves on the sides of the mic.

## Microphone Guidelines

There are not any hard and fast rules about microphone usage. However, here are some helpful guidelines.

• **Dynamic Microphones:** Use dynamic mics on high (loud) sound pressure level instruments (drums), electrical instruments (guitars, amps, electronic keyboards), and loud vocals.

• **Ribbon Microphones:** Use ribbons mics on medium level instruments to give a bass boost or warmer sound (strings, horns, female singers).

• **Condenser Microphones:** Use condenser mics on low sound pressure instruments, acoustic instruments (acoustic guitar, piano), and soft whispering vocals.

• **Exceptions:** There is, of course, an exception to the guidelines. Use condenser mics when you would normally use dynamic mics if you use a pad. A pad reduces the output of the mic and protects the inner electronics from high sound pressure levels (distorting).

## Direct Boxes

Musicians sometimes connect their guitars and keyboards directly to the console. *Direct boxes* may be used instead of mics to convert the high impedance signal of the musical instruments into a low impedance signal acceptable to the console. Direct boxes eliminate the sound of one electrical musical instrument leaking into another open mic. However, it also limits the musicians ability to control their own instruments' sound quality as the guitar amp's tone controls are also removed from the signal flow.

## Consoles

Most *consoles* or "boards" appear to be straight from the bridge of the starship "Enterprise." Consoles act as traffic cops dividing and directing the microphone and electrical instrument signals to various destinations - all at the same time!

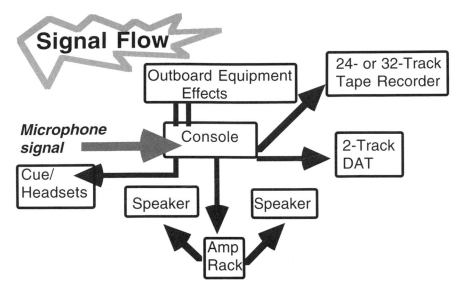

*Figure 8.3 Microphone signals are split at the console and, at the same time, are sent to the: (1) amplifiers and monitor speakers; (2) the effects outboard equipment (reverb, echo, gates etc.); (3) the 24- or 32-track tape machine; (4) the 2-track or DAT to make a copy of the session; and (5) back to the musicians and recording artists through the cue systems and headsets, so they can hear each other and themselves.*

## Multi-track Tape Recorders

*Analog* tape machines record both the amplitude (loudness) and frequency (number of vibrations) of the electronic signal sent by the mics through the console to the tape recorder. *Digital* machines have a computer which converts the microphone electronic signals into the magnetic binary codes of 1's and 0's (pulses and no pulses of voltage) which are then recorded onto the computer disc or recording tape as a magnetic signal. When the codes are played back, the computer re-converts the magnetic signal or lack of signal into 1's and 0's which are then converted back into music. The 2-track tape machines (analog and digital) or the DAT[1] machines are used to mix the 24- or 32- track tape to 2-track stereo. Accepted *master tapes* are usually sent to a mastering lab to be turned into a matrix which can be used to make CDs, cassettes, etc.

## Tape

Let's not forget recording tape! How can a magnetic signal be recorded on a piece of plastic? It can't. Recording tape looks like plastic; yet, it is actually a polyester or mylar base material with *oxide particles* glued on its surface. Oxide particles are tiny pieces of metal, which hold a magnetic signal.[2] Tape is expensive, costing between $175 and $250 per roll. A full album requires four to five rolls of tape.

# Tape Recording Process

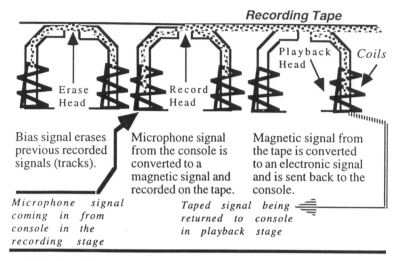

**Recording Tape**

Playback Head   *Coils*

Erase Head

Record Head

| Bias signal erases previous recorded signals (tracks). | Microphone signal from the console is converted to a magnetic signal and recorded on the tape. | Magnetic signal from the tape is converted to an electronic signal and is sent back to the console. |

*Microphone signal coming in from console in the recording stage*

*Taped signal being returned to console in playback stage*

*Figure 8.4 Each track has three sets of heads. The Erase Head uses a high frequency signal (much higher than we can hear) to erase previously-recorded signals. The Record Head converts the electronic signal sent from the console to a magnetic signal that is recorded on the tape. The Playback Head converts the magnetic signal on the tape to an electronic signal that is sent back to the console. Digital tape machines use a different format including an Overwrite Head instead of an Erase Head.*

## Control Room Speakers (Monitors)

In the control room, the microphone signals are once again converted back to soundwaves by the *speakers*. To make sure the speakers and control room acoustics are providing a correct sound (flat frequency response), room equalizers are used to compensate for the "hype of the sound" created by the speakers and control room acoustics.[3]

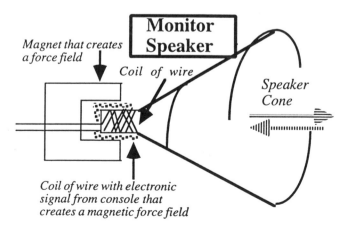

**Monitor Speaker**

*Magnet that creates a force field*

*Coil of wire*

*Speaker Cone*

*Coil of wire with electronic signal from console that creates a magnetic force field*

*Figure 8.5 The electronic signal from the console is sent to an amplifier and speaker crossover network. The electronic signal in the coil of wire creates a magnetic signal that vibrates the speaker cone (similarly charged magnetic force fields repel each other, unlike charges attract) causing soundwaves.*

## Cue System

The *cue system* allows the musicians and recording artists to hear themselves in their headphones.[4] The mic signals sent to the console are simply mixed and returned to the artists and musicians through the cue systems and their headphones. Headset boxes allow the musicians and artists to control the amplitude (loudness) of their own headphones. Most consoles have a minimum of two stereo or four mono cue systems.

## Effects

The *effect sends* are controls on the console used to change the quality of the sound. Outboard equipment adds echo, reverberation, slap, gate, compression, limiting, or harmonizing of the mike signal.

• **Compression:** Used to reduce the amplitude (amount of volume) of a signal in order to record a proper signal on the tape track. Compression is also used to change the quality of the sound of an instrument or vocalist. Most have four compression ratios, various attack times, and release from compression times. It is often used to "fatten up" the sound of a kick drum or bass guitar.

• **Echo:** Long reflections of 50 milliseconds or greater perceived as a repetition of a direct soundwave. Echo is used to make the singer or instruments sound "as if" they were in a different size room than the actual recording studio.

• **Gate:** A switch (threshold) used to terminate a signal based on the amplitude. Gates are used to "block" tape hiss heard between musical notes, ambiance, rumble, and leakage from other microphones. They are regularly used on drums and overdub vocals to "tighten" the sound.

• *Harmonizing:* Offers a variety of special effects including the doubling of an input signal, delay of signal, and changing of the pitch. Doubling allows the engineer to make one instrument or vocalist sound like two. Delay provides echo or reverberation. Changing the pitch allows the engineer to de-tune or tune instruments and vocalists.[5]

• *Limiter:* A compressor at maximum compression. The amplitude of the output is "limited" to the manually-adjusted level of the threshold.

• *Reverberation:* Sound reflections from many sources (several hard surfaces) heard more than 10 milliseconds after a direct soundwave. Reverb is used by engineers to make the vocalists or musicians sound "as if" they were in a large auditorium (hard surfaced, empty, acoustic room) instead of the smaller, acoustically-correct recording studio.

• *Slap:* A delayed sound perceived as a distinct echo, usually a delay of 35 milliseconds or more.

## Types of Sessions

The primary product being created in the studio are recordings of songs for a *demo* or for a *master* that will be released on CDs, DCCs, minidisk, cassettes, or vinyl recordings. Commercials, advertisements, and jingles are also cut.

*1. Demo Sessions promote songs and new artists to the labels. Most demo sessions (short for demonstration) are by music publishers who are recording several songs during the same session.*

*2. Limited pressing sessions restrict the number of pressings allowed to 10,000 for uncharted recordings and 5,000 for trade publication charted recordings (see "Music Business Trades" in Chapter 11).*

*3. Master sessions allow for an unlimited number of pressings.*[6] *Major label artists regularly hire only union musicians and vocalists for sessions.*

*4. Low Budget session scale for non-symphonic Christian label recordings.*

## Scheduling Sessions

Sessions are "booked" in three-hour blocks scheduled from 10 AM to 1 PM, 2 to 5 PM, 6 to 9 PM and 10 PM to 1 AM. The hour between sessions is for tearing down the current session and setting up the next session.

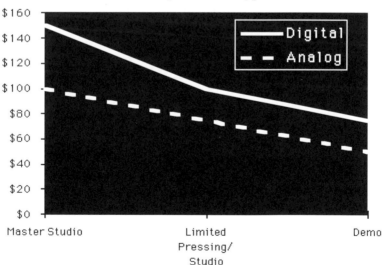

**Studio Rental by hour and type of studio**

*Figure 8.6 Examples are average per-hour rates for renting recording studios. Demo recording studios are commonly low-budget productions; limited pressing sessions use medium-priced productions; master sessions are the most expensive (and best equipped and sounding) productions. In the recording studio, you get what you pay for. Any type of session can be recorded in any studio, master sessions in an inexpensive demo studio, etc. However, pick the best studio for the purpose of the session. Most studios rent in three-hour block minimums.*

## Production Process

The recording production process consists of pre-production, tracking or basic tracks, playback, overdubbing, mixdown and mastering.

## Sage Window

" *... Basically, you're trying to bottle lightning all the time. There's no use putting a record out unless its got some magic on it. And magic doesn't come easy.* "[7]

**– Quincy Jones, Record Producer**

## Pre-production

Marrying the right song to the right artist is essential. The greatest song in the world sung by somebody who can not carry a tune is a waste of time and money. The same is true for matching a poor song to a great performer. The two must fit together in a way that allows the melody and lyrics to reinforce the perceptions consumers hold of the artists. Artist images are tied to the songs selected for an album. The quality of the studio musicians, the recording artist's performance, the production, and engineering all contribute to the final sound and feel of the recording.

## Basic Tracks

The first stage of a recording session in the studio is called *basic tracks* or *tracking*. The rhythm instruments and scratch (rough or practice) vocals lay the foundation for the rest of the instruments and vocals, which are cut later in their final versions. Session instruments can include drums, bass guitar, piano, and electric and acoustic guitars. The recording artist adds a reference or scratch vocal for the musicians to listen to while they play notes which compliment the placement of the sung words. It is re-sung and re-recorded later as a finished vocal.

## Procedure

The session process involves the musicians and vocalists listening to the demo recording of the song, tuning up, and practicing the song at least a couple of times to prepare for the recording. Many of the studio musicians in the music centers of Los Angeles, New York, and Nashville can learn, adapt, and contribute their musical creative talents to the essence of the song in just a few minutes. Basic tracks are recorded once the musicians and vocalists are ready; the audio engineer has set the mic, monitor, and headphone, equalization and effects levels; and the producer is satisfied with the quality of the sound and musical performance during practice.

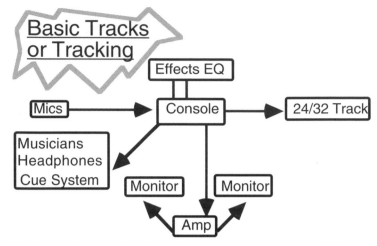

*Figure 8.7 The microphones transduce the soundwaves (music) into electronic signals that are sent to the console, where it is split and sent to the 24-track tape recorder, monitors, effects, 2-track/DAT and back to the musicians and recording artists in their cue system headphones.*

Recording the right amount of signal on the tape is not easy. Too much signal will distort the tape. Too little signal will cause the playback to be noisy. Digital tape recorders record a greater dynamic range, which solves some of the engineer's distortion and noise problems. If most of the musicians play poorly, the recording process is repeated. When the basic tracks are approved by the producer, minor problems are fixed later.

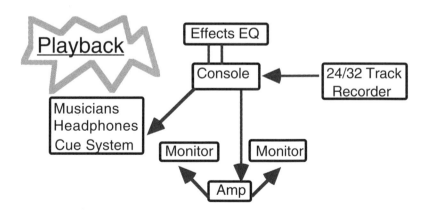

*Figure 8.8 The recorded signal is returned to the console off the playback head of the 24- or 32- track tape recorder. The signal is split at the console and sent to the monitors, effects, 2-track/DAT, and back to the musicians and recording artists in their cue system headsets.*

### Playback

Once the song has been recorded, everyone listens during tape *playback* for mistakes and opportunities to improve their performances. If recorded properly, the "take" becomes a "master."

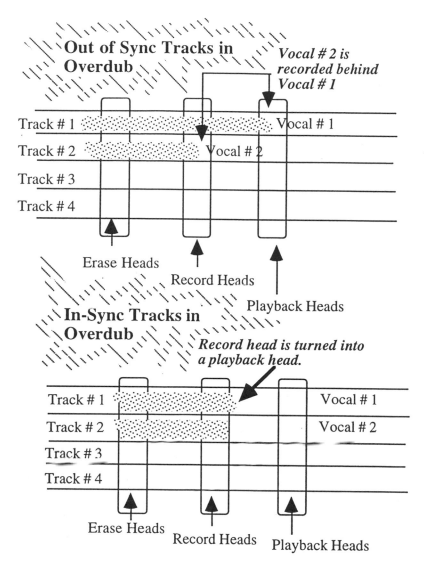

*Figure 8.9  In sel sync, the vocal that was recorded on track #1 is played back through record head #1 which is temporarily turned into a playback head. This allows the second Vocal to be recorded on track #2 in line and in time with the previous vocal that was recorded on tape track #1.*

## Overdubbing

Adding Instrumental parts and vocals to the previously-recorded master tape is called *overdubbing*.  The prior tracks are saved, and the tape machine is placed into sel sync (short for selective synchronization).  Invented by guitarist Les Paul (in 1948), sel sync turns the record heads on the previously-recorded tracks into playback heads.  This allows the new instruments and vocals to be recorded in time with the instruments and vocals that were first recorded.

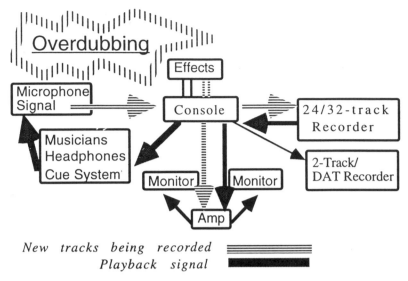

*Figure 8.10 The overdub stage is a combination of basic tracks and playback. The signal is played off the record head in playback (sel sync) and sent to the console where it is split and sent to the monitors, effects, 2-track/DAT, and through the cue system to the musicians' and recording artists' headsets. Once they hear the signal (their previously-recorded tracks), they play or sing their new tracks. The mics transduce the music into electrical signals, which travel back to the console, are split and sent to the monitors, effects, 2-track/DAT and are recorded as new tracks on the 24-or 32-track tape machine.*

## Mixdown

The last stage in the recording process is *mixdown*. After all the instruments and vocals have been recorded and overdubbed, the 24 or 32 tracks are mixed to 2 tracks (stereo). That's what is on our cassettes and CDs. One track of music heard in the left ear and another heard in the right. Some instruments and vocals are heard in both the left and right ears as a mono signal. Producers and audio engineers mix the tracks [8] according to the "style" of the music,[9] create stereo images,[10] and 3-D depth in the mix.[11]

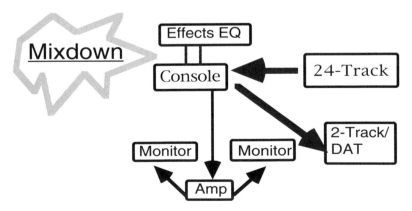

*Figure 8.11 In mixdown, the 24 or 32 tracks of recorded signals are sent to the console to be mixed to 2 tracks. The signal is once again split at the console and sent to the monitors, effects, and 2-track/DAT machine.*

## MIDI Recordings

A trend in the music business is to use *Musical Instrument Digital Interfaces* in conjunction with the recording studio process. MIDI systems include keyboards, synthesizers, sequencers, sound samplers, speakers, computers, controllers and the connecting cords. The equipment is connected together (daisy chaining) and communicates in the digital format of binary codes (0's and 1's) that represent the music.

*Electronic music* is created by using MIDI systems. It is somewhat controversial because one person can take the place of many studio musicians. Drum pads are used instead of real drums and synthesizers instead of strings, guitars, and even vocals. Keyboards are used to create a variety of "real" sounds or "sampled" instruments ranging from acoustic grand piano to full orchestras. *Sampled sounds* are the digitized recordings of actual instruments stored on computer chips. The "sounds" can then be manipulated and digitally "triggered" by touching "pads" and keyboards.

MIDI systems can be recorded directly into PC or Macintosh computer software programs. Most are *icon driven* using a mouse to select a picture on the screen that represents a program function. The computer software packages substitute as a recording studio, offering the musician/engineer the console functions of volume, panning (stereo), equalization, etc., the effects equipment functions of reverb, gates, compression, and harmonizing, and the tape machine functions of recording (up to hundreds of individual tracks), overdubbing and playback. Tracks can be stored on a floppy disk, taken to a recording studio, and transferred to a digital or analog tape machine. Vocals are then overdubbed and mixed to the MIDI-generated tracks for the final product

What is changed when you use a MIDI studio? The equipment! The recording process remains the same with the engineer still completing the basic tracks, playback, overdubbing, and mixdown stages. Instead of using live musicians and recording them onto a tape recorder, the computer samples "digitized stored musical performances" and records them directly to hard disk. The acoustics in the control room are often similar to a recording studio's as the control room is regularly used as a performance studio. Special effects equipment is the same or digitized into the software program in the computer. Signals are compressed, limited, equalized, etc. by patching the signal through effects equipment or by using the effects computerized software.

Knowing these few key terms will help make the recording process clearer Understanding the language of the producer and the audio engineer helps us to communicate "what we want" during a recording sessions.

## Key Audio Engineering Definitions

- *Ambiance* is the "feel" or "sound" of a room that is created by its mixture of hard and soft walls, floors, ceiling, etc.

• *Amp or Amplifier* is an electronic piece of equipment for increasing the loudness of a soundwave or the amplitude (volume) of an electronic signal. Examples include guitar amps, monitor speakers, and operational amps inside the console.

• *Amplitude* is "how loud" a soundwave is or "how much" electronic signal is flowing through a circuit. Amplitude is measured in decibels (dB's).

• *Automated consoles* are computer assisted by using VCA's (Voltage Control Amplifiers) to scan the settings on the console and record their positions onto one of the tape machine tracks or a computer hard disk.

• *Compressors* are outboard equipment used to reduce the amplitude (loudness) of a signal. They allow the audio engineer to record the proper amount of signal and to also change the quality of the sound. They are often used on bass guitars and kick drums to make them sound "punchier" and on singers to help the engineer "catch" increases in amplitude.

• *Crossover networks* are in speakers to separate the frequencies (bass, mid-range, and treble) and send them to the proper speakers.

• *D-1, D-2, & D-3* are formats used in tape recorders (and computers) to convert analog video signals to digital signals.

• *Dry/wet* refers to recording a signal on the tape with or without reverb or "effects" while listening to the signal in the control room monitor speakers and musicians/recording artists headsets with the "effects" mixed in. Dry is no effect, wet is when you are recording the effect.

• *Dynamic range* is the increase or decrease in amplitude of a soundwave. As an example, the dynamic range (loudness) of music is 120 dB.

• *Effects* are outboard equipment (not located on the console) that are often "patched" into the console to change the quality of the signal. Examples include digital reverb, echo, and delay units, noise gates (which cut off the signal at various amplitude levels used to prevent noise), compressors and limitors (which reduce the amplitude or loudness of the signal), and harmonizers (which are used to change the pitch).

• *Editing* is the process of removing unwanted sounds or musical notes by cutting the analog tape with a razor blade and then taping the parts back together, or by using a computer to electronically remove the unwanted information on digital recordings.

• *EQ or equalization* refers to the bass, mid-range and treble controls on the console to change the quality of the sound. Similar examples include the tone controls on your home stereo or car radio.

• *Fader* is a amplitude control on the console moved up and down (instead of left to right like the volume control on your car radio). One hand can manipulate several faders at the same time. Faders control the monitor speakers, cue (signal being sent to the recording artists and musicians headset), and the amount of signal being sent to the tape recorder.

• *Frequency* is the number of complete cycles (soundwaves or vibrations) per second, measured in "Hz" (or Hertz, after the inventor of the concept). We hear 20 to 320 Hz as bass, 320 to 5,120 Hz as mid-range, and 5,120 to 20 KHz as treble.[12]

• *High end* is treble.

• *In the mud* is recording a signal too low, causing the playback to have too much noise.

• *In the red* is recording too much signal on the tape machine which causes distortion.

• *Loudspeakers* are control room and performance studio monitors.

• *Mix* is the process of combining all the recorded tracks on the 24- or 32- track tape machine to 2-tracks (DAT). This is accomplished in the mixdown stage of a recording session. Mixes are also set during the other stages of a recording session for the control room monitors and for the recording artist's and musicians' headsets.

• *Mixer* is a nickname for the console and sometimes the audio engineer who is accomplishing a mixdown.

• *Oscillator* is a frequency or tone generator used to record signals on the tape, align tape machines, and provide special effects when mixed with musical instruments.

• *Pan pots* are controls on the console that "place a signal" into the left side monitor speaker, right side monitor speaker, or center of the signal path.

• *Patching* is when the audio engineer uses "patch cords" to plug in the outboard (effects) equipment, which, in effect, circumvents the normal or hardwired path of the console design.

• **Phase** can be acoustic and electronic. It is an increase or decrease in the amplitude of a signal or soundwave caused by the combining of the signals. It is not uncommon to have both at the same time. Phasing causes a change (positive and negative) in the quality of the signal and can usually be corrected by adjusting the microphones' proximity to each other.

• **Sampling** is a digitized recording of a sound. The sound is stored in the computer chip of effects equipment or keyboards and is controlled by a trigger device called a sequencer.

• **The Board** is another nickname for a console.

• **Tracking or Multiple Recording Parts** are paid an additional 3-hour scale. If one musician is used, then the musician is paid "leader" scale.[13]

• **Windscreens** are the foam rubber devices placed in front or over microphones. They reduce mouth noise (sibilance and popping sounds) and wind distortion.

## Summary

All a great painter needs to paint is a canvas, paint, lots of talent, and some time to create his or her magic. Recordings are different. In the studio, we have a *team of people* who must work together, under time and money constraints, to create their magic - not an easy thing to accomplish. Studio acoustics effect the quality of the recording. Most studios are divided into four rooms or areas: the performance studio, where the recording artist and session musicians perform; the control room, where the producer and audio engineer control and record the microphone signals; the equipment room, where the noise- and heat-generating tape machines and amplifiers are stored; and a storage area, where the microphones, headphones, and additional equipment are kept.

There are six stages to a recording session: *pre-production* to determine the budget, studio musicians, studio, producer, audio engineer and songs; *basic tracks* for recording the rhythm instruments and a scratch vocal; *playback* to make sure the recording is not too noisy or distorted; *overdubbing* to add instruments and vocals to the previously-recorded tracks; *mixdown* to mix the 24 or 32 tracks to 2 tracks or DAT (stereo left and right); and the *mastering process* to convert the 2 tracks or DAT recording into a matrix to press records, CDs or dub to cassettes.

# Chapter Footnotes

[1] DATs are *Digital Audio Tape* recorders. The tape is a smaller version of a cassette.

[2] Electronic signals (from the mics and console) create magnetic signals.

[3] "Hype of the sound" refers to the change in the sound of the monitors caused by the acoustics of the control room. Reflective sound from the acoustics can *phase add* causing the speakers to sound as if they are reproducing more bass or treble.

[4] Session musicians are also considered recording artists. However, in the professional recording studio, there is a distinction made between the session musicians and the royalty (label) artist who is considered *the* recording artist.

[5] Summarized from Audio in Media, Alten (1994).

[6] Major labels rarely press only 5,000 copies. Break-even points require sales (depending on the musical format) of 50,000-plus units.

[7] The Recording Industry Career Handbook by The NARAS Foundation (1995).

[8] The mixing process is the mixing of the loudness levels of the musical instruments and vocals to each other. Echo, reverb and special effects are also added.

[9] Different "styles" of music require different mixing techniques. A traditional country recording often requires the vocals to be much louder than the instruments. A contemporary country mix requires the instruments (including the kick drum and bass guitar) to be much louder than the instruments on the traditional mix. Heavy metal requires the vocals to be below the loudness level of the guitars and snare drums.

[10] Instruments or vocals can be "panned" to either the left or right speaker or anywhere in between.

[11] Depth in the mix is often created by the use of "pre-echo" and is used to help the consumers hear a "placement" of vocals in front of the musical instruments.

[12] See Audio in Media, Alten, pp. 14-17.

[13] AF of M Master Scale Card (1996).

# THE RECORDING TEAM

**Recording Artists
Studio Musicians
Record Producers
Audio Engineers
Recording Budgets**

When we buy a CD or listen to a song on the radio, it's easy to forget that it was created through a team effort. Recording artists may be idolized as superstars; yet, the recordings they are famous for are usually created by a team of very talented studio musicians, backup singers, audio engineers, and record producers.

## Recording (Royalty) Artists

*Recording artists* are more than singers. They are also business people, often incorporate themselves; and still, they have to retain a positive public personality, have the ability to create an image, be capable of schmoozing with record executives, and yes, even sing. However, in the recording studio, only one thing really counts: Can the artist sing well enough to sell records? Successful recording artists make a song come alive by communicating the song's emotional message to potential consumers. The performance must be believable, sellable, true to the message of the song and the persona (image) of the artist. However, as I've already mentioned, being able to sing well is a relative variable and is not the only criteria for success in the music industry.

## Demo Singers

Publishing companies record demos of their songs to "pitch" to major record producers, artist managers, record label A&R departments, and recording artists. The assumption is: the more famous the artist, the more albums will potentially be sold, resulting in greater royalty checks for the songwriters and publishers.

Inexperienced singers find entry-level work at publishing companies singing demo recordings. Non-union members and college interns may earn $10.00 to $50.00 a song; not much money, but singing in a recording studio is different from performing in a choir or on stage. At any rate, the novice studio singer gets some valuable studio experience. The acoustics, lighting, micing, and monitoring are often complex. So, the more experience gained in the studio, the quicker one can use what was learned to become a professional recording artist.

There is also another advantage. As the producers, A&R personnel, and artist managers listen to the demo tapes for a great song, they are also hearing a specific voice on the demo. Singing on demos is a great way to be heard by industry insiders who can make a singing career happen.

## Professional Singing Opportunities

Successful demo singers sometimes become professional singers. Job opportunities include singing for advertisements and jingle companies, as well as harmony tracks for recording sessions and television shows. Professional singers (vocalists) frequently net more money than label recording artists. After all, they just show up and sing. They do not have to support an entourage of road musicians, managers, producers, and label marketing and promotion executives.

## AFTRA

The *American Federation of Television and Radio Artists (AFTRA)* represents vocalists and recording artists in studio sessions, television productions, and live performances. It also represents actors, announcers, sound effects artists, and other personalities working in radio and television.[1] The *Code of Fair Practice for Phonograph Records* is the contractual agreement between AFTRA and the major record labels. The *National Code of Fair Practice for Network Television Broadcasting Agreement* includes pay television, video cassettes and video discs, and the supplemental markets of basic cable and airline in-flight programs. Radio commercials are under the AFTRA *Radio Recorded Commercials Agreement*. The *Television Recorded Commercials Agreement* covers television jingle singers and announcers. Fees vary depending on the number of cities in which the commercials are broadcast.[2]

## Studio Musicians

*Studio musicians* play their instruments to accentuate the marriage of the song to the vocal characteristics of the recording artist. Some of the best musicians in the world are studio musicians. Major record labels and recording artists use *master session studio musicians* for their album projects. Road musicians or concert musicians rarely record albums in the studio with the artists.

## AF of M

All major record labels are *signatories* to the American Federation of Musician's *Phonograph Record Labor Agreement,* which governs the wages, benefits and working conditions of all its members, including studio musicians.[3] *Demo rates* are paid for cutting demo tracks for music publishers, independent songwriters, and non-label recording artists. *Demo recordings cannot be pressed and sold if union musicians participated in the recordings. Limited pressing* scales allow for a maximum of 10,000 albums or units to be pressed for promotion and sales or 5,000 units to be pressed for promotion and sale if the recording makes an entry into the airplay/sales <u>Billboard</u> and/or <u>Radio & Records</u> charts.[4] Sales of more than 5,000 units (with chart action) require the producer and/or label to make additional payments (based upon AF of M scale at the time of the recording). Musicians who participated in the actual recording sessions are paid the difference between the limited pressing rates and master session scale. Studio musicians are paid *master session* rates for recordings by major label artists. The truly great players (who are in demand for session work) are often paid double and triple scale for their services.[5]

## Non-Union Recording Sessions

Anybody can record without using union members. Most non-union sessions are by nonprofessional artists, engineers, and producers who are in the process of developing their creative abilities. However, the best musicians and vocalists are usually union members and most likely will not work for less than union scale. In addition, unions help protect their members from unscrupulous producers, scam artists, and financially-shaky record labels who promise payments but rarely deliver. Finally and as mentioned previously, major labels are signatories to the union agreements and simply cannot legally release any recordings for sale that were created without union members or musicians and vocalists who were paid less than union master scale.

## Record/Session Producer

The *session producer* is the captain of the ship, directing and stimulating the creative elements of the audio engineer, studio musicians, and recording artists. There are three levels of producers: *independent, staff,* and *executive.* Independent producers begin their careers learning the trade by producing demo sessions for publishers and "custom" or "vanity" albums.[6]

Independent producers are, at times, hired by record labels and music publishers to produce *development deals.*[7] The label pays for the studio, musicians, and the producer. If the tracks are exciting or of quality, the label may sign the act and release a single. If the label passes on the artist and production, the cost of the development deal is commonly used as a tax write-off.

In the film business, executive producers put up millions to produce movies. In the music business, *independent executive producers* are at the top of the profession and paid handsomely. Extremely successful producers can almost name their price.[8] They are highly respected for their abilities to produce hit records that make a lot of money. Their success makes them behind the scenes stars within the industry. Mega labels do not want to loose the producer's talents or be in competition with them, so they sometimes make such producers president or vice-president of the label.

## Audio Engineers

Audio engineers mix the creativity of the music to the logical capabilities of the studio's acoustics and equipment to "capture" (record) the recording artists and studio musicians best performances.

- *Entry-level* audio engineers are often college students who are working in a studio as an intern. They are rarely paid for their efforts; however, they are given opportunities to learn the basics and to meet members of the creative team.

- *Second engineers* are a step up in the process. They set up mics, cables, headsets, the console, and alignment of the tape machines. They also run the tape machines and keep the log sheets during the sessions.[9] They occasionally travel with major recording artists on the road because concerts provide a unique opportunity to hone audio and mixing skills.

- *Staff engineers* are sometimes employed at a recording studio. They have the ability to accomplish any level of session, from demo to master session with major recording artists and triple-scale musicians. Staff audio engineers' positions are commonly found in non-music recording centers where great engineers are hard to find. Annual salaries range from $30,000 to $70,000.

- *Independent engineers* are at the top of their profession with a long list of hit records they helped create. They are "on-call" and most often work on master sessions for superstars. Their pay is negotiable, ranging between $500-$1,500 a day plus expenses. Many studios located in music recording centers (Los Angeles, New York, and Nashville) have replaced staff audio engineers with independent engineers. Non-staff engineers are paid by the record company from the artist's recording budget.

## Recording Budgets

The bottom line is that it can cost a lot of money to be in the music and record business. *Let's find out how much it cost to record a master session.* The following matrixes provide some examples of typical recording sessions using AFTRA vocalists, label artists (AFTRA recording fees), AF of M musicians, producer rates, recording studio rental charges, and audio engineer salaries.

## Recording Studio Rental

First, let's figure what it would cost for us to budget a recording studio for a *master session*, *limited pressing session* and *demo session* by the hour (three-hour minimum) and by the day. We can save as much as 20% over the hourly rate by renting the studio by the *daily rates*. However, there is often a minimum of five days rental required to attain daily rates.

| TYPE OF STUDIO | | | PER HOUR | PER DAY |
|---|---|---|---|---|
| **Master Session** | | | | |
| Master | 24/32 | Track digital | $125-$150 | $1,000-$1,500 |
| Master | 24 | Track Analog | $ 50-$125 | $500-$1,000 |
| **Limited Pressing Session** | | | | |
| L/P | 24/32 | Track digital | $125-$150 | $1,000-$1,500 |
| L/P | 24 | Track Analog | $ 25-$125 | $500-$1,000 |
| **Demo Session** | | | | |
| Pub Co. | 24 | Track Analog | $ 50-$125 | $500-$1,000 |
| Pub Co. | 16 | Track Analog | $ 25- $50 | $150-$ 300 |
| Pub Co. | 2/4 | Track Analog | $ 10- $20 | $100——— |

## Label Recording Artists and Studio Vocalists (AFTRA Scale)

The major expenditures for a recording session, in addition to the rent for the studio, are the recording artist(s) (vocalists), studio musicians, producer, and audio engineer. Here are some options for the rates and *union scales* for a master session, limited pressing, and demo session.

A recording artist signed with a major record label is required to be a member of AFTRA and/or be paid AFTRA *recording solo/duo rates*. All major record labels are signatories to the AFTRA Code of Fair Practice for Phonograph Recordings labor agreement. Label recording artists may be paid (and most are) a maximum of three times the solo/duo rate per song on album projects.[10] In addition, a label artist receives royalty points (as mentioned earlier) which are based on record sales. AFTRA has over 40 regional offices and represents TV, film, and theatrical actors, in addition to radio announcers and recording studio vocalists. It is affiliated with the AFL-CIO and has over 70,000 members.

# Master/Limited Pressing Session AFTRA Scale (1996)

*Solo/duo*        $139.25 per song/per hour
            $  15.32 11% for Health & Retirement
**Total**        $154.57 per song/hour


*Group/leader*     $  94.50 Required (more than 3 singers)
            $  10.40 11% for Health & Retirement
**Total**        $104.90 per song/hour


*Group/member*     $  63.00 per song/per hour/per member
            $   6.93 11% for Health & Retirement
**Total**        $  69.93 per song/hour

---

*Note: AFTRA scale rates are the same for **Limited Pressing** sessions as **Master  sessions**.*

---

## Demo Session

*Solo/duo*        $  40.00 per song/ per hour
            $   4.40 11% for Health & Retirement
**Total**        $  44.40 per song/hour


*Group/leader*     $  35.00 Required (more than 3 singers)
            $   3.85 11% for Health & Retirement
**Total**        $  38.85 per song/hour


*Group/member*     $  30.00 Required (more than 3 singers)
            $   3.30 11% for Health & Retirement
**Total**        $  33.30 per song/hour

---

*Note: Scale is per hour or per side (one song), whichever is greater. Limit is 3 and 1/2 minutes playing time and 50% additional scale for each additional minute.*[11]

## AFTRA Scale Per Hour Comparison

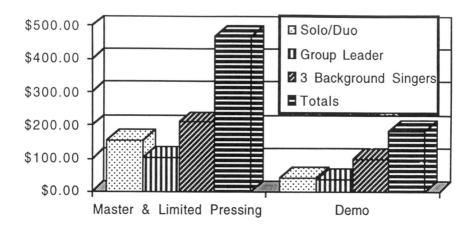

*Figure 9.1 The cost of studio singers can add up. Master and limited pressing sessions require a three-hour minimum call. For an AFTRA master session, the royalty artist is paid a minimum of $154.57 per song or per hour, whichever is greater (prices quoted include basic master scale and health and welfare); the group leader (conductor) is paid $104.89 per song or hour, whichever is greater (including scale and health and welfare); and each additional background group singer is paid $69.93 per song or hour, whichever is greater (including health and welfare). For an AFTRA demo session, the costs are reduced to $44.40 for the royalty artists per song or per hour, $38.85 for the group leader, and $33.30 per group singer (including health and welfare payments).*

## Studio Musician Scale

Studio musicians are represented by the AF of M. Most major record labels are signatories to the AF of M's Phonograph Record Labor Agreement which requires labels to hire union members and/or pay union scale for all their recordings. The AF of M is also affiliated with the AFL-CIO.

All AF of M sessions must have a leader who is paid double the scale of the sideman, excluding pension, health and welfare fees. Demo recordings only require a *two-hour call minimum instead of a three-hour call*. In addition, concurrent sessions are charged $12.00 per session for Health & Welfare. [12]

### MASTER SESSION AF OF M (1996)

| | | |
|---|---|---|
| *Leader* | $543.44 | **per 3-hour** minimum call |
| | $ 54.34 | 10 % Pension |
| | $ 15.00 | Health & Welfare |
| **Total** | $612.78 | for a 3-hour set ($204.26 per hour) |

| | | |
|---|---|---|
| *Sideman* | $271.72 | **per 3-hour** minimum call |
| | $ 27.17 | 10 % Pension |
| | $ 15.00 | Health & Welfare |
| **Total** | $313.89 | for a 3-hour set ($104.63 per hour) |

## Limited Pressing Session

| Leader | | |
|---|---|---|
| | $270.00 | **per 3-hour** minimum call |
| | $ 27.00 | 10 % Pension |
| | $ 6.50 | Health & Welfare |
| **Total** | $303.50 | for a 3-hour set ($101.16 per hour) |

| Sideman | | |
|---|---|---|
| | $135.00 | **per 3-hour** minimum call |
| | $ 13.50 | 10 % Pension |
| | $ 6.50 | Health & Welfare |
| **Total** | $155.00 | for a 3-hour set ($51.66 per hour) |

## Demonstration (Demo) Session

| Leader | | |
|---|---|---|
| | $ 87.90 | **per hour** (2-hour minimum call) |
| | $ 8.79 | 10 % Pension |
| | $ 15.00 | Health & Welfare |
| **Total** | $111.69 | for a 1-hour set ($111.69 per hour) |

| Sideman | | |
|---|---|---|
| | $ 43.67 | **per hour** (2-hour minimum call) |
| | $ 4.36 | 10 % Pension |
| | $ 15.00 | Health & Welfare |
| **Total** | $ 63.03 | for a 1-hour set ($63.03 per hour) |

*Note: Demo sessions have a 2 hour minimum call instead of the 3 hour call required for master and limited pressing sessions.*

## AF of M Scale Per Hour Comparison

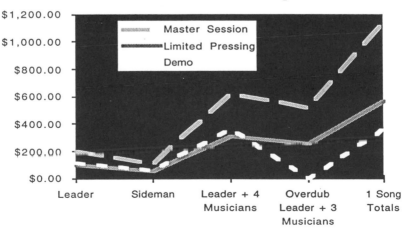

*Figure 9.2 AF of M studio musicians are allowed to record up to 15 minutes of recording time for each three hour minimum call. Using the average of one song per hour, this chart compares the cost of studio musicians for recording one song for a master session (divide the total three-hour master scale of $612.87 for the*

*leader and the sideman scale of $313.89 by 3), limited pressing session (divide the total three-hour limited pressing scale of $303.50 for the leader and the sideman scale of $155.00 by 3), and a demo session (divide a minimum 2-hour call of $223.38 for the leader and the sideman scale of $126.06 by 2). The chart example includes a leader and 4 musicians for the basic tracks and a leader and 3 musicians for the overdub session. Totals allow us to compare a possible average cost of musicians for one song at the master scale, limited pressing scale, and demo rates. As an example, using a leader plus 4 musicians for the basic tracks for one hour and one hour of overdubs with a leader and three additional musicians would average $1,140.93 per song for a master recording, $563.94 for a limited pressing, and $363.81 for a demo recording.*

## Audio Engineer's Scale

The *quality* of the final recorded "sound" on the album is the audio engineers responsibility. Although the producer is in charge of the session, it is the audio engineer's responsibility to capture and/or create the *type of sound* and *musical mix* desired and approved of by the session producer. Audio engineers and a second engineer may act as the producer on demo sessions. They are rarely paid extra for producing the demo session. Successful audio engineers progress to producing limited pressing sessions and then on to master sessions after years of experience.

| **MASTER SESSION** | |
| --- | --- |
| Independent | $300-$500 per 3-hour set, or $1,500 + day |
| Second | $ 75-$125 per 3-hour set |

| **LIMITED PRESSING SESSION** | |
| --- | --- |
| Independent | $ 75-$125 per 3-hour set |
| Second Eng. | $ 30-$ 75 per 3-hour set |
| Intern | $  0-$ 30 per 3-hour set |

| **DEMO SESSION** | |
| --- | --- |
| Independent | $ 10-$ 25 per hour |
| Second Eng. | $  7-$ 10 per hour |
| Intern | College Credit, sometimes minimum wage |

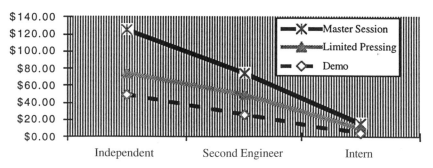

### Audio Engineer Per Hour Comparison Chart

*Figure 9.3  Audio engineers charge according to their reputation and ability to provide a quality recording quickly.*

## Record Producer's Scale

Session producers supervise recording budgets in addition to the creative aspects of the recording project. The selection of the studio, AFTRA background vocalists, AF of M musicians, audio engineer, and songs that will be recorded are part of the producer's duties. Completing the recording of the 10 or so songs on the album without exceeding the budget is crucial. Even more important for the producer and ultimately the royalty artist is the marketability of the album. Successful sales of the recordings (packaged as CDs, cassettes, etc.) provides fame, additional work, and royalty points of 3-7% of the suggested retail price to the producer. Failure, based on a lack of sales, can cost the record label hundreds of thousands of dollars.

---

### MASTER SESSION

| | |
|---|---|
| Executive Label | **$1,000-$4,000 per side**, **plus points** (3-7% of suggested retail price of CDs, tapes). Pension and H & W if Label Executive. No Pension or H & W if Independent |
| Staff Label | **$500-$1,000 per side**, **plus points** (1-3% of suggested retail price of CDs, tapes). Pension and H & W if offered by label. No Pension or H & W if Independent |
| Development Deal | **$0-$500.00 per side**, No salary or points, unless act is signed by label |

---

### LIMITED PRESSING SESSION

| | |
|---|---|
| Indie Custom Deal | **$100-$500 per side**, No points, No Pension, No H & W |

---

### Demo Session

| | |
|---|---|
| Indie Demo Session | **$50-$150 per side**, No points No Pension, No H & W |

---

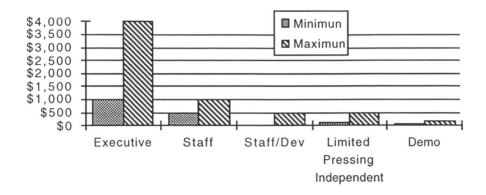

## Session Producer Per *Side* Comparison

*Figure 9.4 Executive producers charge $1,000-$4,000 per song plus points, staff producers $500-$1,000, plus points. Development deal producers often receive a promise of the percentage of sales, if the act is signed, or $500 per side. Independent producers usually earn $50-$500 per song depending on the type of session (master, demo, or limited pressing).*

## Master Session Budgets

Now that we know the basic scales and payment schedules for the recording team members, let's calculate an average cost of a *master session* per song. Expenses, of course, will vary depending on our negotiating skills, the level of musicians, studios, etc. and how much we can accomplish in a typical session. The following are 1996 listings for master, limited pressing and demo recording session related expenses. Note that the royalty artist payment is three times the base scale and that all health, welfare and pension payments are included.

### AFTRA SCALE/PER SONG OR PER HOUR

|  | Royalty Artist | Solo/Duos | Leader | Member |
|---|---|---|---|---|
| Master | $463.70 | $154.57 | $104.90 | $69.93 |
| LP | $154.57 | $154.57 | $104.90 | $69.93 |
| Demo | $44.40 | $44.40 | $38.85 | $33.30 |

### AFTRA SCALE/PER 3-HOUR SET PER PERSON

|  | Royalty Artist | Solo/Duos | Leader | Member |
|---|---|---|---|---|
| Master | $1,391.10 | $463.71 | $314.70 | $209.79 |
| LP | $463.71 | $463.71 | $314.70 | $209.79 |
| Demo | $132.32 | $132.32 | $116.55 | $99.90 |

### STUDIO MUSICIAN MATRIX – AF OF M SCALE/PER HOUR PER MUSICIAN

|  | Leader | Sidemen | Call Requirements |
|---|---|---|---|
| Master | $204.26 | $104.63 | 3-hour minimum |
| LP | $101.16 | $51.66 | 3-hour minimum |
| Demo | $111.69 | $63.03 | 2-hour minimum |

## AF OF M SCALE/PER 3-HOUR SET (REQUIRED CALL)

|  | Leader | Sidemen | Call Requirements |
|---|---|---|---|
| Master | $612.78 | $313.89 | 3-hour minimum |
| LP | $303.50 | $155.00 | 3-hour minimum |
| Demo | $335.07 | $189.09 | 2-hour minimum |

## PRODUCER MATRIX

### SALARY RANGE/PER SIDE

|  | Label/Executive/Indie | Staff/Label | Custom/Indie |
|---|---|---|---|
| Master | $1-4,000 (+ 3-7pts) | $500-1,000(+ 1-3pts) | $0-500 |
| LP | none | none | $100-500 |
| Demo | none | none | $50-150 |

### SALARY RANGE/PER 10-SONG ALBUM

|  | Label/Executive/Indie | Staff/Label | Custom/Indie |
|---|---|---|---|
| Master | $10-40,000 (+ 3-7pts) | $5-10,000 (+ 1-3pts) | $0-5,000 |
| LP | none | none | $1,000-5,000 |
| Demo | none | none | $500-1,500 |

## AUDIO ENGINEER MATRIX

### SALARY RANGE PER 3-HOUR SET

|  | Independent | Second | Intern |
|---|---|---|---|
| Master | $300-500 | $75-125 | none |
| LP | $75-125 | $30-75 | $0- 30 |
| Demo | $0-25 | $7- 10 | Minimum Wage |

### SALARY RANGE PER SONG AVERAGING 4 SESSIONS PER SONG

|  | Independent | Second | Intern |
|---|---|---|---|
| Master | $1,200-2,000 | $300-500 | none |
| LP | $300-500 | $120-300 | $0- 120 |
| Demo | $40-100 | $28- 40 | Minimum Wage |

### SALARY RANGE PER AVERAGE 10-SONG ALBUM

|  | Independent | Second | Intern |
|---|---|---|---|
| Master | $12,000-20,000 | $3,000-5,000 | none |
| LP | $3,000-5,000 | $1,200-3,000 | $0-1,200 |
| Demo | $400-1,000 | $112-400 | Minimum Wage |

## RECORDING STUDIO MATRIX-RENTAL RATES

|  | Type of Studio | Per Hour | Per 3-Hour Set | Per Day |
|---|---|---|---|---|
| Master | 32/24 Digital | $125-$200 | $375-$600 | $1,000-$1,500 |
|  | 24 Analog | $50-$125 | $150-$375 | $500-$1,000 |
| LP | 32/24 Digital | $125-$200 | $375-$600 | $1,000-$1,500 |
|  | 24 Analog | $25-$125 | $75-$375 | $500-$1,000 |
| Demo | 24 (ADAT) | $50-$125 | $150-$375 | $500-$1,000 |
|  | 24 Analog | $50-$125 | $150-$375 | $500-$1,000 |
|  | 16 Analog | $25-$50 | $75-$150 | $150-$ 300 |
|  | 2/4 Analog | $10-$20 | $30-$60 | $100 --------- |

Totals for <u>Hourly</u> Rental Rates Per 10-Song Album – Average of 4 Sessions Per Song

|  | *Type of Studio* | *Set Rate* | *4 Sets Per Song* | *10-Song Total* |
|---|---|---|---|---|
| Master | 32/24 Digital | $375-600 | $1,500-2,400 | $15,000-24,000 |
|  | 24 Analog | $150-375 | $600-1,500 | $6,000-15,000 |
| LP | 32/24 Digital | $375-600 | $1,500-2,400 | $15,000-24,000 |
|  | 24 Analog | $75-325 | $300-1,500 | $3,000-15,000 |
| Demo | 24 (ADAT) | $150-325 | $300-1,500 | $6,000-15,000 |
|  | 24 Analog | $150-325 | $300-1,500 | $3,000-15,000 |
|  | 16 Analog | $75-150 | $300-600 | $3,000-6,000 |
|  | 2/4 Analog | $30-60 | $20-240 | $1,200-2,400 |

Totals for <u>Daily</u> Rental Rates Per 10-Song Album – Average of 4 Sessions Per Song

|  | *Type of Studio* | *Day Rate/4 Sets Per Song* | *10-Song Total* |
|---|---|---|---|
| Master | 32/24 Digital | $1,000-1,500 | $10,000-15,000 |
|  | 24 Analog | $500-1,000 | $5,000-10,000 |
| LP | 2/24 Digital | $1,000-1,500 | $10,000-15,000 |
|  | 24 Analog | $500-1,000 | $5,000-10,000 |
| Demo | 24 (ADAT) | $600-1,500 | $5,000-15,000 |
|  | 24 Analog | $500-1,000 | $5,000-10,000 |
|  | 16 Analog | $150-300 | $1,500-3,000 |
|  | 2/4 Analog | $100- 240 | $1,000-2,400 |

## Album Budgets

By figuring the price of the singers, royalty artists, musicians, producer, studio rental, and audio engineer for *an average song*, we can then calculate and predict the cost of a typical 10-song album at *master*, *limited pressing* and *demo rates*. First, select and add the expenses of renting a studio, AFTRA singers, AF of M musicians, royalty artist payments (at triple scale), a producer and audio engineer. *Then, multiply the total average cost of recording one song times 10.* Again, this process is to establish a *basic budget figure,* and it assumes that the recording of some of the songs on the album will cost more or less than then average song due to instrumentation and audio product requirements of various songs.

For example, let's assume that we hire five musicians (one of them designated as the leader and paid double scale) to complete the basic tracks of a song. **AF of M musicians** cost the producer (or label) roughly $612.78 for the leader, and $313.89 for each of the other four musicians, for a total of $1,868.34. An **AFTRA royalty artist** will be hired to sing the scratch vocals (which will be re-recorded after the musicians have successfully recorded the basic tracks), and we'll pay triple AFTRA scale or about $463.70. The **24-track digital recording studio** must be rented for at least 3 hours (at $150.00 per hour) for a cost of $450.00. The best **producer** we can find will charge us approximately $1,000 for the basic tracks (based on the $4,000 per side rate). Additional recording artist and producer *points* will only be paid after recoupment by the label of all the outstanding expenses. Next, we'll hire an **independent audio engineer** at $500 for the three-hour basic track session. Finally, we'll need to buy three roles of 24-track **digital recording tape** and a **dozen DATs** for a one-time expense of $600.00

## Basic Track Expenditures

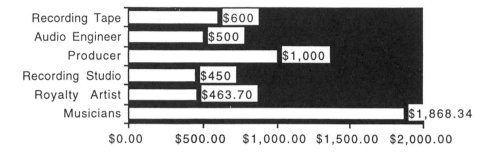

*Figure 9.5 Basic tracks of one song using 1996 AFTRA and AF of M scales totals approximately $4,882.04. Costs include: musicians (four plus a leader at master scale), $1,868.34; a royalty artist (paid triple scale to sing a scratch vocal), $463.70; Studio rental for one session (three hours), $450.00; producer, $1,000; audio engineer $500.00, and digital recording tape, $600.00 (enough for the entire album, charged to the basic tracks).*

Now, let's add a new lead vocal by our AFTRA **royalty artists** and have him/her *stack* it twice. *Stacking* or *multiple tracking* of vocals and instrumental parts is a common practice in the music business. However, the use of union vocalists and musicians in multiple tracking (the doubling or addition of vocal and instrumental parts to an original recording) requires a *new call* (an additional double payment). Cost of the royalty artist is triple scale times three performances (the original and two stacking of the lyrics for a total of approximately $1,391.10. Let's also hire four **AFTRA vocalists**, for our example, to sing harmony parts and then have them stack the parts one additional time. Cost of the harmony singers (one conductor and three group members) times two (the original performance and one vocal stack) is about $629.38. Now add three additional **AF of M musicians** to the overdub session. Cost for the leader and two sidemen is roughly $1,240.56 for the three-hour call. Let's hire our **producer** again for $1,000, the **audio engineer** for $1,000.00 (two sessions or 6 hours) and **rent the studio** for $900.00 (two sessions or 6 hours). [Note that the producer is paid a flat fee and not by the hour or session.]

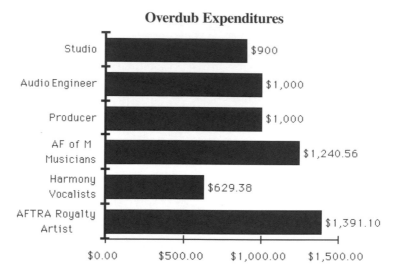

**Overdub Expenditures**

*Figure 9.6 The overdub session is frequently as expensive as the basic tracks. AFTRA royalty vocals regularly multi-track the lyrics which doubles the scale. For our example, the royalty artist sang the same lyrics three times for a payment of $1,391.10. The harmony singers stacked their vocals once for a payment of $629.38. We hired three AF of M musicians to record new parts, $1,240.56. We also hired our producer for $1,000.00; an audio engineer, $1,000.00 (two sessions) and rented the studio for six hours or two sessions for $900.00. Total cost of the overdubbing sessions $6,161.04.*

## Cost of Mixdown

Mixdown is the final stage of the actual recording process. All of the recording has been completed, and it is now up to the producer and audio engineer to weave their magic. As stated previously, the audio engineer and producer will supply special effects, stereo, and mix the 24 digital tracks to a two-track analog or DAT tape. For our example, we'll hire the same **audio engineer** for $500.00, the identical **producer** for $2,000 (which completes the $4,000 per side rate), and rent the **studio** for one additional 3-hour session at $450.00.

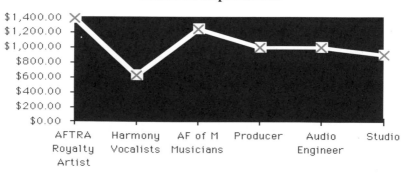

**Mixdown Expenditures**

*Figure 9.7 The final stage of a recording session, mixdown, is often the most creative. The audio engineer and producer work together to create a final mix and 2-track master of the song. Cost for our example includes; the producer who is paid the final $2,000.00 of his/her $4,000 per side rate; the audio engineer $500.00; and the rental of the studio for the final three-hour session, $450.00. Total cost for the mix session, $2,950.*

## One Song Expenditures

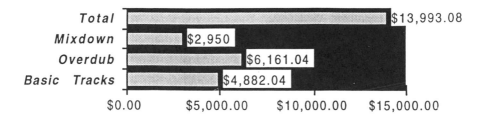

*Figure 9.8 Minus recording tape, the cost for one song (for our project) averaged $13,393.08 ($13,993.08 minus $600). Actual expenses depend on the type of session and the number of musicians and vocalists hired.*

## Average Expenses per 10-Song Master Tape

Now that we have an "average" cost for a master recording of one song, we can estimate a **recording budget** of an *average album of ten songs* by multiplying the per-song total times 10. In our example, each song averaged $13,393.08 to finish, plus we paid another one-time fee of $600 for recording tape. In reality, some songs on a master recording session may cost more or less. Our album of 10 songs adds up to $133,930.80 for the recording session, plus another $600 for the digital tape, for a total of $134,530.80. Of course, limited pressing and demo sessions would be much less expensive. In addition, we could have paid the producer less, rented a less expensive studio, etc. However, in the music business, we often get what we pay for.

## Album Recording Expenditures

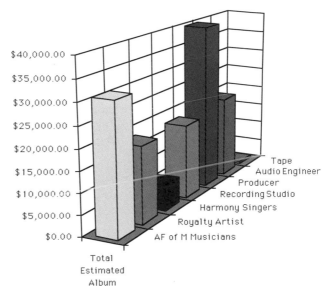

*Figure 9.9 The average cost of recording a 10-song album (in our example) totaled: AF of M Musicians, $31,089.00; AFTRA royalty artist, $18,548.00; AFTRA harmony singers, $6,293.80; rental of the recording studio, $18,000; producer fees, $40,000; audio engineer, $20,000, and recording tape, $600.00 for a sum of $134,530.80.*

## Recording a Demo

When recording a demo, consider:

**(a)** *The studio:* The inexpensive studio may have lousy acoustics, equipment, and lame audio engineers. If that's the case, you are wasting your time and money, because the final recording is still going to sound only as good (or as poor) as the acoustics, equipment and audio engineers. Check out the studio by walking around the performance studio and control room. What does it *sound* and *feel* like to you? Listen to some of the recordings their engineers have completed at the studio - not a demo tape from some other place, but music they have recorded there. Bring in your favorite CD and ask them to play it through their control room monitor speakers. How does it sound? Is the bass, mid-range, clarity, brightness, and presence still there? Finally, ask for references. Call and talk to some of their clients about their recording experiences. Ask to listen to the tape that was recorded in the studio with the engineer you are considering.

**(b)** *Producer:* Who is in charge? If everyone in the band wants to be the spokesperson, little will be accomplished. In the mixdown, the drummer will want to hear more drums, the bass player will want to hear more bass - you get the idea. If you are going to hire a producer, listen to the recordings he or she has completed. Do you like what was done for the recording artist and band? If the producer says they can get you a "deal" or "signed" with a record label, then ask whom have they placed with a label. If the producer wants to charge you money and promise you a major recording deal, be suspicious. Find someone who is talented, someone whose personality you click with, and someone who is honest about what he or she can do for you in the studio.

**(c)** *Budget:* What is the purpose of the recording? If it is to get heard (showcase your songs or talents) by a major label or publishing company, then you will want to record a demo. Do not over-produce the session. If someone in the industry likes your voice, the band, or your material (songs), then they are going to record you over again anyway. Don't waste money on additional instrumental overdubs or background vocals when you are cutting demo tracks.

If the purpose of the recording is to create a custom or vanity album (10,000 or less pressings), you are looking at spending more money to produce and record 10 to 12 songs. You do not have to pay AF of M fees unless you use AF of M musicians or the album is picked up by a signatory record label. That rarely happens, but if it does and the label decides to release the original recordings (which is very uncommon), then the musicians (you and your band) will be compensated the difference between what you were paid in the original recording (even if it was nothing) and the AF of M master recording scale. The same is true for AFTRA scales relating to vocalists.

## Sage Window

*Michael Omartian has produced many hit record-ings, such as "Sailing," "Ride Like the Wind," and "Arthur" (theme from the Dudley Moore movie) by Christopher Cross, "Camouflage," "Infatuation," and "Some Guys Have All The Luck" by Rod Stewart, "Solitude/Solitaire," "Glory of Love," and "The Next Time I Fall" by Peter Centera, and "How Am I Suppose To Live Without You" by Michael Bolton. He has been awarded three Grammys and ten nominations (including Producer of the Year in 1980 and 1984 and Album of the Year in 1984). He has also received the ASCAP award in 1992 for "That's What Love Is For." He has produced hits for Whitney Houston, Roberta Flack, Amy Grant, Sheena Easton, Stephen Bishop, and The Imperials.*

**Michael Omartian,
Record Producer**

**Q. What does it take to be a great producer today?**

**A.** One of the things that makes a great producer, to me, is that despite trends, fads, or whatever seems to be the flavor of the month, a great producer sticks or continues to believe in certain things. Quality will always win out. The short-term producer is someone who finds a groove or some kind of fad and does very well with it, yet they don't have the ability to change when the public does. Great producers have the ability to put together teams of people and be able to hear the kinds of songs that are lasting. I believe in quality, yet I'm not sure whether that means a certain kind of music or just a belief in what you're doing.

**Q. Does musicianship help?**

**A.** There are some producers I would consider to be musicians, and there are other producers who are not musicians. I'm not sure a musician/producer is any better than a non-musician/producer.

**Q. How did you get your first break as a producer?**

**A.** I went to California thinking I was going to be a songwriter, and the next thing I knew, I was a session keyboard player. I think it was helpful being around a lot of artists as a keyboard player. A lot of times, an artist would say, "Hey, try playing this part or that part." I found that through the years it was just a very natural thing, and that turned into arranging, conducting the session as an arranger, and writing the music parts. It took a long time before I found success as a producer, but my first really big production was the Christopher Cross album that came out in '79 and '80. My first production was an album that I did back in '73 called "White Horse." It was a self-produced album on ABC/Dunhill Records. It wasn't until 1979 that I felt I had reached my stride and had figured out a way to stand far enough away from something that I could start judging it, not only by my ears but by the ears of others.

**Q. How do you select the acts you want to work with?**

**A.** For me, selecting acts to work with means not getting the same acts over and over. I think that is what's been the most fun for me; to be challenged by different types of music. Choosing an act doesn't have to be something that's easy to produce. Choosing an act, for me, means something that challenges me, gets me out of my comfort zone, and I think that is important. So, I might try an R&B act, a rock act, or something completely different like a really legitimate choir act.

**Q. How do you select songs for an act?**

**A.** I think material can be derived from various sources; however, my preference is to find someone who has that ability in themselves. Usually, I will work with an artist who is a very competent songwriter; it's indigenous to their character. I feel it's more valid for me to be involved with people who have something to say. A lot of times material is born out of working with an artist as a co-writer, having the artist co-write with others, or, on occasions, we'll find an outside tune that fits the tone of the record. There are two kinds of artists: a great singer like Whitney Houston who tends to want to draw from outside material, and the songwriter/artist who really seems to have an idea of what they want to say.

**Q. How do you determine a budget?**

**A.** I feel that when you're putting together a budget, you just have to really have your budget hat on and really figure it out. I've never been in the situation where it's just down to nickel and dime stuff. I've never had to do that, but there are parameters, there are albums that can be made for $350,000 where nobody at the record company cares how much you spend, and there are other albums where they say, "If you go over $120,000, we've got a problem." There are a lot of ways you can work it; and, if I really believe in the artist, then I'll adjust my fee and do whatever I can to work with them. There never seems to be one amount or one criteria. It's always different. I don't try to put it on musicians because I feel that's their livelihood, that's what they do, and I try not to make them have to compromise. So, if there is anything that has to be compromised, I'll just ask if they'll do it for single scale instead of double scale, which most of my musicians charge. A lot of times, we'll just rotate around in a week and give each guy double scale for the day.

**Q. When you're in a studio and you're producing a session, how do you get the most creative efforts out of all the individual artists at the same time?**

**A.** I'm not sure that is ever achieved. It's very much in the past where you'll map something out on the computer and then bring in live musicians. I think that we find musicians have become so used to hearing a click or some kind of rhythm to play to that they've really figured out a way to do it. It used to be a struggle, but now it's become a part of what we deal with. I did a Vince Gill thing for the movie Maverick where we cut an entirely live track including horns. We had a 12-piece rhythm section, and we made it all happen at once, even his vocals. It turned out to be one of the favorite tracks on the album. You could look around during the session and everyone had a smile on their face. You could hear everything - horn parts - everything going at once. It was a delightful thing to have happen. The way I get the performance out of a singer is that I put absolutely no pressure on them. I say, "Sing me the song, five or six times on different tracks." That way we're not stopping, and we're not interrupting the groove. I just like the singer to have 5 or 6 performances, and then I'll say, "Go sit down" or "Go outside" or "Get a breath of fresh air," and I'll put the 5 or 6 tracks onto one track. Most of the time, they'll never have to sing another note.

*– Michael Omartian, Record Producer*

## Key Terms and Definitions

• *A & B Schedules:* Forms filed by record labels to AFTRA detailing the total scale payments made to label recording artists (designated as "A" vocalists/artists) and to non-royalty artists (designated as "B" vocalists/artists).

• *Contingency Scale:* Payments made to AFTRA non-royalty artists members (who recorded the album) which are made by the record label after the album unit sales have reached levels of 157,000 receive payments of 50% of original scale, and one million units sold payment of 350% scale. Original cast albums of theatrical presentations with sales of 460,000 receive payments of 70% of original scale.[13]

• *Contractors:* AFTRA requires the hiring of a contractor (person in charge of the AFTRA members) who is paid an additional 50%, or for one of the singers to be designated as the contractor when more than three singers are hired. The AF of M requires a contractor to be paid double scale in addition to the leader when more than 12 musicians are called for a session.

• *Cartage:* In the recording business *cartage* is an extra payment (paid by the session producer) for musicians (or a private company) to haul instruments and amplifiers to and from the recording sessions. Insurance coverage is provided on harps, timpani, string bass, accordions, tubas, drums, baritone saxophone, bass saxophone, cello, contrabassoon, contra bass and the clarinet.

• *Multiple Tracking (tracking):* The requirement of AFTRA and AF of M musicians and singers to be paid a new call (or double scale) when recording multiple parts or the same parts to additional tracks.

• *Payment Scale:* For singers of radio and television commercials and jingles the amount paid depends on the size and number of markets that will be using the recordings. Payments for background singers for concert tours depends on the type of act, size of concert draw, and length of tour. Minimum payments range between $1,000-$2,000+ per week, plus a per diem of $150-200 per day for housing and food.

• *Premium Pay/Premium Session:* Terms used by the AF of M and AFTRA to define additional payments for recording work completed between 12 midnight and 8 a.m. and *anytime on holidays or Sunday.* AFTRA premium time includes Saturdays. Payments are 50% additional for AF of M members (double scale on holidays) and 20% additional for AFTRA vocalists.

• *Session Payments:* Full payments are required by AFTRA within 21 days after the session and 15 days after receipt of billing by the AF of M.

• *The Card* is signed by the studio musicians and then sent to the AF of M as proof of working a session.

• *Total Recording Time/Playing Time:* Terms used by the AF of M and AFTRA to limit and define the amount of actual recording time allowed under union contract (15 minutes for musicians *on a three-hour call* and 3 1/2 minutes *per side* for vocalists).[14]


## Summary

Recordings are created by a *team* of very talented individuals including recording artists, studio musicians, producers, and audio engineers. Recording artists and musicians work together to create *musical art* with their vocals and musical instruments. Audio engineers are responsible for the quality of the technical recording. Producers are in charge of sessions, budgets, the musicians and vocalists performance, and the quality of the final product (master tape), which will eventually be turned into CDs and cassettes. Hit recordings take a team effort. However, if the recordings fail to sell, the producer is often blamed for not "delivering" a hit product. The American Federation of Musicians (AF of M) and The American Federation of Television & Radio Artists (AFTRA) represent musicians and vocalists in recording sessions. Both have agreements with all major record labels that require master scale payments on all sessions when the final master tape is pressed into consumer products and released for sale to the public. Producer and royalty artist points are not customarily paid until the label has recouped its debt. It costs a lot of money to be in the *recording side* of the music business. However, that is where most of the money is made, in addition to the fame, glory, etc. Successful artists (including musicians) realize the importance of the publicity, notoriety, and potential income of the recording side of the music business. Fame is often created by radio station airplay and wealth from gold and platinum levels of CD and cassette sales, plus concert performances.

## Chapter Footnotes

[1] A labor union is a "group of people who band together to demand better pay and working conditions" quoted from The Musician's Business & Legal Guide (1991).

[2] For more information, see The Musician's Business & Legal Guide, pp. 168-170.

[3] Labels' signatures also contribute to two other AF of M funds. The Special Payment Fund (*Phonograph Record Manufacturers Special Payments Fund Agreement*) compensates studio musicians for loss of income due to new technology (Midi recordings, digital sampling, etc.). Labels provide bi-annual payments to the fund based on the aggregate sale of 1% of the suggested retail price of all units sold, minus discounts of 15% for packaging, 20% promotional copies, and 50% for product sold through record clubs. The other fund, called the *Trust Fund Agreement*, is also based on record sales. The purpose of the fund is to increase the appreciation of live music performances by providing free concerts to the public. The Music Business Handbook & Career Guide, Baskerville (1990).

[4] AF of M Limited Pressing Recording Scale Rate Card Addendum "A" (1996).

[5] Enterprising recording artists, producers and musicians will often cut non-union tracks. In addition, many states have "right-to-work laws" which allow for non-union recording. However, most non-union recordings are used only for "pitching" songs and showcasing "potential" recording artists. If a label signs an act, it will usually re-cut the tracks with union musicians or pay the difference between what the musicians were paid and union scale.

[6] Custom albums are non-label productions paid for by the recording artist or band. They are demo recordings to showcase the recording artists or songs, which are then "pitched" to a record label.

[7] Development deals are offered by record companies to recording artists and bands that appear to have the potential talent to become major recording artists and songwriters.

[8] A few top independent executive producers are paid $20,000-50,000 per side. They are as famous (inside the industry) as the artist they produce. They are sometimes hired to produce one or two cuts on a new artist's album.

[9] Logs are written notes about the songs being recorded. Notes include length of the song, problems that need to be corrected in the overdub stage, and equalization and effects settings. Logs are stored in the box with the master tape. They are used in later recording sessions to alert the engineer and producers of necessary issues.

[10] American Federation of TV & Radio Artists Record Agreement Master Scale Card (1996).

[11] Ibid.

[12] AF of M Recording Scale Card (1996).

[13] Music Business Handbook & Career Guide, Baskerville (1990), p. 269.

[14] American Federation of Television & Radio Artists Record Agreement Master Scale Card and The American Federation of Musicians Master Recording Scale Rate Card (1996).

# 10

# MARKETING MUSIC

**Mastering**
**Pressing Platforms**
**Distribution**
**One-Stops**
**Rack Jobbers**
**Retail**

Once labels have spent the money to record an album, they still need to spend additional money to press, market and distribute the albums to generate sales. Indeed, the *marketing of the music* is just as important as the *creation of the recorded music*.

**Risky Business**

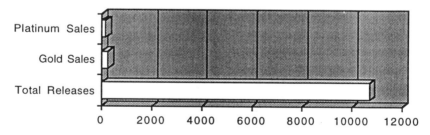

*Figure 10.1 In 1993, of the 10,686 albums and EPs (extended play) released, only 239 achieved sales of 500,000 units (a gold record), and, of those, only 149 achieved sales of a million or more units (a platinum record). With such low success rates, marketing techniques of the artists and their recordings become even more important for the bottom-line profits of the labels.[1]*

## Mastering

If the recording team of musicians, recording artist, audio engineers, and producers have done their jobs, the creativity of the recording session has been "captured" on tape. The *2-track tape or DAT* is sent to the *mastering lab* to be processed, then pressed into CDs, minidisks, and duplicated onto cassette tapes,

DCCs, etc. The tape will be turned into a *matrix master* for either an analog (vinyl records and cassettes) or a digital matrix master for CDs, minidisks, and DCCs. The analog process converts the magnetic signals on the tape into grooves in a lacquer disc, which are then sprayed with a nickel composite that hardens. The disc is later used to press grooves into vinyl records. This process is almost ancient history now because most of the albums sold are CDs.

The 1630 and PM-CD (pre-mastering) processes (two different processes, either one will work) convert the digital signal on the 2-track or DAT to a *digital master matrix* (which looks similar to a U-matic 3/4 inch video tape). The pressing plant transforms the digital master matrix into a glass master that contains "spikes." The "spikes make "pits" in the plastic CD during the pressing process. A laser beam scans the grooves in the CD and identifies the "pits" as 1's and the space between the "pits" as 0's. The computer chip in your CD player converts the 1's and 0's (which are the binary code) back into music. Typical cost of mastering, which is paid by the record labels and charged back to the artist's budget includes:

---

### Mastering of CDs, Minidisk, DCCs, etc.

- Mastering process ($1,000 per album) for CDs .........$1,000

### Mastering of Cassettes

- Mastering process ($250 per high-speed tape dub).......$ 250

---

## Manufacturing

The six mega entertainment organizations own or share CD, minidisk, cassette, etc., manufacturing plants. The *negatives* (the results of the mastering process) are sent from the mastering labs to the pressing plants, which are located in regional population clusters within the United States, Asia and Europe. Placing the manufacturing plants close to the population reduces shipping cost of the products to the distributors and eventually to the retail outlets. Excluding mechanicals and shipping, CDs cost the major labels approximately 45¢; roughly 15¢ for the actual CD disk and about 30¢ for the paper insert and plastic jewel box. However, manufactures still have to pay a small royalty (of a few cents) to the inventors and patent holders of the CD pressing process, Philips Electronics, Thompson, and Discovision.[2]

## Product Platforms

Next, the "negatives of the master tape" are used to "press" several different types of "sellable" platforms including:

*1. Cassettes* (analog tape): A magnetic copy of the recording is stored in the metal particles on recording tape. It is an inexpensive process. The limitations include: noise, distortions, and a limited frequency response.[3]

**2. Compact Discs (CDs)**: Plastic discs that have "pits" and "spaces between the pits" that are scanned by a light beam and converted into binary codes of 0's and 1's. The codes are then "read" by the computer chip in the player and converted into the original sounds of the recording. Advantages include a greater dynamic range and frequency response, as well as no noise or distortion. The primary disadvantage is the higher cost per unit to the customer.

**3. CD-ROM:** Allows for the storage of pictures and full-motion video, as well as music in a digital format. Advantages include the same quality found on CDs plus the additional storage space required for text and video.

**4. CD-I** (Compact Disc Interactive): Allows the computer operator to change or select various options in the music program. Users can "remix" the sound quality of the tracks.

**5. Chips:** Used in greeting cards and novelty items.

**6. Digital Audio Tape** (DAT): Stores a digitized version of the master recording on DAT cassettes. Professional music producers often use DATs to store copies of their final mix masters.[4] An advantage is improved quality of sound compared to two-track analog reel-to-reel tapes and analog cassettes.

**7. Digital Compact Cassette** (DCC): The consumer version of DAT developed by Phillips Electronics. DCCs allow consumers to copy CDs and play them back on digital cassette players.

**8. Direct TV:** Satellite-delivered *music television* is currently seen worldwide on cable channels BET, CMT, MTV and VH-1. However, in the future, interactively will allow consumers to order products as well as view them.

**9. Minidisk:** Developed by Sony, these 3-inch CDs allow consumers to make digital copies of their standard size CDs. Minidisk players have a lower sampling rate, which causes a minor reduction in playback quality. However, the playback is still better than on analog cassettes. Advantages include better-than-analog reproduction quality and a small convenient size for portability.

**10. 3DO** : A competitive format to CD-I. Matsushita recently purchased part of the California company which uses a double-speed disk for clarity of music and interactive games.

**11. Vinyl Recordings:** The passé technique of the old 45 rpm single and 33 1/3 rpm long-play flat vinyl discs. Sales have decreased to the point that vinyl records are used only for niche jazz and genre markets. An advantage is a distortion in the reproduction quality of sound often interpreted as a "warm" sound.

*12. Internet and On-line Services*: It is entirely possible that within 15 years the record store as we know it, will cease to exist. Internet sales will be billed as part of our monthly phone bill. Recorded music can already be downloaded and ordered (for home delivery) through the Internet and on-line computer services. America Online, Compuserve, Microsoft Network, and others offer downloading of music samples and direct-mail ordering at the touch of a button. Software includes *Netscape* for browsers who can find most of the labels' home pages on the *worldwide web*.

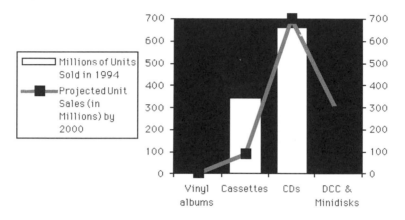

*Figure 10.2  Platform format sales are projected to shift in the United States' market by the year 2000. Vinyl albums sales are projected to decrease from 1 million units in 1994 to zero. Analog cassettes are projected to decrease from 345 million to 90 million units. CDs are projected to increase from 662 million to 700 million units sold by 2000. DCCs/Minidisks are projected to increase from 1 million units sold in 1994 to 280 million by 2000.[5]*

## Product Distribution Systems

After pressing the master tapes into *consumer products*, the CDs, minidisks, and video tapes are shipped by *distribution companies* to *retail outlets*. The megas have their own distribution companies: *BMG Distribution* ships Arista, RCA Records and others labels; *CEMA* distributes EMI products; *MCA* sends its own MCA and Geffen Records; *Polygram* ships Polygram, A&M Records and others; *Sony Music* issues CBS, Columbia, Epic Records, plus others; and *WFA* distributes Time Warner's major and affiliate labels including Atlantic, Elektra and Warner Bros. Records.[6] *Independent record distributors* (who add an additional 5%-10% to the cost of consumer product) act as middlemen between the mega distribution companies and various niche markets. They also distribute small *independent record labels'* products to retail outlets.

## Record Labels' Distribution Systems

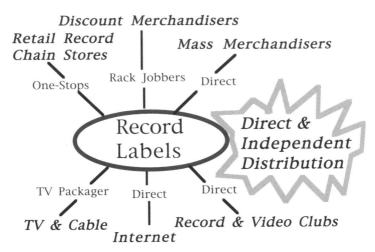

*Figure 10.3 Record labels use several distribution "systems" to deliver their recordings (in the form of cassettes, CDs, etc.) to consumers. Examples include discount merchandisers, retail record stores, record & video clubs, mass merchandisers, broadcasters, and the Internet.*

## Wholesale/Retail Markups

Record labels determine the *suggested retail price* of the CDs, cassettes, etc., that are placed *for sale* in various retail outlets. Retailers often ignore the suggested price in favor of their own marketing strategies. *However, the suggested retail price is used to determine the wholesale price.* Retail outlets use the range between wholesale (what they paid for the product) and retail (the price they sell the product to the public) to generate profits. A CD with a suggested retail price of $16.95 is usually sold by a wholesale distributor to a retail outlet for $10.72 to $11.20.[7]

### $16.95 CD Price Distribution

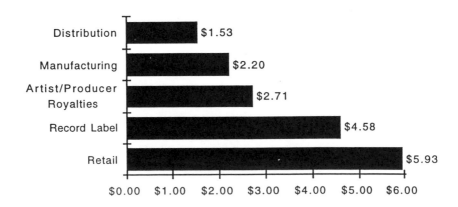

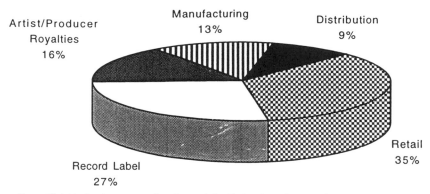

Artist/Producer
Royalties
16%

Manufacturing
13%

Distribution
9%

Record Label
27%

Retail
35%

*Figure 10.4 Markup between retail outlets and distribution depends on: (a) the type of distribution (retail, department stores/racks, or one-stops); (b) the type of platform the music is recorded on (CDs, cassettes, DCCs, minidisks); and (c) the sales propensity of the artists (a hot superstar, a high-ticket item, known artist with current radio airplay) or title albums with recurrent radio station airplay. However, as an example, the typical distribution for a CD with a suggested retail price of $16.95 is: retail outlet, $5.93 (35%); record label, $4.58 (27%); royalty artist(s) and producer royalties, $2.71 (16%); manufacturing (which includes pressings, inserts, jewel boxes, labor, AF of M Trust Fund & mechanicals), $2.20 (13%) and; distribution $1.53 (9%). Cassettes have a similar retail breakdown except for a 5% skew toward retail, which creates a 40% potential retail markup.*[8]

## Pricing Strategies

Different types of retail outlets have various pricing policies strategically aimed at the stores' specific type of customer. Correspondingly, the same hit CDs or cassettes frequently found discounted at a Kmart, Wal-Mart or Target are full price at a Tower Records or Peaches. The *demographics* or types of consumers who purchase recordings from the department discounters, are not the same types of consumers who shop in record chain stores. The younger, non-married record buyers are often found shopping in chain stores. The slightly older, married, family types (who shopped in the chain stores when they were younger) now pick up their music selections while shopping for other items at the local Kmart, Wal-Mart or Target. Thus, different types of record distribution systems have developed to supply the various type of retail outlets.

## Rack Jobbers

*Rack jobbers* supply recorded music to the discount merchandise department stores (Wal-Marts, Kmarts and Targets). The distributors own their racks and then rent the floor space by giving the stores a percentage of the profit from each unit sold. Profit margins are usually lower (8-12%) because most of the inventory are hit recordings by known artists. Turnover is faster (quicker sales) than in the chain record stores, which makes the discount department stores a valued industry retail outlet.

## Rack Jobber Profits

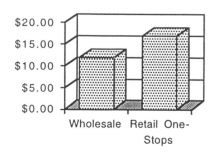

*Figure 10.5 The range between retail and wholesale for rack jobbers is much less than the 30-40% of the one-stops and retail chain stores. Rack jobber markups average between 8-12% with a CD wholesale price of approximately $11.88 and a retail selling price averaging $12.59 at your local Kmart, Wal-Mart or Target. The same CDs are $15.95 to $16.95 in chain stores.* [9]

## The Handleman Company

Handleman's is the most significant music *rack jobber* in the United States. The company was founded in 1934 as a prescription drug wholesaler. In the 1950's, it moved into pre-recorded music distribution. In 1976, Handleman's introduced *The Retail Inventory Management System* (RIMS) which is a product sales and management tracking systems. Using RIMS, Handlemans stocks only the CDs, cassettes, video tapes (movies) and books it predicts will become huge successful sellers. Handleman started distributing video tapes and CDs in the 1980's and, in 1989, formed its own direct retail side of the business with its Entertainment Zone retail stores.[10]

## Handleman's 1995 Sales

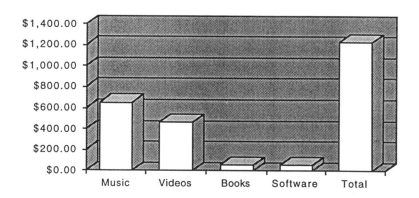

*Figure 10.6 Handleman's 1995 gross sales includes: music, $653.4 million (53% of total sales); videos, $461.6 million (38%); books, $57.6 million (5%); and computer software, $53.4 million (4%).* [11]

## One-Stops

Chain stores (Sam Goody, Peaches and Tower, as an example) stock a wide variety of music titles, video tapes, books and magazines. They supply "the hits" *plus* the types of recordings favored by smaller niche markets. *One-stop distributors* (who are really wholesalers) supply the hits and niche records, etc., to the chain stores, thus the name "one-stops." To cover the cost of the larger inventory, chain stores (regularly called *retail* by the labels) charge slightly more for all of their products, which adds an additional cost to each unit (at the retail level).

## Musicland

Musicland is the largest music retail chain store outlet in the U.S. It has over 800 mall stores using the names Musicland and Sam Goody. Started in 1956, Musicland has continued to *grow the business* by purchasing (in 1978) all of the existing Sam Goody music stores located in suburban malls. It continued to expand by acquiring the Harmony Hut and Licorice Pizza music stores in 1984 and the Musicden store chain in 1987. Musicland's newest marketing strategy is multimedia superstores located in strip outlets. Its Media Play retail outlets offer over 200,000 items ranging from CDs to comic books.[12]

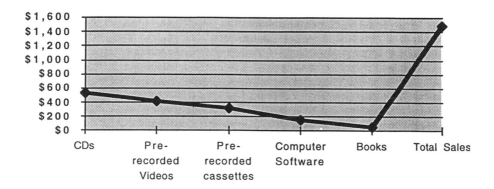

*Figure 10.7 The largest retail music chain store system in the U.S. is Musicland. Its 1994 sales gross revenues were: CDs, $534 million (36% of total revenues); pre-recorded videocassettes, $413 million (28%); audiocassettes and other pre-recorded music, $315 million (21%); computer software and related items, $160 million (11%); and books, $57 million (4%), for a total of $1.479 billion.[13]*

## Direct Mass Merchandisers

*Mass Merchandisers* are the newest retail trend in the music business. Most were started as music retail outlets or stereo stores, but as the music and video technology improved, so did the size and inventory of the stores. Now, they are considered *entertainment superstores* that offer consumers everything from CDs to refrigerators. Most acquire their pre-recorded music directly from the mega distributors, however, a few still attain some of their pre-recorded music from one-stops. The stores offer a genuine marketing advantage to the mega's by providing them with a place to sell more than pre-recorded music. Most sell (in addition to CDs and cassettes) large quantities of movies, magazines, books, video tapes, and other entertainment-related items, including: computers, video camcorders, TVs, VCRs, car stereos, keyboards, and even home appliances. As previously stated, we know that rack jobbers and one-stops have also started their own superstores, including Musicland with its entry *Media Play* and Handleman's with its new superstores, *Entertainment Zone*.

*Best Buys* was originally founded in 1966 as The Sound of Music home and car stereo stores. It changed its name in 1983 and went public in 1985. The popularity and sales of home VCRs allowed Best Buys to expand into the first home electronics superstore. Later, management changed to the Toys "R" Us and Home Depot sales technique of consumer self-help, reducing the sales force one-third. It found that consumers could select their own home stereo equipment without sales help or "pressure." [14]

*Circuit City* is the nations largest retailer of appliances and consumer electronics. The stores (under the name of Wards) were started in 1949 to provide TVs to local consumers in the South. Wards expanded by acquiring many appliance retailers in the 1960's and 1970's. It opened its first appliance superstore in 1975, developed an advance computerized sales systems, and, in 1991, was the first home electronics store to offer the IBM PS/1 computer. Circuit City offered pre-recorded music in 1992 and started its successful used car CarMax dealerships in 1993. In 1995, 20% of its sales where in audio and pre-recorded music. [15]

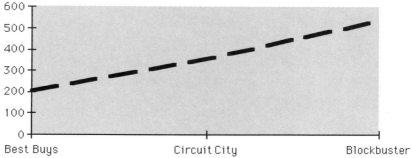

Figure 10.8 Leading music mass merchandisers (who sell their products in superstores) include: Best Buys (204 stores), Circuit City (356), and, Blockbuster Music Stores (542). [16]

*Blockbuster* is the nations largest video retailer. It is owned by Viacom, who paid $7.6 billion for it in 1994 and combined it with its Showtime Network and Paramount theme parks to form *The Blockbuster Entertainment Group*. Blockbuster was started as an oil and gas software computing company (under the name of Cook Data Services) in 1982. It was sold in the 1980's during the downswing of the oil business. The new company started as a computerized video rental chain in 1985. Wayne Huizenga bought the company in the late 1980's and grew the company through many acquisitions. Blockbuster has 4,035 video stores and 542 music stores throughout the U.S. and 15 foreign countries. [17]

## Mom-and-Pop Stores

Once the main avenue of retail recorded music to the public, the privately-owned *mom-and-pop record stores* have, for the most part, given way to the chain stores and the discount rack jobbers. Mom-and-pop stores are supplied by one-stops. However, because the stores carry a smaller inventory, sell less product, and use the one-stop middleman distributors, the average cost of the CDs, cassette, etc. to the public are habitually priced higher in order to produce a profit.

**Product Return Rates**

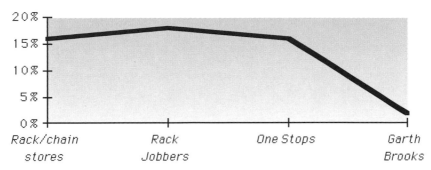

*Figure 10.9 Returns of unsold and consumer-returned recordings average between 16-18%. However, "hot artists" will often have much lower return rates averaging approximately 2-5%.*[18]

## Other Types of Retail

In addition, there are still some privately-owned *novelty shops* which offer dated and hard-to-find titles, record rentals, and resale items. Rentals and resales are generally disliked in the industry because the store owner is the only money maker. Royalties normally paid to the label, songwriters, and others in standard sales transactions are not paid in rental and resale transactions.

## Record Clubs

*Record clubs* offer the industry another funnel in which to sell products to consumers. *BMG Direct* and the *Columbia House Record Club* have been increasing in both size and popularity. The labels use the difference between the retail and wholesale prices to spur memberships. The advantage to the record labels is the 20-40% markup they save by not having the products sold through a retail outlet.[19] The disadvantage is the amount of money they pay in album giveaways (for example, 8 CDs for a penny) to motivate record club memberships.

## Music Sales by Distribution

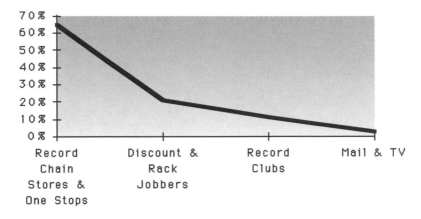

*Figure 10.10 Recent recorded music sales in the U.S. consists of 64.4% at record stores and one-stops, 20.7% at rack jobber discount stores, 10.7% through record clubs, and 3.8% through direct mail and TV orders.[20]*

## Television Outlets

*Cable TV channels*, including QVC, sell CDs, cassettes, and artists' novelty items. TV reaches a different type of music consumer than retail outlets. Marketers have discovered that through *per inquiry advertising* they can sell "oldies," classical and non-traditional recordings. *Broadcast stations* provide their late-night, unsold advertising time to independent marketing companies in exchange for a percentage of the money made on each order.[21]

### Cable TV increases in subscriptions and revenues

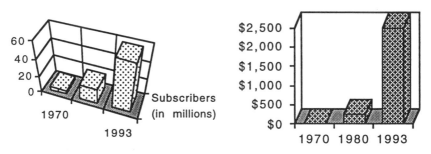

*Figure 10.11 Cable TV systems have increased significantly in popularity in the last few years. Subscriptions increased from 4.5 million in 1970 to 17.7 in 1980 and 58 million in 1993. Gross revenues increased from 345 million in 1970 to 2.5 billion in 1980 and 22 billion in 1993.[22] TV sales, considered part of mail orders, approximate 3.8% of all record sales.*

## Sage Window

"*The Internet is an example, I think, of how fast change can come. In two years, it's gone wild and exploded.*"[23]

**– Rupert Murdoch, Chairman of News Corp.**

## Interactive Outlets

As technology continues to improve, interactive marketing techniques are also being developed. Many cable TV stations now provide 30-plus channels of digital music, giving consumers an opportunity to order the recordings they hear. CD-ROMs with samples of the latest releases (that you can purchase) are being offered to consumers who own computers with CD players. America On-line, CompuServe, Prodigy and the Internet offer music products. Interactive cable TV channels dedicated to various music genres may soon be offered on the information super highway.[24]

## Home Pages

Most major record labels provide direct computer access to their *home pages* through the Internet's Wide World Web. Samples of the labels latest releases, artist videos, bio's, pictures, and tour schedules can be downloaded. CDs and cassettes can be purchased (charged to a credit card) for a price somewhat less then the prices commonly found in retail chain stores. America On-line, CompuServe and others offer access to the web which then allows access to the labels' home pages.

## Free Goods

Record labels offer *free goods* (free albums) to retail outlets in exchange for hanging posters, advertisements, and playing the music in their stores. No song mechanicals are paid on free goods. Sometimes, labels negotiate the number of *non-royalty bearing units* that can be used as free goods on each album project. Artists' royalties are often paid at the 50% level after all project expenses have been recouped on additional free goods. Free goods are also provided to retail stores to increased unit sales. As an example, a store that purchases 100 CDs may be given another 25 units free. The stores make huge profits on the free goods as they were provided free of charge from the label. Free goods may also be exchanged for unsold albums. Instead of returning money, the label sends new and different albums in exchange for unsold product.

## Packaging Discounts

*Packaging Discounts* are applied by the labels to cover the cost of "packaging" products. Different levels of discounts are applied to various platforms negotiated in the original artists' deal. The percentage discounted is figured on the labels' suggested retail price. Discount levels can be negotiated in the artist's contract with the label. Specific maximum levels of discounts include 25% for CDs, 20% for cassettes, and 50% on record club and discounted albums.

# Packaging Discounts & Free Goods

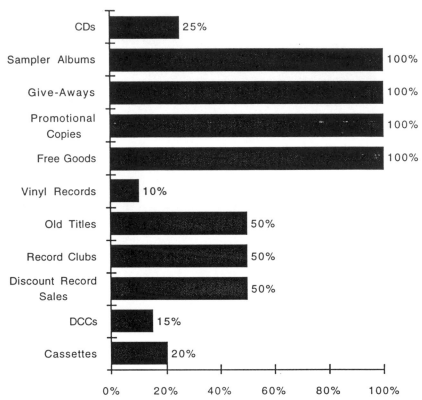

*Figure 10.12 Labels habitually deduct a packaging charge of 10-15% of the suggested retail price for cassette tapes, DCCs, and vinyl records and up to 25% for all CDs. Discount record sales, record clubs, or "old titles" sales are paid 50% to 75% of the negotiated royalty rates. Ordinarily no royalties are paid on free goods which are often used to create sales incentives for distributors and retail outlets. No royalties are paid on promotional releases, give-aways, record club member bonuses, "free" records, and sampler albums which are supplied to radio, TV stations or movie companies for promotion.[25]*

## Pressing/Distribution Budget

In Chapter 9, *The Recording Team,* we explored the cost of recording a 10-song album at master session rates. For our experiment, the total cost of the *recording budget* totaled $134,530.80. Accordingly, let's continue our example and figure the cost of pressing 200,000 units (of which 100,000 will be CDs and the other 100,000 will be cassettes). First, let's turn the *master tape* into a "negative" that can be used to press CDs and a "high-speed master dub" to make consumer cassettes. The *mastering process* will costs us about:

| | |
|---|---|
| ***Mastering of CDs*** | |
| Mastering process ($1,000 per album) for CD's$ ......................1,000 | |
| ***Mastering of Cassettes*** | |
| Mastering process ($250 per high-speed tape dub)$ ...................250 | |
| **Total** ..................................................................................**$1,250** | |

## Mechanicals

From the copyright law, we learned that the labels have to pay the *copyright owner* for the right to copy or press the songs they use on an album. For a 10-song album, we'll figure both the *statutory rate* and *controlled composition rate*. Full payment will be budgeted; however, labels ordinarily hold 50% of the payment *in reserves* until all the records are sold. *No mechanicals are paid on free goods and promotional copies.* For our example, we'll establish that 25% of the pressings will be used for free goods and promotional purposes. With a statutory rate of 6.95¢ ($0.0695) per song and ten songs on the album, the total cost of mechanicals per-album equal 69.5¢ ($0.695).

| *Statutory Rate of 6.95 cents Per Song* |
| --- |
| **100,000 CDs** (-) 25% (free goods) = 75,000 x 69.5¢ per 10-song album. Total mechanical royalties at statutory rates  = **$52,125,00** |
| **100,000 cassettes** (-) 25% (free goods) = 75,000 x 69.5¢ per 10-song album  = **$52,125.00** |
| **Total = $104,250.00** |

If we negotiated the mechanical license at the *controlled composition clause rate* (of 75% of the statutory rate), we would owe a lower mechanical fee to the music publisher(s). The controlled composition rate is 5.21¢ ($0.0521) per song times the ten songs on the album for a total of 52.1¢ ($0.521) per album.

| *Controlled Composition Clause* *(75% of Statutory Rate or 5.21 cents Per Song)* |
| --- |
| **100,000 CDs** (-) 25% (free goods) = 75,000 x 52.1¢ per 10-song album  = **$39,075.00** |
| **100,000 cassettes** (-) 25% = 75,000 x .52.1¢ per 10-song album  = **$39,075.00** |
| **Total = $78,150.00** |

## Pressing of Platforms

Sales of CDs, cassettes, DCC, minidisks, etc. (platforms) must be estimated and pressed. For our example, we decided to press 100,000 CDs and 100,000 cassettes.[26] We'll assume that we can pay the major label cost of 45¢ per CD and 30¢ per cassette.

| CDs per unit cost: | |
| :--- | ---: |
| **45 cents** for a major label which includes the insert and box with order of 20,000 plus. | |
| **75 cents** for an independent label. | |
| **$1.25-1.50** for vanity labels with orders of 5,000 or less units. | |
| 45 cents x 100,000 | **Total $45,000.00** |

| Cassettes per unit cost: | |
| :--- | ---: |
| **30 cents** for a major label which includes label and box with order of 20,000 plus. | |
| **60 cents** for an independent label | |
| **90 cents-1.50** for vanity labels with orders of 5,000 or less units. | |
| 30 cents x 100,000 | **Total $30,000.00** |

## Example Sub-Total

In our example, the label has spent $288,930.80 to create a product (recording of a master tape in the studio, the pressing of CDs, cassettes, etc., plus mechanicals). Next, we'll look at the *promotion* and *publicity* required to alert the public and hopefully motivate sales.

| Creative/Production Sub-Total | |
| :--- | ---: |
| Master Recording | **$134,530.80** |
| Mastering Process | **1,250.00** |
| 100,000 CDs | **45,000.00** |
| 100,000 cassettes | **30,000.00** |
| Mechanicals (Controlled Composition) | **78,150.00** |
| | **Creative Total $288,930.80** |

## Key Distribution and Retail Terms

• *Account:* A store or distributor which orders product from the record label.

• *ADI (Area of Dominate Influence):* Major American metropolitan areas and regions are structured into approximately 250 different ADIs. Labels and researchers use the ADIs to track record sales.

• *Billing:* The total dollar amount of sales of product ordered by an account over a fiscal year.

• **BDS (Broadcast Data Systems):** The most commonly used and accurate method of tracking the number of times a single is played on radio. A digital "fingerprint" emitted by each single is detected by the BDS reporting stations.

• **Cutouts:** Records retail has not been able to sell (due to overestimated sales projections, change in buyer habits, etc.) are marked and sold at or below cost to retail discounters.

• **Deadlines:** Record labels have specific deadlines to meet for each album project. Examples are, the date of pressing, date of shipping, and in store dates. Projects are cycled on 4-5 deadlines per month.

• **Depth of Stock:** The amount of inventory in a particular store or region of the country.

• **Devalued Product:** Usually catalog or older titles that have been reduced in price from the original suggested retail price in order to revitalize sales.

• **Discount Department Stores:** The Kmarts, Wal-Marts, and Target stores supplied by rack jobbers.

• **End Caps:** The racks located at the end of the aisles used for price and position to increase unit sales. Labels pay for the end caps.

• **Front-line:** Priority album projects that are new and active in the marketplace.

• **Guide Figure:** A figure used to predict the amount of record sales. Over-estimates cost the labels money as unsold products on the racks. Under-estimates mean that products are not on the racks when the customers want them, causing the loss of a sale.

• **Instore or Street Date:** The date at which certain products can be sold in stores.

• **List Price:** The suggested or recommended retail price for a product. It is the figure the *RIAA* (Recording Industry Association of America) uses to calculate annual gross sales.

• **Price and Position:** An agreement made between the record company and the store, which agrees to sell the product to the store for less and position it in a better place within the store. The purpose is to increase record sales by placing the product into a high-traffic, point-of-purchase location. Record labels compensate the store by providing free or reduced prices on additional stock.

• **Rack vs Retail:** Rack products are units sold in discount stores. Retail are the units sold in chain stores such as Tower Records and Peaches.

• **Retail Deal:** An opportunity for an account to buy for a limited time only the product at a discounted rate. Used as a motivation for stores to purchase additional stock on a new product.

• ***Reissues and Re-releases:*** Albums that are released anew because the recording artist has once again become popular, a living legend, or died. Albums are also repackaged by themes, as in "artists of the 40's greatest hits," "stars and hits of the 60's, 70's," etc. Niche artists recordings (who often receive little to no radio station airplay) are sometimes very successful with re-packaged albums sold through TV advertising.

• ***Sell-Through:*** The difference between shipments and the actual SoundScan sales. As an example, an 80% sell-through exists if 100,000 units were shipped and 80,000 units were sold.

• ***Shipments:*** The number of units (CDs, cassettes, etc.) shipped from a pressing plant to a distributor and finally to the retail outlets.

• ***Units on Order:*** The number of units of product ordered by an account but not yet shipped.[27]

## Summary

The marketing of music (recorded products) is considered just as important as the actual recordings. It is up to the marketing department to make sure that the recordings (which are stored on different types of consumer platforms; cassettes, CDs, DCCs, etc.) are made available to the public. Most of the labels use their own affiliated mega entertainment organization distribution system to "deliver" the products to retail outlets. The suggested retail price depends on the type of artist, the platform the music is stored on, the type of distributor, and the type of retail outlet. Marketing is regularly tied to rack jobbers and one-stops who place the label's CDs, cassettes, etc. into retail outlets. Racks are for mass merchandising and provide a lower profit per unit sold. One-stops add an additional step and, therefore, offer a wider variety of stock at a slightly higher unit price. Kmart, Wal-Mart, and Target stores are considered rack jobbers, which provide a limited stock of "hit" releases at a discounted price. Record stores, such as Tower Records, are supplied directly by the label's distributor or through an additional one-stop distributor. Chain stores provide a wider selection of music products at a higher price. Recordings can also be marketed and purchased through record clubs, TV commercials, and computer on-line systems. Typical *suggested price* breakdowns include retail, 35-40%; record labels generally, 27%; royalty artist(s) and producer points, 12-16%; manufacturing and labor for the art, design, and actual consumer product, 13%; and distribution, 9-14%. Retail is often much less then the suggested 35-40% markup as each type of retailer (rack jobber, one-stop, direct, mass merchandiser) determines their own pricing strategy.

| Type of Distributor | Retail Outlet | Examples |
|---|---|---|
| Rack Jobbers (8%-12% of Retail) | Discount Merchandisers | Kmart, Wal-Marts, etc. |
| One-Stops (15%-20% of Retail) | Retail Record Stores | Tower Records Sam Goodies, etc. |
| Direct | Record & Video Clubs (No retail outlet; direct to consumers) | BMG Direct Columbia House |
| Direct | Mass Merchandisers | Best Buys BlockBuster, etc. |
| TV Packagers (Per-Inquiry/Stations paid 40%-50% per sale of CD or Cassette) | TV & Cable TV | Local TV/Cable Stations |
| Direct | Internet (No retail outlet; direct to consumers) | World Wide Web Home Pages |

These new books are recommended for additional information on entertainment marketing:

Marketing in the Music Industry
by Charles W. Hall & Frederick J. Taylor
Simon & Schuster
ISBN 0-536-59487-2

Music in the Market
by Don Cusic
Bowling Green State University Popular Press
ISBN # 0-87972-694-6

## Chapter Footnotes

[1] That Glaze In Buyers' Eyes Is Shell-Shock From Release Glut, Billboard Magazine, (May 7, 1995) and RIAA Release (1995).

[2] "Pennies That Add Up to $16.95: Why CD's Cost So Much," Neil Strauss, The New York Times (July 5, 1995).

[3] "Frequency response" means the bass, mid-range, and treble sounds may or may not be reproduced equally to the original recording. As an example, cassettes are not able to reproduce low bass or treble frequencies. See Audio In Media, Stanley R. Alten (1994).

[4] See Chapter 5.

[5] MBI World Report (1994), industry sources (1996), and "RIAA Report Shows Stagnant '95 Shipments for Music, Video," Paul Verna, Billboard Magazine (March 2, 1996).

[6] All you Need To Know about the Music Business, Donald S. Passman (1994).

[7] "Pennies That Add Up to $16.95: Why CD's Cost So Much," Neil Strauss, The New York Times (July 5, 1995).

[8] Ibid. and industry sources (1995).

[9] Ibid.

[10] Hoovers Company Profiles and The Reference Press (1996).

[11] Ibid.

[12] Ibid.

[13] Ibid.

[14] Ibid.

[15] Ibid.

[16] Ibid.

[17] Ibid.

[18] Industry sources (1994).

[19] Record labels recoup 40 to 50% of the suggested retail price of an album.

[20] MBI World Report (1993).

[21] Called PI or per inquiry advertising.

[22] Based on industry figures as reported in Cable World, BPA Publication (1995).

[23] Rupert Murdoch, News Corp. Chairman at a seminar for music and radio programmers (1996). Interview by Charley Rose, Reuters/Variety (1996).

[24] As the megas merge with the telephone companies and cable TV systems, interactive shopping will become a reality. See "The Future on the Information Super Highway," Time (April 12, 1993).

[25] Industry Sources (1995).

[26] Copies of cassettes are made by high-speed duplication. The term "pressing" from the days of pressing vinyl records is still used as a generic term for the turning of a master tape into various platforms.

[27] Ibid.

# 11

# PROMOTION

**Radio**
**Music Videos**
**Trade Magazines**

## Promotion

There are primarily *three methods of promotion* record labels use to *alert the public and industry insiders* of the recordings and artists they have signed. Promotion, in the music business, involves *radio station airplay, trade magazine advertisements*, and *music videos*.

## Radio station airplay

Radio station airplay is essential for the successful sale of the label's CDs, cassettes, and other platforms. However, radio stations are in the business of selling advertisements, not recordings. Consequently, labels have promotional people at the label and outside regional promotional people (street promotions) who personally visit stations to meet with program and music directors. The phone calls and visits help build a "consultation relationship" which provides information about the recordings' successful airplay at other stations, plus free dinners, lunches, concert tickets, etc. The purpose is to help the station *build a larger audience* by playing the label's recordings. The larger audience allows the station to charge more money for its advertising time. The station's airplay of the recording alerts the public of the recordings which will, hopefully, stimulate sales.

## Radio Station Formats

Various musical formats are used to attract niche audiences who are most likely to purchase various goods and services from advertisers. The larger the proven audience, the more money the station can charge for its advertisement time.[1]

# Radio Station Music Formats

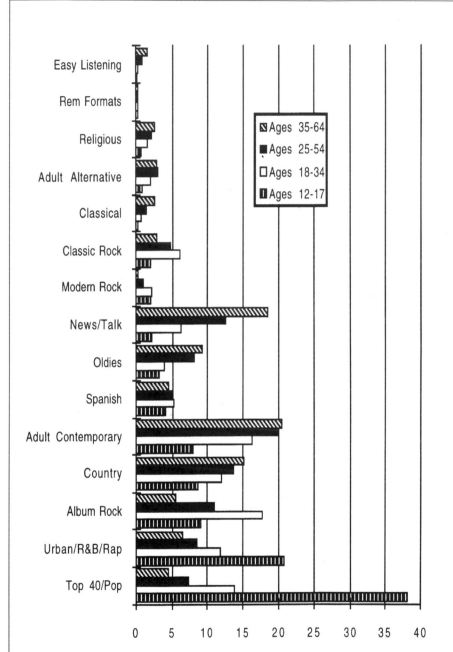

*Figure 11.1 There are approximately 15 types of music on the nation's 10,000-plus radio stations. Gender, age, politics, culture, beliefs and other variables appear to influence the types of music or entertainment people most enjoy. The above graph indicates the percent of people (at different ages) who listen to varisous types of radio formats. As an example, approximately 38% of the people who listen to top 40/pop radio broadcasts are 12 to 17 years old.*

## Radio Format Examples

| | |
|---|---|
| **Top 40/Pop** | Mariah Carey, Celine Dion, Janet Jackson, Anita Baker, Whitney Houston, Tom Petty, Enigma, Yanni, and Bryan Adams |
| **Urban/R&B/Rap** | Mint Condition, Salt-n-Pepa, Prince, So So Def's Da Brat, Heavy D & The Boyz, Zhane, Janet Jackson, Snoop Doggy Dogg, Tag Team, Jody Watley, Bonnie Raitt, R. Kelly, Toni Braxton, Jodeci, and Baby Face |
| **Album Rock** | Stone Temple Pilots, U2, Collective Soul, Tom Petty, Pearl Jam, R.E.M., Nirvana, Eagles, Black Crowes, Alice in Chains, and Aerosmith |
| **Country** | Garth Brooks, Alan Jackson, Wynonna, Reba McEntire, George Strait, Alabama, Willie Nelson, Vince Gill, and Trisha Yearwood |
| **Adult Contemporary** | Vanessa Williams, Boyz II Men, Heart, Amy Grant, Vince Gill, Luther Vandross, Phil Collins, Mariah Carey, Michael Bolton, Ace of Base, Madonna, Sting, and Bonnie Raitt |
| **Spanish (Latin)** | Gloria Estefan, Selena, Placido Domingo, Gipsy Kings, La Diferenzia, Julio Iglesias, Fama, Mazz, and Jon Secada |
| **Oldies/Adult Standards** | Often programmed as music theme stations including the big band sounds of the 1940's, and popular recording artists of the 50's, 60's and 70's, including The Glen Miller Orchestra, The Beatles, Elvis, The Rolling Stones, BB King, Rod Stewart, and Fats Domino |
| **News/Talk** | Rush Limbaugh, Howard Stern |
| **Modern Rock** | Crash Test Dummies, Nirvana, Offspring, Toad The Wet Sprocket, Smashing Pumkins, Cracker, The Cranberries, Live, Pearl Jam, Metallica, and Counting Crows |
| **Classic Rock** | ZZ Top, Eagles, Eric Clapton, Pink Floyd, Aerosmith, Bob Dylan, Van Halen, Traffic, Alman Brothers, and John Mellencamp |
| **Adult Alternative** | Simple Minds, Cranberries, Nine Inch Nails, Golden Palominos, Oasis, and Green Day |
| **Classical** | The Benedictine Monks of Santo Domingo De Silos, and professional artists such as Perlman, Pavarotti, Cecilia Bartoli, and The London Philharmonic Orchestra, performing Gershwin, Vivaldi, Beethoven, Mozart, Bach, Chopin, and Strauss |
| **Religious** | Includes two major formats: *Gospel Music* with |

artists such as Bill Gaither, The Cathedrals, Edwin Hawkins, Bebe & Cece Winans, The Oslo Gospel Choir, and Ricky Van Shelton, and *Contemporary Christian Music;* Amy Grant, Carmen, DC Talk, Point of Grace, Pam Thum, Kathy Troccoli, Michael W. Smith, Gary Chapman, and Steven Curtis Chapman

**Easy Listening**          Instrumental versions of successful top 40 recordings often re-recorded by orchestras or MIDI computer programs. Artists include soft rock favorites Anita Baker, Vanessa Williams, Tony Bennett, and Frank Sinatra

**Remaining Format**        Includes college radio stations; *Jazz artists*, Tony Bennett, Cassandra Wilson, Kenny G; *Dance Music artists* CeCe Peniston, M People, Mad Lion, and Crystal Waters; *New Age artists* Ottmar Liebert Yanni, Charo, Danny Wright and Enya, and; *World Music artists* The Gypsy Kings, Clannad, Ali Fark, Zap Mama, and Ray Cooder.[2]

## Crossovers

A *crossover hit* is a single played on more than one radio station format. The advantage is the increase in different typologies of listeners, which tends to increase album and concert ticket sales. Crossover artists include Janet Jackson, Mariah Carey, Bonnie Raitt, and Anita Baker, artists who attain both R&B and Top 40/Pop radio airplay. Madonna's records are played on Classic Rock, Adult Contemporary, Top 40/Pop, and Urban R&B stations. Amy Grant is played on Contemporary Christian, Top 40/Pop, and AC stations.[3] Gloria Estefan attains airplay on Top 40/Pop stations in addition to AC, Urban/R&B, and Spanish-formatted stations. PBS' All Things Considered places music between news breaks. Rush Limbaugh adds various types of rock music cuts between his talk show segments and commercials.[4]

## Payola

Paying money for radio station airplay (payola) is not new. In the mid-1800's, songpluggers compensated entertainers to sing their songs by paying or sharing the song's print royalties. In the 1950's, payola was a common industry practice until a congressional committee started to investigate it.[5] *Alan Freed*, a popular radio DJ, who courageously played the original rock and roll recordings by black artists instead of white artists' *cover tunes*, was indicted. His sentence was later suspended, but his career was finished.[6] *Dick Clark* was never charged, yet he was forced out of any businesses (mostly music publishing) that might have given the "appearance" of a conflict.[7] That action probably cost him millions in lost song revenues over the years.

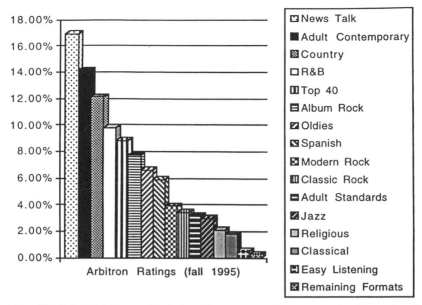

*Figure 11.2 Fall 1995 Arbitron ratings indicate the percentage of listeners (age 12 and over) who select-
ed various types of radio formats. News/talk radio with a 16.9% rating is preferred over all musical formats.
Adult Contemporary ranked second nationally with 14.1%. Other formats include: Country, 12.1%; R&B
9.8%; Top 40, 8.8%; Album Rock, 7.7%; Oldies, 6.6%; Latin, 5.9%; Modern Rock, 3.9%; Classic Rock,
3.4%; Adult Standards (big bands, etc.), 3.2%; Jazz, 3.0; Religious, 2.1%; Classical, 1.8%; Easy Listening,
.5%; and all remaining formats, .5%.*[8]

Because radio station airplay is so important to the ultimate success of a
record, labels had, in the past, showered money and gifts on the stations' music
and program directors. The Harris congressional committee changed that practice. Currently, exchanging money and other bonuses for radio station airplay
is illegal. The law requires all radio station employees to disclose any gifts to
the station owners, and then the station must announce to the public the specifics
of the gift. Failure to disclose an attempt of payola can lead to commercial
bribery charges, lawsuits, loss of broadcast licenses, and jail sentences.[9]

## Radio Demographics

*Figure 11.3 According to
Arbitron ratings of radio station
formats (winter 1993), age is often
an important factor in determining
audience listening habits. Top 40
radio stations are selected by
38.2% of 12-17-year-olds and
only 4.5% of adults 35-64. Radio
stations with Urban formats are
favored by 20.8% of 12-17-year-
olds and only 6.5% of 35-64
adults. News/talk radio is preferred by 18.5% of the 35-64-
year-old adults compared to only
2.1% of the 12-17-year-olds.*[10]

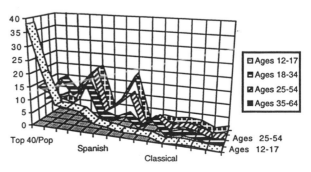

## Street Promotion

Record labels not only have to place their recordings into retail outlets, they also need to motivate unit sales. Radio airplay notifies the public of an artist and of their latest recordings. To avoid payola and yet attain radio station airplay, record labels often hire *independent record promotion companies.* Their job is to motivate the station to play the label's records. The independents culture "friendships" and business relationships with radio station music and program directors. They act as *consultants* who "advise" the stations on which records to play to increase the size of a radio station's listening audience.

Promotion men and women provide *legal payola,* such as lunches, dinners and concert tickets, *as business expenses* to build consulting relationships. They *track* the success of new releases at other radio stations in similarly-sized markets and then relay the information to their client stations. Successful promoters are often hired by the labels to supervise the labels' national promotional efforts. Past friendship and association with radio station personalities and music directors are used by label promotions to *campaign* for the station to add a new recording to their playlist.

## Most Listened to Radio Formats

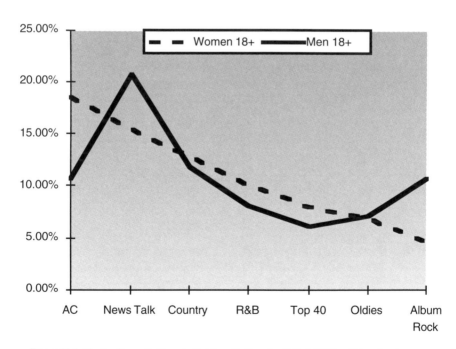

*Figure 11.4 The top five radio formats (Arbitron Ratings for Fall of 1995) as listened to by women and men age 18 and over include: news/talk, 15.4% women, 20.8% men; adult contemporary, 18.5% women, 10.7% men; album rock, 4.6% women, 10.7% men; country, 12.8% women, 11.8% men; R&B, 10% women, 8.0% men; and oldies, 6.8% women, 7% men.* [11]

## Radio Promotion Budget

Radio promotion is customarily a frenzied two-week campaign for air-play on reporting radio stations (stations that report their airplay activities to the trade magazines). In our recording experiment, the total cost of the *creative expenses* (recordings, mechanicals, pressings, etc.) totaled **$288,930.80**. Now, let's promote our recording by hiring a street promotions firm to attain radio station airplay (if possible). Labels usually budget about half of their creative (production) budget for radio promotion. In our case, we'll round off the $144,465.40 (50% of our $288,930.80 creative/production budget) to $150,000.00.

| *Radio Promotion* | |
|---|---|
| Two-week promotional campaign budgeted at approximately 50% of creative expenses | **$150,000.00** |

### Least Listened to Radio Formats

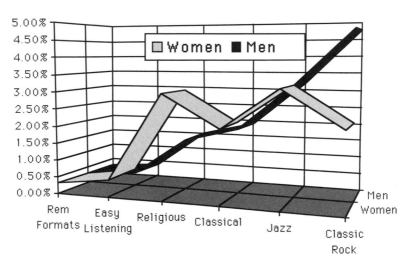

*Figure 11. 5 The least listened to music on radio stations (fall of 1995) are selected by less than 5% of the listening audience. Formats include classical at 2.1% for women and 1.9% for men; religious programming, 3.0% women, 1.5% men; easy listening, .5% women, .4% men; jazz, 3.2% women, 3.2% men; classic rock, 2.2% women, 4.8% men; and all remaining formats .3% women and .3% men.[12]*

## Trades

The second method labels use to promote a recording is *purchasing advertisements in trade magazines*. The "trades" are used by industry insiders to notify and "hype" the label's artists and recordings. As an example, Billboard's circulation is approximately 55,000. However, subscribers include the industry insiders and radio stations who help make the industry's recordings successful. Record labels, artist managers, producers, booking agents, concert promoters, music video producers, actors, agents, radio stations music programmers, and retail outlets use *trade magazines* to make their industry-related business decisions. At the same time, they also plant stories to promote their artist's image and company. The trades chart radio station airplay and record sales in addition to the industry-related articles. The major music industry trade magazines are:

**_Billboard Magazine_**
1515 Broadway, New York, N.Y. 10036 (212) 764-7300

*Billboard Magazine* "charts" radio station airplay and record sales and combines the two together to provide the industry with a reliable report card of sales and airplay.[13] Record sales figures are compiled from a national sample of retail stores and rack sales provided by *SoundScan*, which monitors the bar code on the album's jacket and reports the number of retail sales to a main computer.[14] Additional reporting systems are also used. Record labels use the information to investigate the location and number of records actually being sold and returned. Radio airplay is determined by *reporting stations* that are called and monitored to determine which records are actually being played. *Broadcast Data System* (BDS) offer electronic monitoring devices that digitally report a radio station's airplay.[15] Stations are selected from a panel of leading broadcasters in various radio markets. The stations are monitored 24 hours a day, 7 days a week.[16] Recordings are then ranked by the total number of airplays noted by the BDS system during a particular week.[17] Billboard uses the BDS system to report "The Hot 100 Airplay" chart which ranks 188 stations in four sub-formats of top 40 radio.[18] Billboard also charts musical genres including classical, country, jazz, R&B, adult contemporary, dance music, rap, and the sale and rental of video tapes and laserdiscs.[19] Billboard is also used by the industry to report and promote artist signings, structural and personal changes, mergers, acquisitions, legal issues, and other related stories.

**_Top 40 Airplay Monitor_**
**_Country Airplay Monitor_**
**_R&B Aiplay Monitor_**
**_Rock Airplay Monitor_**
1515 Broadway, New York, N.Y. 10036 (212) 536-5294

Small "sample" of actual recordings are stored digitally in the BDS system. A *detection* is confirmed when the music from a radio stations' broadcast matches the digitized music stored in the BDS's digital *fingerprinting system*. The *Monitors* chart the BDS reports for various radio station formats and airplay. Also included are lists of singles receiving the strongest increases in airplay during a given week. The titles of songs and number of airplay occurrences from approximately 100 radio stations are enclosed in each publication. Industry-related stories are also provided.

### Gavin
### Gavin Yellow Pages of Radio Today
140 Second Street, San Francisco, CA 94105 (415) 495-1990

The *Gavin Report* was founded by Bill Gavin in 1958 to focus primarily on the radio and recording side of the music business. It charts radio station airplay of Top 40, Rap, Urban, A/C (Adult Contemporary), Jazz, AAA (Adult Alternative), College radio station airplay, and Rock. Gavin charts include the name of the act, song title, label, plus the rankings from the last two weeks, previous week and current week. The charts also report the number of stations reporting, how many of the stations have added the recording to their play list, and whether the recording is receiving heavy, medium, or light *rotations*.[20] Gavin reports radio station sales, personalities, promotions, legal issues, and related music and entertainment-industry-related stories.[21] Gavin's secondary publication, the *Gavin Yellow Pages of Radio Today*, offers classified ads and a listing of regional radio stations by broadcast formats, phone numbers, address, and recent added recordings.

## Consumer/Music Industry-Related Publications

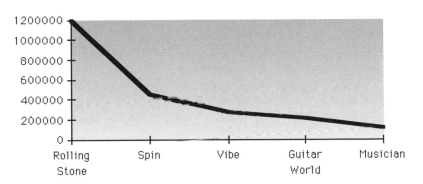

*Figure 11.6  Leading consumer music industry related publications includes: Rolling Stone with a 1995 circulation of 1.2 million; Spin, 450,000; Vibe, 275,000; Guitar World, 208,000; and Musician, 112,000.*[22]

### Radio & Records
10100 Santa Monica Blvd.,5th Floor  Los Angeles, CA 90067 (310) 553-4330

*Radio & Records* considers itself the radio industry's newspaper. Its charts include News/Talk, CHR, UC, Country, AC, Rock, Alternative, Progressive and NAC. R&R reports a variety of stories including: transactions, personnel and executive hires, and music-industry-related news. R&R reports the Arbitron results for select radio markets, radio station airplays by artist and song title, and the music video charts for the leading music video channels.

> **MBI**
> Music Business International, C/O Spotlight Publications, Ltd.,
> 8th Floor, Ludgate House, 245 Blackfriars Road
> London, SE1 9UR, United Kingdom (+44) (0) 71 921 5981

*Music Business International* considers itself to be the "business magazine for the global music industry."[23] It is often packed with international music and entertainment *business personalities*, statistics, sales, airplay, and insightful reviews of new European releases.

> **Music & Media**
> PO. Box 9027, 1006 AA Amsterdam, The Netherlands
> (+31) 20.669 1941

*Music & Media* claims to be Europe's weekly radio trade magazine. The sales and airplay charts from each country are listed in addition to the typical industry-related stories. European single and album releases are reviewed. Individual country charts are merged to establish the Euro Hot l00 singles and Album charts.

## Trade Magazine Expenditures

The cost of "buying" advertisements in trade magazine varies, however, the following are some examples from Billboard.

> **Billboard Magazine**
> **Full-page, black & white advertisement** (approximately        **$6,500**
> **Four-color full-page, advertisement** (approximately)        **$8,500**

For our recording example, we'll buy the full black & white page the first week, and the full 4-color page for the second week. In reality, the labels would also buy ads in several of the other trade magazines.

> A full-page, black & white and a full-page, 4-color trade magazine advertisement (approximately)        **$15,000**

## "I Want My MTV"

*Music videos* are used to alert the public about a new act or recording. Radio had a "lock" on the music industry's connection to the public until *MTV* appeared in 1981. With the words, "Ladies and gentlemen, rock and roll," MTV changed the way audiences experienced music.[24] For the first time, the public started to hear and see the new recording artists that radio had refused to play.[25] The popularity of the acts on MTV forced radio to play the MTV artists and their recordings.[26] The most popular national video networks include: *Black*

*Entertainment Television* (BET), *Country Music Television* (CMT), *Music Television* (MTV), *The Box*, *The Nashville Network* (TNN), and *Video Hit-One* (VH-1). Smaller systems include: *MTV-Latino*; broadcasting Spanish-language videos to Latin America; *MTV-Europe*, the European version of MTV; *CMT-E*, the Nashville Network's European version of Country Music Television; The *Americana Network*, transmitting country music videos from Branson, Mo.; *MOR Music TV* of St. Petersburg, Florida, middle-of-the-road videos with a variety of artists; *Power Play Music Video Television*, with 5 hours weekly; *Lightmusic*, with 3-1/2 hours of programming per week; and *JBTV Music Television*, with 1 hour of programming per week.[27] *Viva* is a new German music video cable channel that supplies the mega entertainment corporations with another European outlet. The channel gives MTV-Europe its first European rock music video competition and airs a minimum of 25% German-language music videos.[28]

## Music Videos

*Music videos* have become the second most important outlet (second to radio) for new artists to notify the public of their recordings. The artists and label share in the production expenses of music videos, however, in reality the labels usually "loan" the artists the money up-front. If the records do not sell enough to "break-even," labels are saddled with the total production expenses. Some music videos (i.e., Michael Jackson) have been rumored to cost more than a million dollars. However, most music videos fall into three production ranges:

| | |
|---|---|
| **Low Budget Videos**<br>Band or artist performing on stage | $20- 30,000 |
| **Mid-Range Budget Videos**<br>Band playing, plus location shots | $50- 60,000 |
| **High Budget Videos**<br>Band playing, actors, location shots, special effects | $80-150,000 |

For our example, we'll budget two $50,000 music videos
**$100,000**

**Robert Deaton, music video producer**

### Sage Window:

**Q.** Let's talk about the process of creating a music video.

**A.** Well, what normally happens is the Video Commissioner in Creative Development at the label contacts us. They say, "We've got a single coming up on such and such, the budget is this, and we want to shoot it between these dates. They'll send over a copy of the recording, and then we have to develop an idea or concept for the video.

## The Concept

**Q. So, you initiate the idea or theme of the video?**

**A.** Right. We just live with it, think about it a while, talk about it, and then my partner George Flanigen and I choose the best idea.

## Treatment

**A.** Once we've decided on a concept, we'll write it out on four or five pages describing everything we want to do. If there's a story, it describes the story; if it's to be shot in black & white, gold, or in color, we explain why. We describe the type of lighting, soft or hard. Everything is explained in order for the label to gain a clear understanding of what we are proposing. At the same time, we know that the label has probably bid three other video production companies to submit treatments. So, it's a competitive thing and our treatment has to sell our idea.

**Q. Do you supply storyboards?**

**A.** No. We don't do storyboards. It would just take too much energy, time and money to do storyboards on a music video.

**Q. What happens once the label has accepted your treatment?**

**A.** Once we're awarded the job, it's really up to us to decide the location. We'll have an idea of where we want to shoot. So, if it's in Albuquerque, New Mexico, L.A., Seattle, or here on a stage, it's in our pitch (treatment).

## Budget

**A.** Industry-wide the general price is always in flux, but average guidelines are $50,000 to $60,000 for a medium-level video and $80,000 to $150,000 for a high-budget project. However, for superstars, it can easily reach one to two million. There's no difference in price between black & white and color as we still have to hire the same number of crew and rent the same amount of lights. Location shots are more expensive. A band playing in a club, where we don't need to add much special lighting is less expensive.

## Equipment

**A.** We rent all of our gear, and we shoot all over the country. One project we're shooting 16mm, another super 16mm, and in another video we may be shooting 35mm.

**Q. Do you prefer 35mm?**

**A.** We prefer 35mm, but 16mm is very clean.

## Location Shots

**A.** What we do first is get in touch with a location scout. We'll tell them what we're looking for, they take pictures of places that fit our descriptions and send them to us. Then, when we fly into the location, they show us the locations we picked out of the pictures. Sometimes, we find what we want from the pictures, and other times, we have to get in our cars and travel around the state until we find what we need.

## Talent

**A.** We use a casting director wherever we go. We'll tell them what we want, the kind of person, the kind of looks, etc. They videotape a hundred or so people, and then we select the cast from the videotape.

**Q. How many people are on a shoot?**

**A.** Normally, there's between 20 and 30 people on each crew. The cost of the crew depends on how many we need to hire (lighting people, etc.) and for how many days we need them.

**Q. Do you employ a DP?**

**A.** Sometimes, I'm the director of photography. I do 25% of the shoots, and we'll bring in a DP for the other 75%. I also direct, but I don't direct and DP at the same time.

**Q. How much does a DP usually charge?**

**A.** A good DP is about $2,500 a day. A good gaffer (lighting person) is about $450 to $500 a day.

**Q. How about a sound person?**

**A.** About $350 per day.

**Q. How about your actors and actresses?**

**A.** We normally hire non-union. We pay $200 to $500 a day plus expenses.

## Shooting Schedule

**Q. How long does it take you to shoot a video?**

**A.** It depends on the budget. If you're shooting a $50,000 budget, you're going to be shooting one 14- to 15-hour day. If we're shooting an $80,000 to $150,000 budget, it's either 2 or 3, 14- to 15-hour days.

**Q. Are you using the video camera inside the film camera?**

**A.** Yeah, video-assist. It's good for the director to have. Otherwise, the director really has no idea if they are getting the performance they need out of the talent. By the way, did you know that Jerry Lewis invented video-assist?

**Q. No way! The comedian?**

**A.** Yeah. What happened was that Jerry started directing a lot of his movies, and he couldn't tell whether he got the performance he wanted or not. So, he invented video-assist by putting all his performances on a videotape using a camera located inside the film camera.

**Q. How do you get the performance you are looking for (as the director) out of the actors?**

**A.** Hopefully, we've casted well and don't have to worry about it. I tell them things they need to know about the role they're playing in each particular scene. In Martina McBride's video, when the little girl is going out the door, I gave the mom direction by saying, "Your little girl doesn't know this, but you know this is possibly the last time you're going to see her."

**Q. How do you motivate the recording artists to act? How do you make them look good on film? How do you make them comfortable and turn them into actors?**

**A.** What we like to do is work with an artist or at least meet, talk, and just sit around with an artist. By their personality, we can often tell whether they're going to be able to pull off the acting job.

### Post Production

**A.** The exposed film is sent to the lab to be processed into a negative. Then, we take the negative to a post-production house to transfer it to videotape.

**Q. Is it digitized?**

**A.** Yes, D2 digital which is digital tape. At the same time, we also make a three-quarter-inch dub for rough cuts. Sympte code is put on the tape to accomplish on-line editing. We do a rough cut on 3/4 inch. Sometimes, we use the AVID random access computer editing system. We just punch in a number, and the footage is instantly located. We're not actually editing on the tape, we're editing in the computer. We'll take the numbers of every scene edited and of all the scenes that made it into the video. Then, we'll actually conform the master to a broadcast master and deliver it on D2 to the label.

**Q. What's the future of music videos?**

**A.** I would like to see the day when consumers buy the record and the videos at the same time. We're contractors. We're contracted to do a job, and we get paid for that job. When it gets to the point where videos are bought (as in a record store on CDV), then we will start to receive royalties.

**Q. How do students get a start in the music video business?**

**A.** The only way to get into this is to do it. Get experience while you're in school. The only reason to be in this business is because you have to in your heart and soul. 'Cause, if you're doing it for the money, then don't do it, because it's too hard of a business. Have lots of energy and don't take "no" for an answer.

**Q. How about education?**

**A.** Education is important, but at the same time, get work experience with production companies. That's what I did. Get experience while you're in school or someday you're going to turn in your resume to someone, they're going to look at your degree and say, "Well, that's great, but you don't have any experience." Go to school and then do what I did. At nights, I was on shoots. I worked on shoots. I was working cameras. I was working it for free. I was working for pizza. I was doing whatever it takes, and that's what it takes to be successful.

*– Robert Deaton, Music Video Producer*

### Music Video Networks

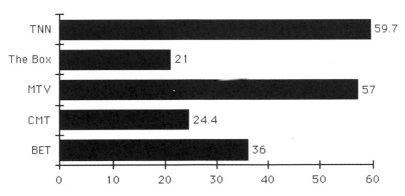

*Figure 11.7 The number of households hooked up to a music video channel can be misleading. As an example, BET has 36 million subscribers; CMT, 24.4 million; MTV, 57 million; The Box, 21 million; and VH-1, 48.8 million.[29] However, the actual number of viewers watching at any given time is usually less than 1/2 of 1% of the number of households hooked up. For example, the maximum number of TVs tuned into MTV at any given time is actually 319,000; the maximum number of households tuned into VH-1 is 123,000. Additionally, there is research that appears to indicate that in many of the homes the TVs are only turned on and nobody is watching.[30]*

## Movies

Imagine the shower scene in the movie "Psycho" without the music. Music is often used in films to build suspense or as an emotional break. Recorded soundtracks are used to *cross promote* the movie through radio station airplay and promote the music by viewing the movie.

## Music Beds

*Instrumental music* is used as an emotional foundation in news inserts, situation comedies, station identifications, and dramatic thrillers. Bands often perform *live to tape* (which means delayed) on the network talk shows in an effort to create excitement and various moods. Examples include Jay Leno, David Lettermen, and a number of cable network shows which are shot live and delayed for later broadcasts. Broadcast television, cable, and movie *trade magazines* include:

## Media Trades

### *Electronic Media*
c/o Crain Communications
740 N. Rush St., Chicago, IL 60611-2590
(312) 649-5200

*Electronic Media* is used by broadcast TV and cable stations to make programming decisions. *Nielsen* ratings are used to chart the viewers' acceptance of network programming. Article subjects include legal issues, station management policies, and industry personalities. TV station and production company stock fluctuations are listed. In addition, program syndicators use the magazine to promote their latest offerings.

### *Variety*
Cahners Publishing Co.
475 Park Ave. South, New York, N.Y. 10016
(212)779-1100

*Variety* is the Billboard Magazine of the movie and film industry. It's the premier trade paper of the Hollywood and world studios, agents, actors, producers, and want-to-be's. Industry insiders use it to promote and market their products and themselves. Advertisements are used to notify the industry of new movie releases, to motivate gossip and hype, and to promote potential Oscar nominations. Variety's *Weekly Box Office Report* displays the weekly gross revenues, number of screens, average dollar income per week per screen, the increase or decrease of revenues generated, the number of weeks the movie has been in release, and the gross cumulative amount of money the film has earned. Additional stories cover the video rental business, industry personalities, and the music industry.

## Key Radio Terms

• *AM (Amplitude Modulation):* The sound (music) is created by varying the amplitude of the radio wave.

• *Air Personality:* Radio announcers and disc jockeys who are employed by radio stations to play music and entertain listeners. Research indicates a desire for "live" personalities at the radio stations instead of "taped" programming. However, research also indicates that listeners do not want air personalities to "talk" over the music.

• *Antenna:* The height of the antenna affects the range of the broadcast signal. The signal is line of sight; the higher the antenna, the greater the broadcast radius.

• *Arbitrons MSA's and TSA's:* Arbitron assigns all radio stations in 261 radio markets to a Metro Survey Area (MSA) and a Total Survey Area (TSA). Arbitron conducts research for the stations to determine characteristics about a station's listening audience.

• *Call-Out Research:* Research firms provide radio stations and record labels with the results of their call-out research. Typically, 100 to 150 people (in a local area) are called, asked, and paid to meet at a central location. The respondents listen to the "hooks" (ordinarily 5-10 seconds of the main theme of the song) from new, current, and recurrent recordings (older recordings that are still "worthy" of airplay). Respondents are asked to rank the hooks (on a seven-point scale) based on how much they "like" the recordings. Radio stations pay the research firms for the information and customarily play only the highest ranked recordings.

• *Drive Time:* The time when most people are in their cars driving to or from work. Times include 7 AM to 9 AM and afternoons from 4 PM to 6 PM. Stations run more commercials during drive time and charge maximum rates due to the larger listening audience.

• *FM (Frequency Modulation):* The sound (music) is created by varying the frequency of the radio wave.

• *Nielsen DMA's:* The A.C. Nielsen Company has developed its Designated Market Areas (DMA's) which are used to divide the country into non-overlapping markets. Radio stations that do not fall into the Arbitrons MSA's are listed in the Nielsen DMA's.

• *Program/Music Director:* Radio stations employ program or music directors to select the records they air. Smaller stations use the trade magazine charts, listener requests and local record store sales tallies to determine their play lists. Larger market stations regularly use national consultants and research firms to determine their play lists.

• *Syndicated Programming:* Networks often provide live and/or tape delayed music programs based on research, music formats, and special themes. Live programs are provided over microwave and satellite links. The tape delay programs (for example, "American Top 40") are commonly mailed to the stations on CDs or cassette tapes.

• *The "Burn" or "Fatigue" Factor:* Current recordings are often tested by research firms to determine the listeners' "tiredness" of the recording. A 20-plus % response rate indicates listener fatigue, which may also indicate a desire by the listener to change the station.[31]

• **Watts:** The stations broadcast power; the greater the power, the larger the broadcast signal and the area it covers. AM stations are licensed from 250 to 50,000 watts. FM station wattage varies from 3,000 to 50,000 watts.[32]

## Summary

Radio station airplay, trade magazine advertisements, and music videos are the three main types of promotion used by the music industry to alert the public of their new recordings and signed artists. Radio stations are not in the record business - they are in the advertisement business. They play music to attract an audience in order to sell advertisements. Radio station formats were developed to attract various types of niche audiences who prefer the type of music the station airs. Call-out research is used to determine which recordings are potential "hits" and which recordings have been over-played. Consumer demographics (age, education, etc.) are used to correlate the listeners to various types of music. Trade magazines chart the retail sales and radio station airplay of the label's recordings. Advertisements are regularly placed in the trades to attract the attention of industry insiders and radio station program directors. Music videos are the third type of promotion. Acting, producing, directing, financing, marketing, scripting, and distribution (which have been unique to the film industry) are now used to budget, shoot, and edit music videos. If you want to shoot film or learn about the movie business, in addition to university programs, contact:

**Dov S-S Simens' Hollywood Film Institute**
5225 Wilshire, #410
Los Angeles, CA 90036
(213) 933-3456

## Chapter Footnotes

[1] The Arbitron Co. samples radio station audience demographics and listening habits and then sells the information to radio stations. The stations use the "rating" to determine their advertisement rates and to insure advertisers of the estimated number of people who will hear their advertisements during dissimilar times of the broadcast day.

[2] "The Year In Music 1994," _Billboard Magazine_ and radio formats as listed in R&R (1994).

[3] AC is the Adult Contemporary format.

[4] PBS is the Public Broadcasting Service.

[5] The Encyclopedia of The Music Business, Harvey Rachlin (1981).

[6] "The History of Rock & Roll, Part One" Showtime Productions (video tape) (1985).

[7] The Encyclopedia of The Music Business, Harvey Rachlin (1981).

[8] Arbitron Format Share Fall '95, Billboard Magazine (March 9, 1996).

[9] The loss of a station's broadcast license (which is originally granted by the United States Federal Communications Commission) will put a station off-the-air and, in effect, force the station out of business.

[10] "Arbitron Co. formats (Winter 1993)" as reported in Billboard Magazine (June 5, 1993).

[11] "Format Share by Demographic Group, Fall '95 Arbitrons," Billboard Magazine (March 9, 1996).

[12] Ibid.

[13] Called the "Hot 100 Singles," Billboard Magazine (1994).

[14] *SoundScan* currently reports about 60% of all record sales.

[15] Called a digital "fingerprint."

[16] Called "gross impressions," Billboard Magazine (1994).

[17] "Monitor Power Playlists" Billboard Music Group, BPI Publications (1994).

[18] Billboard Magazine (1994).

[19] Ibid.

[20] Used by Gavin to figure a recording's "Hit Factor," which is the percentage of reporting stations that will play the recording on a heavy or medium rotation, Gavin (1994).

[21] Gavin Report (1994).

[22] "1995 The Year in Music," Billboard Magazine, pp. YE-6 through YE-84 (December 23, 1995).

[23] Music Business International (July, 1993).

[24] "Inside MTV," R. Serge Denisoff, Transaction Publisher (1991).

[25] Radio wanted to play only the "known recording artists and their hits." The assumption was that unproven artists could reduce the size of the audience, causing the radio station to loose advertisement money.

[26] Radio was locked into playing the hits by established artists. MTV introduced unknown acts to the public through the music videos. MTV audiences called local radio stations requesting the MTV acts and songs. The calls forced the stations to add many of the MTV artists to their playlist, breaking radio's monopoly to the public.

[27] "Billboard Video Monitor," Billboard Magazine (1994).

[28] "German Music Biz Welcomes Viva," Billboard Magazine (1994).

[29] R&R (January 20, 1995).

[30] Nielsen ratings as reported in "MTV Experiments To Hold Viewers," Billboard Magazine (1993).

[31] The Eagle Group research report at the Country Music Radio Seminar (CRS 27), Nashville, TN, (March 2, 1996).

[32] Radio Datatrak, Bethlehem Publishing (1994)

# 12

# ARTIST MANAGEMENT

**Imaging Talent & Product
Management Team
Booking Agents
Publicity**

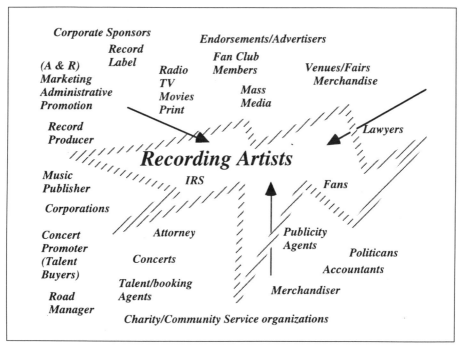

*Figure 12.1  It seems that once you're famous everyone wants a piece of you.  The mass media wants your story, image, etc. for their newscasts and tabloid TV shows; corporations and advertisers seek endorsements; music business promoters, record labels, and music publishers what you to sing their songs, promote their albums and appear in their concerts; community and charity organizations want your time and endorsements; lawyers and accountants want to represent your time, image, and money; musicians and singers want to be on your next record and play on your concert tour; and once you've made a little money and paid all the bills, the IRS wants their piece of the pie.*

The music business is a topsy-turvy, high-pressure, competitive business. Millions of dollars change hands every day based on how successful the industry's creative and business systems work together. However, most consumers do not care about the intimate details and legalities of "how the industry operates." They are only interested in the label's recording artists and their music. Or, to put it a better way, most consumers are interested in the *public image* of the artist. The music industry and most of the artists themselves use their public images as marketing *icons* to motivate concert ticket and recorded music unit sales.

## Popularity

Huge income brings out the long-lost relatives and the unscrupulous. Fame brings the sacrifice of a private lifestyle to over-zealous fans. At times, it seems that everyone wants a piece of the action, which really means a piece of the artist's money, time, or fame.

## Artist Representation

Artist managers bring representation, administrative supervision, surrogate control, and sanity to a recording artist's complex image and long-term career. A business plan for the business side of the artist's career and a strategic management plan that links the business and creative sides of the artist's career together are developed. Career plans and goals are established based on the perceived commercialization of the artist's image and talents.

## Management Team

Managers are hired and fired by artists. It is best not to hire a friend or relative because they will have to make many important business decisions that will effect the artist's income and long-term career. They have to be able to say "no" to friends and family, as well as shady business offers. Once the manger is in place, then he or she will hire several talented individuals who will work under their supervision to accomplish specific duties in the name and "best interest" of the artist. The management team commonly includes a *business manager*, *booking* or *talent agent*, *road manager*, *attorney*, *publicist*, *road musicians* and *office personnel*.

## Booking or Talent Agents

Business managers are really Investment advisors. It is best if they have a degree in finance, plus a successful track record in investments and money market funds. Otherwise, you're turning over your money to someone who only claims to know what they are doing and, unfortunately, may loose your hard-earned commissions and royalties. Booking or talent agents are *franchised* by the unions they represent. AFTRA approves of agents who represent their members seeking employment as vocalists in recording sessions and as newscasters and TV personalities. Agents commissioned by the AF of M represent musicians employed as recording artists, session musicians, and concert or other live performers. *Equity* agents represent actors and actresses pursuing employment in any type of unionized live theater. Finally, SAG (Screen Actors Guild) represents actors and actresses seeking employment in any type of film media (as opposed to video which is covered by AFTRA), such as movies, TV shows and commercials. Union-franchised booking agents are ordinarily limited to 10% commission rates.

## Attorneys

Attorneys structure deals for artists under the supervision of the personal manager. Accordingly, some attorneys become very powerful and act as personal managers after they have established themselves in the business. Attorneys charge hourly rates ($150-500 per hour) or are placed on a *retainer,* which is a monthly minimum fee based on a negotiated number of hours of work per month.

## Publicity

Publicity is often thought of as *free promotion*. However, stories, in trade and popular press articles are usually supplied by a staff or hired publicists. TV show appearances, radio station interviews, etc. are regularly *arranged* by label representatives or hired publicists. Thus, artist managers, record labels, professional musicians and event specialists, hire publicists as part-time or full-time employees from public relation firms to plant stories and articles featuring their clients in the professional trades and consumer mass media.

The publicists assimilate images which have been created, molded, or, hopefully, enhanced by the artist's manager and label representatives and then write stores, news articles, and press releases. It is always better to have an image that is true to the essence of the artist instead of a manufactured image which may be perceived as contrived. Then, the publicist alerts the media to cover the events (which are often created by the management and label representatives) as news or entertainment stories. The stories are then released to the print and broadcasting mass media with the hopes of stimulating a positive correlation between the artist's name and public perceptions. Increases in the public's awareness of an artist and acknowledgment of an artist's creative talents often transfer into record sales and record label profits.

## Press Kits and BIO's

*Press kits* help establish authenticity of the artists. They are assembled by publicists and management to alert the press and mass media of a new artist and of an established artist's new recordings. A black & white photo-

graph (*publicity photo*) is included. A one-page *bio* of demographic information, artistic and creative accomplishments, and copies of previous *press
releases* to the trades and consumer press are enclosed.

## TV Appearances

Broadcast television is still used to market recording artists, musicians,
and their music. Variety, late-night and morning talk shows promote artists
and their products. *Publicists* are hired to help "place" stories about the
artists in the trades and consumer press. They also help generate interest in
their artists which can be used by the label and the artist's manager to
"book" the act on a television variety/talk show. Appearances on popular
TV shows reinforce the status of the act and inform the public of new recordings being released.

## Publicity Budgets

The amount of money to spend on publicity varies greatly. It often
depends on the *star factor* (name and image strength of the artist), *sales projections* (how many units the label expects to sell), and *consumer perceptions* (notification of the release of a new album and/or press release to build
an artist's image or to counter negative news stories, etc.). Maximum publicity budgets are often limited to 25% of the creative (production) budget.
As an example, we've already spent **$288,930.80** on our ongoing recording
project. Twenty-five percent or an additional **$72,232.70** needs to added to
cover publicity.

---

### *Publicity*
Label and independent publicity budgeted at about 25% of
creative/production expenses                              **$72,232.70**

---

## Road Managers

Road managers are responsible for all the daily business decisions dealing with concerts and personal appearances. As a result, road managers handle the local press, questions and concerns from promoters, local radio stations and record retail promotions. In addition, they make hotel and restaurant reservations and handle any issues of concern between the recording
artist(s), band members, roadies, and tour support. Accordingly, road managers report directly to the artist and personal manager, and they are the local
communication link between the artist, the promoter and the manager of the
venue.

## Gate Keeping

Artist managers act as *gate keepers* for the artist. They seek out only the
industry insiders who can help *improve the artist's image* and career. At the

same time, managers filter out individuals and companies whose association with the artist or the artist's image would not benefit the artist. Only the industry insiders, public, corporations, and media personnel who fit into the goals and strategic management plan are given access to the artist and permission to associate themselves with the artist's image.

## Additional Duties and Responsibilities

To be a successful manager you will need to:

- *Find a talented artist.*
- *Help develop an image and persona for the talent.*
- *Develop at strategic management plan.*
- *Get a record deal.*
- *Line up a backup band and concert tour through a booking agency.*
- *Invest profits from records and concerts for the artist.*
- *Manage all business decisions and appearances (time).*
- *Negotiate complex contracts.*
- *Find a corporate sponsor.*
- *Help in the selection of songs for album projects.*
- *Hire a publicist to "plant" stories and news articles and provide appearances on TV talk shows.*
- *Approve employment opportunities.*
- *Supervise accountants, attorneys actions, financial advisors, road managers, publicists, and band members.*
- *Hire a vocal coach and media trainer. Media trainers are professionals who teach artists how to answer questions in interviews, look their best on TV, etc.*

## Non-Management Duties

Managers are *not employment agents* and will ordinarily only *approve* of work "pitched" to them by booking agents (for concert tours), publicists (for articles and radio, personal, and TV appearances), record labels (for approval of recording issues and promotional concepts, etc.) and other business offers. Accordingly, managers are not often songpluggers, record producers, or record label executives. And if they were, the artist should be concerned about how much time they are allotting to the artist's career.

# Artist Management Organization Chart

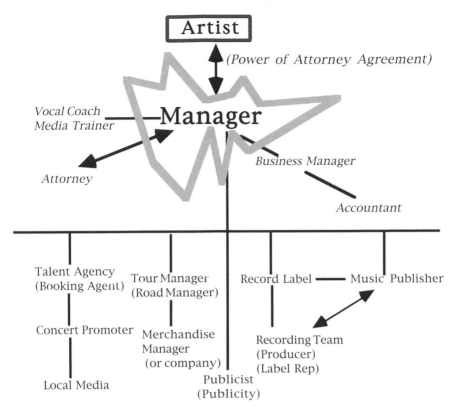

Figure 12.2 Artist managers bring order to the daily chaos caused by success in the music industry. Managers legally represent artists through a power-of-attorney agreement. It provides managers with the legal privilege and obligation of controlling the business and career decisions of the artist. Examples include: record label agreements, music publishing, and music producer selections; mass media promotion and publicity through a hired or label publicist; concert appearances supervised by the road manager and arranged by a talent agent through a concert promoter; and merchandising, corporate sponsorship, endorsements, charity and community service.

## Artist-Manager Relationship

The artist-manager relationship is built on *trust*. The artist has to have confidence in the manager's ability to make the decisions that will enhance his or her career. The artist is busy being an "artist." They need someone to take care of "the business" of being an artist. Hence, the need for a manager. Good managers are plentiful, however, great ones are hard to find.

## Power of Attorney Agreement

A *power-of-attorney agreement* permits the manager to lawfully represent (to the very best of their ability) the artist(s) in all business decisions. Examples include the right and obligation to:

1. *Have an attorney structure contractual agreements,*
2. *Accept, endorse, collect bills, royalties, and checks,*
3. *Defend the artist in lawsuits and against claims,*
4. *Deliver receipts and legal papers, and*
5. *Hire a management team to represent the artist.*

## Commissions

Managers are typically paid 15-25% of an artist's royalty base, such as record deals, concert tours, movie appearances and corporate sponsorships. They do not receive a percent of everything an artist is paid, only what is negotiated (called a *commission base*) between the artist and manager.

## Stage Names

Artists often pick a stage name other than their actual birth name with which to perform or create an image. Examples include:

| Stage Name | Original or Birth Names |
|---|---|
| Pat Benatar | Patricia Andrejewski |
| Tony Bennett | Anthony Benedetto |
| Victor Borge | Borge Bosenbaum |
| David Bowie | David Roger Jones |
| Boy George | George Alan O'Dowd |
| Cher | Cherilyn Sarkisian |
| Patsy Cline | Virginia Patterson Hensley |
| Alice Cooper | Vincent Furnier |
| Elvis Costello | Declan Patrick McManus |
| Bob Dylan | Robert Zimmerman |
| Whoopi Goldberg | Caryn Johnson |
| Tom Jones | Thomas Woodward |
| Chaka Khan | Yvette Stevens |
| Carole King | Carole Klein |
| Huey Lewis | Hugh Cregg |
| Madonna | Madonna Louise Ciccone |
| Demi Moore | Demi Guynes |
| Chuck Norris | Carlos Ray[1] |

## Sage Window

"The first act I managed was *Tag Team*. Their single "Whoomp There It Is" has sold over five million copies. It also broke Elvis' "Don't Be Cruel" and "Hounddog" for the most consecutive weeks on Billboard's Hot 100 Singles Chart. I've recently negotiated a co-publishing and co-production deal with Curb Records. We're developing several R&B/rap acts.

**Q: How did you help Tag Team become so successful?**

**A:** The most important thing you can do for an act is exploit all their talents. Being there and listening to what they want to do and helping them translate that into what could really happen is important. First, you evaluate the artist and assess their talent. At the time I met Tag Team, "Whoomp!" had already been released. My focus was to take what had become a solid regional hit and explore every avenue available to help expand Tag Team and their single into new markets.

Pam Browne,
Artist management:
Tag Team

**Q: How do you do that?**

**A:** You talk to the act and find out what their priorities are. What are they most interested in? I might be interested in one direction, and they may be interested in something entirely different. *Famous Artists* booking agency (one of the biggest agencies for R&B acts) had booked several dates with Tag Team before I became their manager. I flew to New York and met with one of their agents to establish a good working relationship. Several weeks later, *Famous Artists* booked Tag Team as the opening act for the Budweiser Superfest (a major R&B concert tour).

**Q: What is your role with the group?**

**A:** I act as an advisor to all the artists I manage. Some artists need more guidance than others. The members of Tag Team are very astute and are great businessmen. I encourage them to make the final decisions. I tell them honestly and frankly what I think based on my experience, and what I think the perception of the industry is going to be. It's up to them to make that final decision because I don't have to live with it, they do.

**Q: How did you get them the Adam Family Values movie soundtrack?**

**A:** The *William Morris Agency* called me (we worked with them on several soundtracks) and said that Paramount Pictures needed a theme song for the movie. The movie was about to be released and Paramount wanted a theme based on "Whoomp!" After negotiating a deal with Paramount, Tag Team flew to Los Angeles and co-wrote the theme (Addams Family... "Whoomp!") in one night with the soundtrack's producer.

**Q: Has the movie soundtrack helped record sales?**

**A:** Yes, it has helped record sales because I'm sure some people may not have heard of Tag Team before they heard the song or saw the video on MTV.

**Q: Do you target the white audience now?**

**A:** No. We knew "Whoomp!" was a great song with a phrase that became a national anthem. Our indication of its crossover status occurred when we reviewed BDS (monitors radio airplay) and Soundscan (monitors point of purchase record sales) reports which are reported by city and region. These reports revealed that Tag Team's airplay and sales were phenomenal in rural and non-urban areas.  Additionally, Tag Team received three tremendous career boosts which helped "Whoomp!" maintain its position as the number one selling pop single for 1993 and 1994.  First, "Whoomp!" was selected by the Chicago Bulls and other professional sports teams (e.g., Dallas Cowboys, Philadelphia Phillies, New York Giants, New Orleans Saints, etc.) as their theme/rallying song.  Second, ABC licensed "Whoomp!" as the theme song for ABC's 1994 preview of its fall line-up (these commercials ran all summer prior to the 1994 television season).  Third, Disney recorded its first rap album for children, "Mickey Unrapped," and Tag Team was invited as the only rap act to perform on the album (they sang a parody of "Whoomp!" called "Whoomp! There it Went" with a music video featuring Tag Team and Mickey, Minnie, Goofy, Donald Duck, etc.).  Whoopi Goldberg also appeared on this album.

**Q: How much do you use the trades and the media reports to help you?**

**A:** They are important guides to let us know how the public is perceiving us and where sales and radio airplay are occurring.

**Q: What advice would you give to someone who wants to be an artist manager?**

**A:** Become involved in the music business any way you can.  Join some of the professional organizations.  Attend any functions that BMI, ASCAP, or SESAC or anyone in the business is giving.  Register for entertainment or music seminars.  In addition to learning a great deal, these seminars provide excellent opportunities to meet industry insiders and develop vital networking contacts.

*— Pam Browne, Artist Management: Tag Team*

## Key Artist Management Contractual Terms

Artist/Management *agreements* regularly include the following collective points:

•*Assignment:* The *appointment of the manager* to represent the artist.

•*Commission Base:*  The *negotiated artists' revenue sources* that will earn the manager a commission.

•*Commission Rate:* The *percent of the commission base* that is paid to the manager for his or her service.  Commission rates are usually 10% to 25% of the commission base, however, Col. Parker received 50% of Elvis Presley's earnings.

•**Creative Representation**: Artists grant a *power of attorney* to managers, and managers accept it as a mutual agreement to exhibit common interest in the development of the artist's creative talents, recording, performing, and professional career.

•**Exclusivity**: *The artist is represented solely by the signed manager.* In addition, the artist will often be required to agree not to perform any of the legal duties assigned to the manager in the power-of-attorney agreement without any prior written consent from the manager.

•**Gross Monthly Earnings**: The gross monthly earnings are usually the total monies made by the artists from recording royalty points, bonuses or salaries, profits from concerts and merchandise sales, music publishing and songwriting royalties, commercial endorsements, acting or movie, television performances, and profits from shares in capital ventures.

•**Limitations**: The *power of attorney agreement* is usually limited to matters reasonably related to the artist's career as a musician, songwriter, publisher, and performing artist.

•**Payment of Services**: All monies from the artist's performances, record sales, and commercial endorsements are paid to the manager or the artist's accountant or business manager, as approved by the manager. The manager usually collects his or her negotiated percentage of the commission base and then has the business manager invest or place the remaining portion of the monies collected into the artist's accounts or businesses.[2]

## Summary

Successful musicians and recording artists rarely have the time to be anything other than an "artist." Yet, to be successful in the music business, career decisions (based on sound business principles) have to be made every day. Personnel managers (known as artist managers) are hired by artists to represent them in most of their business and career decisions. Power-of-attorney agreements give the manager the lawful right and power to negotiate business decisions in the best interest of the artist. In return, managers are usually paid 15% to 25% of the artist's income based on various factors agreed upon by the artist and the manager.

Great managers can open the doors to success in the music industry. Poor management can damage long-term career opportunities. Accordingly, the artist-management relationship should be built on trust and respect for one another's knowledge, personalities, qualifications, creative and business talents.  Managers cannot seek employment for the artist they represent. They can only offer guidance and approval of the artist's daily agenda, recording contracts, concert appearances, movie deals, finances, personal appearances, images, hiring and firing of employees, corporate affiliations, etc.

Managers form and supervise a management team consisting of the following: an attorney (normally placed on a monthly retainer), a talent or booking agent (who is franchised by the AF of M and commonly receives 10% of gross income from arranged concert appearances), a business manager (to invest the artist's money - hopefully, an expert in money markets and finance), a publicist (to arrange, write and place news stories about the artist in the commercial press and tabloid TV), a road manager (who is the communicative link between band members, roadies, promoters, venue managers, and the media), and a merchandise company (who will supply tour support merchandise for all concert dates).

Two new books are recommended for additional information on artist management.  They are:

**Managing Your Band**
Artist Management: The Ultimate Responsibility
by Dr. Stephen Marcone
HiMarks Publishing Company
P.O. Box 2083, Wayne, NJ 07474-2083 Fax: 201-595-2217

**This Business of Artist Management**
By H. Lee Heatherington & Xavier M. Franscogna, Jr.
Billboard Books
1515 Broadway
New York, NY 10036

## Chapter Footnotes

[1] "The World Almanac and Book of Facts 1995," Funk & Wagnalls Corporation (1995).
[2] Industry sources.

# 13

## CONCERTS

**Concert Promotion**
**Booking Agents**
**Bid Sheets**
**Ticketmaster**
**The Serious Music Scene**

Record labels want their signed artists *out on the road* performing their hit recordings as a promotional tool to stir up record sales and, of course, profits. In addition, recording artists need to generate revenues to pay for their management team. Record sales provide royalties *after recoupment* of all related label expenses. As a result, most active recording artists need to be on the road performing in order to pay their bills.

### Promoters

*Concert promoters* work independently from the record labels to create their own entrepreneurial businesses. They provide their expertise, money, social and business connections to create *concerts* that help generate the positive cash flow opportunities needed by many performing artists and the album sales desired by the labels.

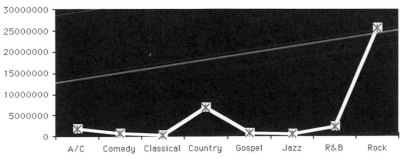

**Concert Attendance by Format**

*Figure 13.1 Rock and country music concert performances had the highest attendance in 1995. A/C paid attendance summed 1,737,063; comedy, 663,742; classical music, 171,494; country music, 6,762,232; gospel music, 726,574; jazz, a surprising 386,664; R&B, 2,269,226; and rock had the highest number of concert ticket buyers with 25, 652,815.*[1]

## Concert Promotion Process

Once they determine which acts to book (employ), promoters match the artists (who are out on tour and available) with the venues that have open dates. At the same time, *booking agents* who represent the artists are calling regional promoters, corporations and venture capitalists (who may act as promoters) to generate *concert dates* for their artists. It's a huge gamble. Bad weather, an artist's poor health, or some other uncontrollable situation can negatively effect the final concert attendance. A poor turnout may cost independent promoters thousands of dollars. Successful concerts can profit hundreds of thousands of dollars in one evening. It's easy to see why the concert promotion business is truly considered *a risky business*.

### Concert Gross Incomes

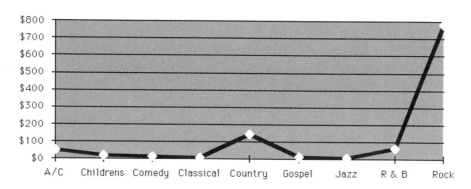

*Figure 13.2 Gross income from 1995 concert performances includes A/C with $49,079,540; children's concerts $24,955,520; comedy, $16,097,386; classical, $6,430,097; country, $142,260,548; gospel, $13,819,695; jazz, $7,905,266; R&B, $66,549,060; and rock music concerts grossed more than 3/4 of a billion at $780,027,596.*[2]

## Virtual Corporations

*Virtual corporations* are often established to run and supervise concert tours. They are *sole-purpose* companies set up to run the tour, ticketing, and merchandising. Promoters run the businesses out of their hotel rooms using multiple phone lines and fax machines. The corporations often gross millions of dollars during the tour, and when the tour is finished, the companies are closed and "out-of-business."

## Stones 94-95 Concert Tour Income

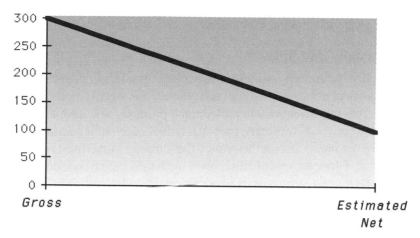

Figure 13.3: The Rolling Stones' 1994-95 concert tour was supervised by a Virtual Corporation run out of hotel rooms. The company oversaw the Stones' tour, all the arrangements, its 250 employees, and its $1.5 million-a week budget. Gross income for the tour was approximately $300 million, of which the Rolling Stones collected about $100 million.[3]

## Deposits

*Bookings* (scheduling) of tour dates by the booking agent must be approved by the artist's manager. A down-payment (*called a deposit*), usually of 50% of agreed upon price, is required from the promoter to finalize the deal. The money is placed into an interest-bearing account. At the night of the concert, as the band is on stage playing, the road manager, tour accountant, and promoter tabulate the concert receipts in the back office. The down payment is subtracted from the money owed the band. Full payment for the band's/artist's performance is required at closing.

Successful promoters are known by industry insiders who continue to reschedule their acts with trustworthy promoters. Successful promoters are offered entire national tours, regions, or clusters of cities to reduce the band's risk of working with amateur promoters.

## Profit Margins

Promoters subtract their *total projected expenses* from their projected *gross ticket sales revenues* to determine their *break even points and profit margins.* They must project how many tickets they can sell at various prices. That total is the projected gross ticket revenues (income). Then, using the "bid sheet" promoters must correctly determine their projected expenses. The projected expenses are then subtracted from the projected gross ticket revenues to determine profitability. Profit margins are based on how many "seats or tickets" must be sold to break even or to make a profit. Most concerts require 80-85% of all tickets to be sold to break even financially. Major acts may require 95% of all tickets to be sold before profit margins are achieved. In addition, concerts are sometimes scheduled in smaller cities between major concert venues. The concerts (called pick-ups) offer the band (or artists) a way to pay their expenses between the more profitable concerts.

## Guarantees and Splits

Clearly, the concert business is very risky. If a band or artist (through their booking/talent agent) is charging more money for a performance than the projected ticket sale revenues will provide, the promoter will have to offer a lower guaranteed price. Accordingly, promoters often negotiate a *guarantee price* plus a *split of the profits* in order to reduce the gamble. Advertisement budgets are rarely cut. However, record labels want the bands (artists) out on the road promoting their latest albums, so, co-promotional "deals" (which help promote the band's concert appearance) are often arranged with the promoters and local radio stations. However, what if it rains or snows? What if there is another concert (by another promoter) the same week as yours (people often have a limited income and may attend only one)? What if a band member gets sick? What if the artist makes a negative public statement or is caught (by the press) doing something illegal? The concert may still have to be played and the attendance may suffer, which means the promoter gambled and lost money.

## Bid Sheets

Promoters use a bid sheet to determine their break even points and projected expenses. The following generic bid sheet lists many of the items promoters must consider and budget *before* they sign a contract to employ an act, buy advertisements (on the radio and in the print media), and rent or lease a venue.[4]

## Sage Window:

**Walt Lederle**
**Mid-South**
**Concerts**

**Q: How do you decide which acts to select?**

**A:** We have an active, working relationship with most of the agencies that are representing multiple acts (booking agencies). Some handle as few as half a dozen acts to agencies as large as the William Morris Agency which handles thousands of acts. We are in daily communication with them. If we see an act or we hear about an act that's going out on the road, we immediately call the agent and say, "Hey, we want a piece of that. We'd like to take a crack at it. Give us your best shot, and we'll give you our best shot." We'll make an offer.

We subscribe to SoundScan, and, of course, we're on-line with all the trades too — PollStar, Billboard and Amusement Business. They immediately show the box scores of acts, which is a summary of how they are doing in which venues.

# Sample Bid Sheet

Artist _____

Date _____

Venue _____

| | | |
|---|---|---|
| ***Talent*** | | ***Totals Expenses*** |
| Headliner | $_____ | |
| Support Act #1 | $_____ | |
| Support Act #2 | $_____ | |
| **Total Talent Bid** | | $_____ |
| ***Venue*** | | |
| Additional (All-In's) | $_____ | |
| **Total Venue** | | $_____ |
| ***Tickets*** | | |
| Printing (non-tm) | $_____ | |
| Ticket Master | $_____ | |
| **Ticket Cost/Commission** | | $_____ |
| Advertising | | $_____ |
| ASCAP/BMI/SESAC License | | $_____ |
| Box Office Advances | | $_____ |
| Box Office Commission | | $_____ |
| Catering | | $_____ |
| Cleanup/Setup | | $_____ |
| House Staff | | $_____ |
| Insurance/Bond | | $_____ |
| Local Transportation/Limousines | | $_____ |
| Lighting Equipment/Spotlights | | |
| (If not included in venue) | | $_____ |
| Medical/Ambulance | | $_____ |
| Misc. | | $_____ |
| Piano Tuner | | $_____ |
| Stage Rental | | $_____ |
| (If not included in venue) | | $_____ |
| Sound Equipment | | |
| (If not included in venue) | | $_____ |
| ***Security*** | | |
| Uniform | $_____ | |
| T-Shirt (security) | $_____ | |
| **Total Security** | | $_____ |
| ***Union Operators*** | | |
| Electrical | $_____ | |
| Forklift | $_____ | |
| Lights | $_____ | |
| Stagehands | $_____ | |
| Spotlights | $_____ | |
| Audio Engineer | $_____ | |
| **Total Union Scale Personal** | | $_____ |
| ***Total Projected Expenses*** | | $_____ [5] |

## The Deal

**A:** A guaranteed figure of money is established, and then there's a formula that kicks in once we break a certain dollar point. In other words, then it goes into a percentage deal. The percentage may be as high as 85/15. It varies from act to act. Sometimes, there's a flat guarantee without a split. Sometimes, there's a flat percentage point without a guarantee. It all depends on the artist's agency, their management, and how they plan on negotiating the tour.

**Q: What's your profit margin?**

**A:** It fluctuates. It can be a couple thousand dollars on a show, it can be in the five-figure digits, or it can break even. When it's all said and done, when we consider all the factors that go into putting on a concert, if you break even, you've done the city a service by bringing talent and putting on the show. The public was entertained, and if you have sponsors in your building, you've done a service for them. You may have done a lot of work for hardly any or no money, but that's part of the game.

## Contracts

**A:** Contracts are there to obviously provide details of the agreement to the promoter. The contract is there to say, "Yes, we will pay 'x' amount of dollars for the services of this band that will play so many hours at this particular venue, at this particular date, at this particular time." The contract is lengthy, and it's detailed. It's not like contracts were 20 years ago. The lawyers have gotten hold of it, and I guess it's for everyone's protection. Once that's put to bed, then the contract also has stipulations about how we are to advertise the act's likeness and what we're to provide when they get here. That's the part of the contract that is known in the business as a rider. It spells out everything from what type of staging we are to provide to what they want for breakfast, lunch, and dinner.

Promoters are usually required to put a deposit down just to show earnest; that we are indeed serious about it, but, again, when you're dealing with the agencies on the scale that we do (we have very good relationships with them), usually it's a phone call and a fax. It could go as late as 3 or 4 weeks before any money is transferred and the deposits are actually delivered. On the other hand, we may be required to set the deposit down immediately with the final negotiations.

**Q: I assume that somebody who's a new concert promoter is probably going be paying all of it up front.**

**A:** Yeah. And, even to this day, when I do a show in a different market, I may be required to pay full up front.

**Q: How are you going to promote the show?**

**A:** Probably 70% radio, 20% print, and 10% television. We can slice that up further when we start doing posters, handbills, and other "grassroots" promotions. Those are general figures. My product, a live concert, is an extension of a radio station's programming. When my commercial plays, the listener hears music, usually the greatest hits of the artist being advertised. Your typical radio advertisers, soft drinks, beer, car dealers and restaurants don't have the attention attraction my "live in concert" ad does. Just as the concert patron's motivation is to see and hear their favorite performer, the radio spot is designed to stir that same emotion to urge people to buy tickets to the event.

**Q: How about the record companies. Are they going to give you any support at this point?**

**A:** Yes, they are. The record company's goal is to sell records, whereas my goal is to sell concert tickets. So, there's a happy medium to be met there. They want the public to buy the records, and what better way to do that than to help the radio stations promote the event. They will help the radio stations with product. In other words, if the Eagles are in town Monday night, they'll provide the radio stations with some product (30 CDs to give away). And that's how the promotions work. They will actually call me and say, "Hey, our artist is in town, and I'd like to go ahead and buy a block of your best tickets." And, in doing so, they will, in turn, give them or sell them to the radio station, and the radio station utilizes them for promotion.

## Merchandising

**A:** Merchandising is an integral part of the concert industry. When people attend a concert, they're going to experience an emotion and get as much good feeling out of seeing and hearing their favorite artist as they can. However, when they leave, all they have is a memory and that ticket stub. So, merchandising has come into play, and it's rare when you see an act that doesn't have at least a couple different styles of t-shirts. Basically, there are companies such as EMI, Brockum, FMI, Nice Man and Winterland which have sprung up to provide the bands with their merchandise. They produce all the merchandise for the band and send a representative on the road to manage the merchandise and seller, count it, provide sellers and tables, and so on and so forth. They inventory it all, sell what they can, and then match it up with the dollars. It's a big revenue stream, and it's a big part of the concert industry.

**Q: I assume that at a really big concert, they're making almost half as much off of the merchandising as they are on the concert.**

**A:** Yeah. The Rolling Stones, for instance, was a marketing phenomenon on their "Voodoo Lounge" tour. They hit the ground running before the tour even went out. They had stuff on The Home Shopping Channel. Honestly, there were over 100 items with The Rolling Stones' likeness on it. Everything from the $300 jackets to a Rolling Stones Harley Davidson motorcycle.

*– Walt Lederle, Mid-South Concerts*

## Ticketmaster

*Ticketmaster* dominates the concert and now sports business. Some call it a monopoly. Others, call it good business. However, their command of the business has caused concerns by major acts (including R.E.M. and Pearl Jam) and the United States Justice Department, which was investigating its business practices until mid-1995. Ticketmaster charges a "service fee" of $3.00-6.00 to consumers when they purchase a ticket. It controls all tickets sold at over 3,000 U.S. venues and tickets sold by more than 50 professional sports teams. It built its business by offering many of the venues front money (in some cases millions of dollars) for the exclusive right to sell tickets to all the events scheduled at the venues. ETM Entertainment Network is Ticketmaster's main competitor. However, Ticketmaster, in the past, has purchased most of its competitors through mergers and buyouts. In addition, Ticketmaster is already offering services over *America Online* and will soon be combining with BlockBuster and The Sony Corp. in other ticketing ventures.[6]

## U.S. Music Products Industry

The success of the recorded music business appears to have stimulated a positive cash flow for the *music products industry,* which is defined as the retail sale of *musical instruments and other various products.* With over 6,000 specialized music products, retailers sell everything from sheet music to guitars, saxophones, and MIDI computer systems in their stores. In addition, portable keyboards and *karaoke machines* are sold by mass merchandisers and consumer electronic outlets. Retailers are represented by The National Association of Music Merchants, better known as NAMM.

> ### NAMM
> (The National Association of Music Merchants)
> 5140 Avenida Encinas, Carlsbad, CA 92008-4391
> (619) 438-8001
> Fax(619) 438-7327

### The Music and Sound Industry Summary[7]
#### (Sales in Millions of Dollars)

| Instrument/equipment | Gross Sales (1988) | Gross Sales (1994) |
|---|---|---|
| • Fretted Products | $378.7 | $665.8 |
| • Sound Reinforcement | $355.0 | $609.2 |
| • Acoustic Pianos | $568.8 | $605.2 |
| • Wind Instruments | $335.3 | $439.4 |
| • Printed Music | $309.6 | $400.1 |
| • Single Unit Amplifiers | $194. | $311.6 |
| • General Accessories | $205.0 | $298.4 |

- Microphones ............................................... $145.2 ............ $259.2[8]
- Percussion ................................................. $148.3 ............ $151.4
- Portable Keyboards .................................... $340.0 ............ $151.4
- Multi-Track Consumer Recorders ............... $ 70.0 ............ $128.7
- Digital Pianos ........................................... $ 82.5 ............ $124.2
- Keyboard Synthesizers ............................... $169.0 ............ $122.6
- Signal Processing Units ............................. $ 64.3 ............ $122.6
- Karaoke Products ...................................... $ 18.8 ............ $116.0
- Home Organs ............................................ $ 97.2 ............ $ 85.9
- Cables ...................................................... $ 52.5 ............ $ 78.1
- Sound Modules ......................................... $ 36.3 ............ $ 68.8
- Institutional Organs .................................. $ 58.6 ............ $ 56.2
- Software Products ...................................... $ 46.0 ............ $ 54.1
- Stringed Instruments ................................. $ 38.3 ............ $ 54.1
- Other Electronics Products[9] ....................... $ 38.7 ............ $ 34.6
- Drum Machines ......................................... $ 00.0 ............ $ 19.7

**Total** ......................................................... **$3,753.0** ........ **$4,977.7**

## Serious Music Market

The music business is much more than the record biz, CDs, cassettes, and rock stars. The *serious music markets* of symphony orchestras, opera, Broadway theater, and dance companies should not be overlooked. Many opportunities are available for classically-trained, consummate musicians and vocalists.

## Membership and Sponsors

Symphonies, orchestras, and various types of choral groups are financed by private and public organizations, churches, universities, public and private grants, donations, businesses, and local volunteer organizations. Many serious music organizations are dependent on these political, social, and music-supporting groups to provide financial support for the local musicians. Memberships (which provide opportunities for socialization) are sold by direct-mail response lists. Memberships and ticket sales are offered at social functions, musical presentations, through phone numbers listed in the advertisements, news stores, public service spots, and by direct mail. Memberships usually include tickets to musical performances *and* social functions. Local symphonies, operas, etc. are marketed through the mass media by using their public service spots (on radio and TV) to announce performances and by providing stories and pictures (about the performances or performers) to the print media.

The *American Symphony Orchestra League* represents approximately half of the 1,600 symphony orchestras in the United States. It is a non-profit society (founded in 1942) which provides education workshops, fellowship, and communicative organizational support to symphony and chamber orchestras.

## Endowment For the Arts

The *Endowment For the Arts* is a government agency that provides matching funds to tax-exempt artistic organizations including symphonies and opera companies. The agency has become controversial due to its awards to debatable non-musical artists.

## Trade Magazines

Trade magazines that report on the music concert and live performance business include the following:

---

### *Amusement Business*
BPI Communications (Mail Box 24970)
49 Music Square West, Nashville, TN 37203 (615) 321-4250

---

*Amusement Business* magazine covers the world's live entertainment and arena business. Founded by William H. Donaldson in 1894, the magazine was known as Billboard Advertising and sold for a dime. In 1896, the magazine changed its name to The Billboard and reported stories on amusement parks, roller rinks, burlesque shows, vaudeville acts, circuses, vending machine sales, and the record business. In 1960, The Billboard split into Billboard Magazine to cover the record business and Amusement Business to cover the live entertainment business.[10] AB's *Boxscore/Concerts* reviews the nations concert scene by reporting the gross amount of money earned at each concert, the gross ticket sales, the headliner and supporting acts, the attendance, the capacity of the venue, number of shows, ticket prices, the promoter's name or organization, the venue, city, and dates of the concerts. Artist managers use the information to have their booking agents arrange tour dates with other successful acts. Concert promoters use the information to infer which acts are playing to sellout audiences in different parts of the country. Record labels check the attendance against regional record sales.

---

### *Pollstar*
Promoters On-Line Listings
4697 West Jacquelyn Ave. Fresno, CA 93721
1-(800) 344-7383  Fax 1-(209) 271-7979

---

*Pollstar* is continually used by industry insiders to make their concert business decisions. Promoters use the agency rosters to select and locate the artists they may want to book into their venues. Venues use the trade to publicize their auditoriums to acts, managers and promoters. Domestic and international stories detail the lifestyle of acts and their successful enterprises. To make business decisions, Pollstar provides a summary chart of radio station airplay (by formats); a listing of recent concert revenues (by the average gross); the number of shows per week and per act; a summary of album sales (by artist, title, and label); and a listing of touring acts' scheduled concerts.

## Concert Promotion Terms

• *Billing:* The location or placement of the act's or artist's name (logo) on tickets, advertisements, and press releases. *Top billing* means that the name of the artists will be on the top of the venues' billboard or marquee, larger print than other acts' or artists' names on tickets, and first mention on radio promotion spots.

• *Break-Even Points:* The point in financial statements where the income (monies gained) from the event (concert, recording contract, etc.) equals the cost or total expenses for the event (or cost of recording, promotion, marketing, etc. of the recording).

• *Cartage:* In the recording studio, *cartage* is the cost of renting and delivery of musical and sound equipment from an independent company. In the concert business, *cartage* is the cost of garbage removal after the concert.

• *Comp Ticket:* Complementary ticket to a concert often provided to radio station and local important music insiders to promote an event. The number of tickets is usually supplied by the promoter and approved by the artist's manager.

• *Concessions:* T-shirt, hats, records, CDs, belts, and other types of merchandise endorsed by the artists are considered concessions. Private companies for 15-25% of the gross income of total sales provide the merchandise, shipment, sales personal, booths, tables, etc. for the acts they represent. Concession sales locations and the percentages of sales (for allowing the sale of merchandise in a venue) are negotiated by the booking agent and approved by the artist's manager.

• *Firm Offer:* A firm offer is a *signed contracted agreement* which includes the concert dates, time of appearance, negotiated price for the acts' performance, and a deposit consisting of a cleared check or money order that will be placed into a secured account.

• *Four Walls:* The most basic levels of service a venue has available to the concert promoter and act are listed under the term "four walls" or "four walling." The amount of electricity available (amps), heating, air conditioning, lights, and personnel, including house security, are listed on the contractual agreement between the venue and concert promoter.

• *Gross Potential:* *The GP* is the maximum amount of money that will be generated by the concert if all tickets are sold.

• *Guarantee:* The minimum amount of money the artist or act will perform for is considered the guarantee. Often, artists will accept a guarantee plus an additional split of the profits. The bigger name acts demand a larger guarantee and larger percent of the promoter's profits.

• *Headliner:* The main attraction or most famous act to perform at the concert. Headliners are paid more money to perform than supporting acts.

• *Load In:* The actual unloading and setting up of the musical instruments, sound, staging, and lighting equipment. It usually takes hours to complete the set-up.

• *Load Out:* The actual breaking down of the musical instruments, sound, staging, and lighting equipment after a concert has been completed. The load out is usually *completed in minutes* instead of hours.

• *Local:* The local *I.A.T.S.E union*, whose members are hired due to contractual agreements with the venue. Workers usually include staging, set builders, lighting riggers, spot and audio operators, and technicians.

• *Opening Act:* The *first act* to appear at a concert. However, the act or artists must be approved by the headliner's manager in order to prevent unknown talent from performing and causing a negative reaction (by association) to the major artist.

• *Rider:* A rider is an additional set of instructions for the promoter regarding specific artist requirements. Riders usually include the size of the stage, lighting, etc. and may even include the type of food, drinks, and color of m&m's the artist want supplied to the dressing rooms.

• *Splits:* A percentage (*PC*) of the profits or money collected from the gate (entry) after the concert expenses have reached the break-even point.

• *Packaging:* Packaging means two similar issues: (a) the selection of bands or artists who will tour together and attract a similar type of audience, and (b) the actual accumulation of cities and dates for the tour.

• *PR:* Public relations, which are usually provided by a hired publicists.

• **Presenter Station:** Promoters and labels offer local radio stations the opportunity to "act" as the radio station that is "bringing the concert to the city" in exchange for a reduced advertisement rate and/or a number of free promotional spots.

• **Representation:** Booking agents who exclusively represent artists and acts for the purpose of acquiring personal appearance commitments (concert dates) from local promoters. Agents usually arrange national concert tours by calling local promoters. Final approval of concert dates are made by the artist's manager.

• **Rigger:** Usually an *I.A.T.S.E union* member who strings the lights and sound systems, often from the ceiling in large venues.

• **Roadies:** Members of the touring acts who load in and out (and often set-up, operate, and break-down) the musical instruments, lighting and sound equipment. The amount and type of work roadies can accomplish depends on: (a) the *I.A.T.S.E union agreements* with each venue, (b) the contractual agreements made with the promoter and artist's manager, and (c) specific items listed in the artist's rider. Roadies are also responsible for loading and driving the trucks to each venue.

• **Road Manager:** The road manager (who acts as an assistant manager to the artist's manager) supervises the band on the road and makes the final decisions associated with concert issues and local contacts including the promoter, press, radio, union's shop steward and the venue's administration.

• **Scaling:** The *assignment of ticket prices* to different types and seat location in a venue.

• **Shop Steward:** The leader and administrator of the local *I.A.T.S.E union.*

• **Ticket Manifest:** A computerized list of every seat (and ticket price) in a venue for a specific act or artists for each concert date.

• **The House:** The venue.[11]

## Summary

Concerts provide record labels with another way to publicize their artists and recordings. However, the concert business is really a separate industry with its own set of entrepreneurial businessmen and women. Concert promoters risk their own money on the whims of the public's fancy to attend a staged event (a concert). Booking agents represent various acts. Their job is to call on the promoters to "book" the act into various tours and venues.

The concert promoters use bid sheets to determine their profit margins and to negotiate the cost of the act(s). Front money (a deposit of 10% to 100% of the cost of the act) is sent to the booking agent with the signed contract and placed into an interest-bearing account. Booking agents are paid 10% for acquiring concert dates for the acts they represent. Acts often share the risk with the promoter by accepting a guaranteed amount of money and then splitting the profits. Typical splits range from 50/50 to 85% to the act and 15% to the promoter. A rider is the actual contract that stipulates how the act's likeness may be advertised. They also detail everything that must be provided for the act, from the type of mineral water in the dressing rooms to the size of the performance stage.

## Chapter Footnotes

[1] "Boxscore Database," calendar year 1995 Amusement Business (1996).

[2] Ibid.

[3] "Top 40" Robert La Franco, Forbes (September 25, 1995), pp. 136-7.

[4] Industry Sources.

[5] Ibid.

[6] "Will Ticketmaster Get Scalped: The Justice Dep. and rivals question its dominance," Linde Himelstein and Ronald Grover: Business Week (June 26, 1995).

[7] "1995 Statistical Review of the Music Products Industry," 1995 Music USA, The National Association of Music Merchants (NAMM) (1995).

[8] Estimates mics, sold only through music merchant retails (NAMM Survey).

[9] Includes sequencers, samplers, controller keyboards, and professional electronic pianos (NAMM Survey).

[10] "Amusement Business" marks 100 years of covering live entertainment industry, Nashville Business Journal, Elizabeth Murray (1994).

[11] Industry sources.

# 14

# MUSIC BUSINESS ECONOMICS

**Break-Even Points**
**Major Markets**
**Secondary Market**
**Emerging Markets**

Let's finish our *recording budget project* by determining how much *money we spent* and how many *units* we need to sell to break-even. Previously, we spent **$288,930.80** by recording, mastering and pressing (including paying for mechanicals) 200,000 units (100,000 CDs and 100,000 cassettes).

## AF of M Trust Fund and Special Payment Fund

Next, we need to contribute to the *AF of M's Trust* and *Special Payment Funds*. Record labels who are signatories to the Phonograph Record Labor Agreement are required to contribute royalties to these two AF of M funds. Both funds are paid twice a year by the labels. The Trust Fund provides payments to musicians for free public performances (music in the parks, etc.). The Special Payment fund helps support musicians who are losing work due to new recording technologies. Trust Fund fees are currently set at $0.0020475 based on a fixed suggest retail price of $8.95 for cassettes (1.8¢ per cassettes sold) and $10.95 for CDs (2.24¢ per CD sold).[1] Free goods, promotional copies and the first 25,000 units (per album) are exempt. Payments are required for five years after the original release date of each album project.[2] *Special Fund rates are the same as the Trust Fund.* Therefore, when combined, the Trust and Special Fund contributions total about 3.6¢ for cassettes and nearly 4.5¢ per CD.

For our project, we pressed 200,000 units, of which 50,000 are classified as free goods and promotional copies. An additional 25,000 units are exempt from the special and trust fund payments, which leaves us with 125,000 units (62,500 cassettes and 62,500 CDs) on which we have to pay S&T royalties. As a result, our Trust Fund and Special Payments will be $0.036 (3.6¢) times 62,500 for cassettes ($2,250) and $0.045 (4.5¢) times 62,500 for CDs ($2,812.50). Combined, our S&T payments total **$5,062.50**.

Special and Trust Fund Payments...............................................**$5,062.50**

## Project Business Sub-Total

To promote our new album, we need to add **$150,000** for radio promotion (approximately 50% of the creative/production budget), **$15,000** for a black & white and a 4-color, full-page ad in <u>Billboard Magazine</u>. Let's also spent **$100,000** for the production of two music videos. Next, let's hire a publicist and pay the label maximum of 25% of our production expenses of $288,930.80 or **$72,232.70**.

Now, let's examine what it costs to market, promote and publicize our new album release.

### *Business Sub-Total*

| | |
|---|---|
| Radio ..................................................................................... | $150,000.00 |
| Trade Magazines Advertisements............................................ | $ 15,000.00 |
| Music Videos ........................................................................ | $100,000.00 |
| Publicity ............................................................................... | $ 72,232.70 |
| Trust and Special Payment Funds.......................................... | $ 5,062.50 |
| **Business Total** ................................................................. | **$342,295.20** |

In our trial run, the creative/production expenses sub-totaled $288,930.80. The marketing, promotion, publicity, etc., sub-totaled $342,295.20. Therefore, the complete package of creating our master tape, pressing 200,000 units, marketing, promoting, and publicizing our artist and album totaled **$631,226.00.** A lot of money! Still, it fits into the industry's average of $500,000 to $1,000,000 to break a new act.

### *Creative/Production Sub-Total*

| | |
|---|---|
| Master Recording ................................................................ | $134,530.80 |
| Mastering Process ............................................................... | $ 1,250.00 |
| 100,000 CDs........................................................................ | $ 45,000.00 |
| 100,000 cassettes................................................................ | $ 30,000.00 |
| Mechanicals (Controlled Composition).............................. | $ 78,150.00 |
| **Creative Total**.............................................................. | **$288,930.80** |

### *Sub-Totals*

| | |
|---|---|
| **Business Sub-Total**............................................................ | **$342,295.20** |
| **Creative Sub-Total**............................................................ | **$288,930.80** |
| **Total Cost of Project** ..................................................... | **$631,226.00** |

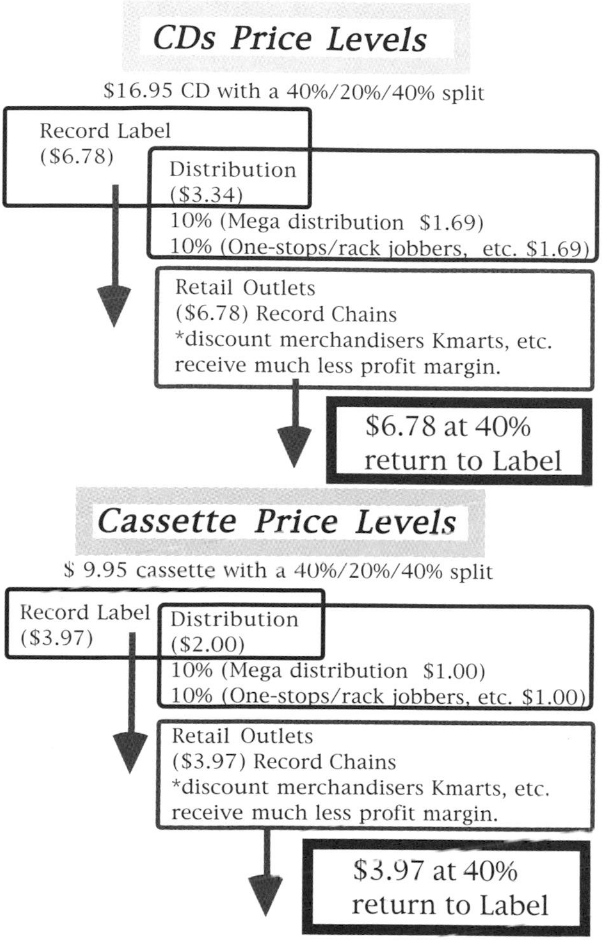

## CDs Price Levels

$16.95 CD with a 40%/20%/40% split

Record Label
($6.78)

Distribution
($3.34)
10% (Mega distribution  $1.69)
10% (One-stops/rack jobbers, etc. $1.69)

Retail Outlets
($6.78) Record Chains
*discount merchandisers Kmarts, etc.
receive much less profit margin.

$6.78 at 40%
return to Label

## Cassette Price Levels

$ 9.95 cassette with a 40%/20%/40% split

Record Label
($3.97)

Distribution
($2.00)
10% (Mega distribution  $1.00)
10% (One-stops/rack jobbers, etc. $1.00)

Retail Outlets
($3.97) Record Chains
*discount merchandisers Kmarts, etc.
receive much less profit margin.

$3.97 at 40%
return to Label

*Figure 14. 1 The monies gathered from the suggested retail price of CDs, cassettes, etc. fall into the typical marketing ranges of 40% (retail), 20% (distribution), and 40% manufacturing (label's 40%). Labels (excluding distribution, which is often a two- or three-step process, depending on the type of distributor) receive 35-40% of the suggested retail price to pay for all related label expenses.*

## Break-Even Points

*Break-even points* are defined as the number of CDs, Cassettes, or *units* that need to be sold for the label (or us) to *recoup expenses*. To find the break-even point for our recording, we need to divide the amount of money returned to us (through the sale of albums in retail outlets) into our total debt of **$631,226.00**.

## Margins

Labels use their own distribution systems and then rely on one-stops, rack jobbers, indie distributors, record clubs, internet outlets, and TV packagers to "deliver" their CDs, cassettes, etc. into commercial markets. Yields or the margins of monies gathered from the suggested retail price of CDs, cassettes, etc.

fall into the traditional marketing ranges of 40% (retail), 20% (distribution), and 40% manufacturing (label's 40%). However, we know that the 40% of retail is severely reduced by the mass merchandisers (Blockbusters, Best Buys) and rack jobbers (Kmarts, Wal-Marts) as a marketing scheme to increase sales.

In addition, the *distribution process* is often a two- or three-step operation. First, the labels have their own mega distribution systems including: WEA (Warner Bros.), Sony, PGD (Polygram), BMG, CEMA (EMI/Capital), and UNI (MCA). Next, the rack jobbers and one-stops take their chunk of the distribution pie (often splitting the 20% with the mega's distribution wing). Finally, the one-stops (now acting as independents) and true independent distributors (there are still a few around who supply mom-and-pop stores) add an additional charge to cover their inclusion into the distribution process.

## Unit Break-Even Points

Unit break-even points are established by averaging the sum of the label's share (40% CD and cassette) of the suggested retail price. As in our example, the suggested retail prices are $16.95 and $9.95 for a total of $26.90. To get the *suggested unit retail price,* divide by 2, which equals $13.45. To figure the label's unit yield (approximately 40% of the suggested retail price), add the $6.78 plus $3.97 (40% returned to the label by the distributor on a CD and cassette) and divided by 2. The average *unit return* is $5.38. Now (for our ongoing record budget project), to determine how many "units" we must sell to recoup our expenses, divide the *average unit return* ($5.38) into our total debt of **$631,226.00**.

> Unit break-even point (assuming all pressing will eventually be sold)
> $5.38 into **$631,226.00**            **= 117,335 Units**

## CD and Cassette Break-even Points

Different types of artists sell better in different types of platforms. As an example, artists who appeal to an older demographic sell more cassettes than CDs. Accordingly, let's ponder the break-even points (for our example) in CDs and cassettes sales.

> **Break-even point for CD sales**
> ---
> $6.78 per CD sold (40% recoupment from retail) divided into total debt of **$631,226.00**            **= 93,102 CDs**

> **Break-even point for cassettes sales**
> ---
> $3.97 per cassette sold (40% recoupment from retail) divided into total debt of **$631,226.00**            **= 158,999 Cassettes**

## Signing Bonuses

Ordinarily, recording artists are not paid royalties (*points*) by the labels *until* the sale of the CDs, cassettes, etc. allow the labels to recoup all of their debt. *Front money* paid directly to the artists as a signing bonus, in addition to the creative and business expenses, are rare. Generally, only superstars are offered signing bonuses. Nevertheless, recording contracts are structured around the *total amount of funds* the label will provide to the artist for their album.[3] The money is budgeted to pay for the recording of the master tape, tour support (buses, musical instruments, sound and lighting equipment) and producer fees. Any money left over is considered the artist's. Once the labels have paid the artist's debt through unit sales, royalty points kick in for the artist and producer.

## Royalty Points

Points are a percentage of the suggested retail price for the CDs, cassette, etc. As an example, 1 point equals 1% of the $16.95 or 16.9 cents. Labels set aside a certain percentage for all royalty points (averaging 8-10% for new artists, 11-14% for established artists, and 15+% for superstars). *Producer's royalties are paid out of the royalty points set aside for the artists.* A recording artist with 15 points negotiated from the label and a 5-point commitment to a producer, would split the 15 points (10 to the artist and 5 to the producer). In addition, the producer is paid their per-side (per song) fee for producing the album (which is charged back to the artist and recouped by the label). One last comment about points: *Successful album sales commonly activate a negotiated escalation in royalty points.* As an example, artists with an album that reaches gold or platinum are frequently awarded an additional 1 2% royalty.[4]

## Packaging Charges

Most labels still place *packaging charges* into recording artist's contracts. The charges are suppose to cover the cost of "packaging" recordings. Except, it is really used to reduce royalty rates and to cover the high cost of marketing new artists. Packaging charges habitually range from 10-25%. They are applied to the suggested retail price of CDs, cassettes, etc. and create a new *royalty base* for the artist. As an example, if an artist has a 25% packaging charge in their contract for CDs, royalty points are figured not on the suggested retail price of $16.95 but on the new royalty base of $16.95 minus 25% (packaging charge) or $12.71. In effect, this process reduces an artist's 10% royalty (once all the album debt has been recouped) from $1.69 per CD sold to $1.27. In addition, remember that no royalties are paid on free goods and promotional copies, which are usually limited in the artist's contract to 15-25% of all pressing. Also, let's not forget *Uncle Sam* who wants a large percentage of any profits to be paid as income and business taxes. Now, that we've spent all that money to create, market and promote our record, where can we sell it?

## Financials

Financial breakpoints on a CD with a suggest retail price of $16.95 and a 40% retail, 20% distribution, and 40% label split include: $6.78 to retail (of which a large percentage is often discounted by mass merchandisers and rack jobber outlets); $3.39 to distribution (which is often split equally between the mega distribution systems, rack jobbers and one-stops, etc.); and $6.78 that is returned to the label. Financial outlays from the 40% returned to the label are estimated as: 61¢ packaging discounts; 67¢ manufacturing of jewel box, disc, plus artwork; $1.76 (13% of retail) set aside for artist and producer royalties (amount negotiated and paid after recoupment is completed); song mechanicals, 52¢ (controlled composition) or 70¢ (statutory rate); AF of M Trust and Special Fund payments 5¢; marketing, promotion, and publicity, $1.50; and profits after recoupment, $1.67.[5]

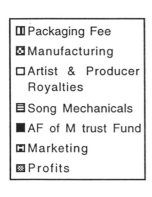
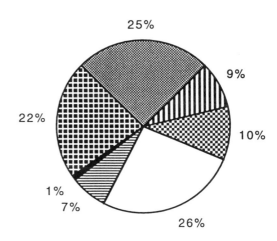

*Figure 14.2 Excluding distribution and retail, record label expenses include the packaging discount fees of about 10% (depending on platform format); manufacturing, 9% (including the cost of pressing the recordings onto CDs, minidisks, cassettes, etc., the artwork, jewel box, and shrink wrap); artist and producer royalties roughly 13% of retail or 26% of wholesale; song mechanicals, 7% (depending on the number of songs on the album and the controlled composition clause); the AF of M Trust Fund and Special Payment Fee, generally less than 1%; marketing (including promotion and publicity, nearly 22%; and, hopefully, profits of about 25% per unit.[6]*

Artist royalties are combined with any monies set aside for profits to pay for recordings, signing bonuses (which are becoming rare), tour support, and other funds advanced to the artist. In addition, after the monies from album sales pay for all the "bills" accumulated by the artists (production, manufacturing, marketing, promotion and other expenses approved by the label), then, and only then, are profits sustained by the label and artist and producer royalties paid. Also, once album sales show a dividend, the label still has to pay administrative, staff salaries, office space, business expenses and taxes out of the profits. The manufacturing, artist, producer royalties and mechanicals are frequently considered *below-the-line* or "fixed" per-pressing expenditures. The marketing, promotion, packaging discounts, etc. tend to fluctuate depending on the success or failure of sales and are thus considered "above-the-line" or "non-fixed" expenditures.

## World Music Markets

The world of recorded music sales is defined by *major, secondary,* and *emerging markets.* Major markets are the United States, Japan, Germany, the United Kingdom, and France. Sales in the five countries summed approximately 70% of all world recorded music transactions. As an example, in 1993, major market recorded music sales were in the *millions of units* (except for singles, which were in the hundreds of thousands) and revenues were counted in the *billions of dollars.*[7]

## Major Markets

| Country | Singles | LP | Cass. | CDs | Units/Millions | $/billions |
|---|---|---|---|---|---|---|
| (1) USA | 108.4 | 1.2 | 339.5 | 495.4 | 944.5 | **9.8** |
| (2) Japan | 145.3 | 0.6 | 14.0 | 191.8 | 351.7 | **5.0** |
| (3) Germany | 36.0 | 1.6 | 47.2 | 152.8 | 238.5 | **2.6** |
| (4) UK | 56.2 | 5.0 | 55.7 | 92.9 | 209.8 | **1.9** |
| (5) France | 20.8 | 0.2 | 31.2 | 86.61 | 38.8 | **1.8** |

### Major Markets by Sales of Units and Revenues

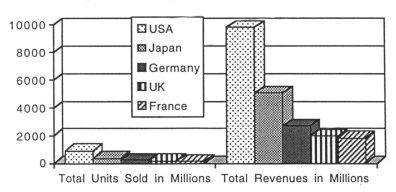

*Figure 14.3 Major markets countries include the United States with 1993 sales of $9.8 billion, 50% of the sales of the five major market countries. (In addition, the U.S. market is about 30% of all world markets.) Other major market countries include; Japan, $5.08 billion and 19% of the major markets; Germany with $2.7 billion, 13%; the UK with $1.97 billion, 11%; and France with $1.84 billion, 7%.*[8]

## Secondary Markets

*Secondary markets* include Canada, the Netherlands, Mexico, Australia and Spain. Sales are in Millions of units and millions of dollars.

| Country | Singles | LP | Cass. | CDs | Units/Millions | $/Million[9] |
|---|---|---|---|---|---|---|
| (6) Canada | 1.1 | 0.00 | 28.3 | 38.8 | 68.2 | **897** |
| (7) Netherlands | 5.7 | 0.30 | 1.6 | 34.1 | 42.2 | **618** |
| (8) Mexico | 0.5 | 0.60 | 40.9 | 20.2 | 62.2 | **572** |
| (9) Australia | 10.2 | 0.02 | 10.1 | 26.4 | 46.7 | **545** |
| (10) Spain | 0.8 | 5.30 | 19.6 | 25.0 | 50.7 | **493** |

## Emerging Markets

The smallest, yet fastest growing markets for recorded music are in the *emerging markets*. They are primarily third-world developing countries and the maturing countries in South America, Africa, and Asia. Trends appears to indicate that the dominance of American artist record sales in foreign markets is declining. As a result, the six mega entertainment organizations are increasing their investments in foreign markets and artists.

### Emerging Foreign Markets

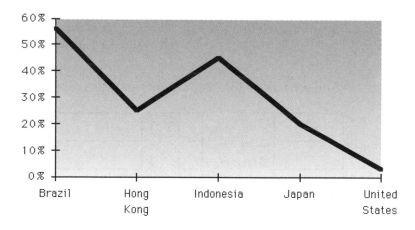

*Figure 14.4 Estimated figures from the first six months of 1995 indicate the rapid increase in album sales overseas compared to the U.S. market. It is important to remember that the overseas markets are much smaller than the American market, however, the huge increases of sales overseas (as high as 55%) compared to the U.S. (about 3%) appears to indicate a shift in future market trends away from the U.S. market and American artists to foreign markets and artists.[10]*

## American Market

The *Recording Industry Association of America* (RIAA) researches the recording market for its label-affiliated members.[11]

## Share of Recorded Music Sales by Format

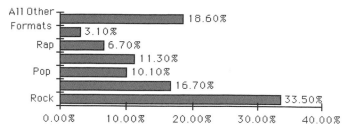

*Figure 14.5 Rock music commanded a 33.50% share of the 1995 12.3 billion U.S. recorded music market. Country music sold 16.7%; pop, 10.10%; urban contemporary, 11.30%; rap, 6.7%; and gospel, 3%. Jazz and classical music (commonly averaging about 3-4% of all sales, combined with all other music formats totaled the final 18.6%.* [12]

## American Recorded Music Sales

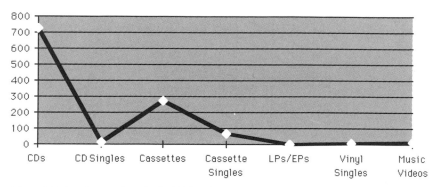

*Figure 14.6 American market sales for 1995 totaled 1.1 billion units. Platform sales included CDs, 727.6 million; CD singles, 17.2 million; cassettes, 272.6 million; cassette singles, 70.7 million; LPs/EPs, 2.2 million; vinyl singles, 10.2 million, and music videos, 12.6 million.* [13]

## American Market Sales by Musical Genre

*Figure 14.7 Rock, pop, and jazz sales have suffered from the increase in the popularity of country music, urban contemporary, and rap music. Sales of rock music has decreased from 42.9% of total sales in 1989 to 32.6% in 1993; pop dropped from 14.4% to 11.7%; and jazz from 5.7% to 3.3%. Country music sales has jumped from 6.8% of total sales in 1989 to 17.5% in 1993. Urban contemporary and rap have climbed to 9.9% and 7.8% of total 1993 sales.* [14]

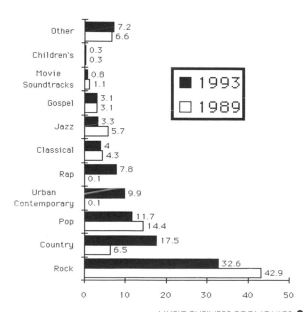

## Silver, Gold, Platinum and Diamond Awards

Silver, gold, platinum, and diamond record awards are presented by the RIAA to record labels for various levels of unit sales. The awards are based on the number of albums sold and the population of the country. Labels usually purchase the album awards and pass them on to the recording artists, studio musicians, producers, and others associated with the success of the products. The United States does not award silver and diamond certifications.

### Silver, Gold, Platinum and Diamond Awards

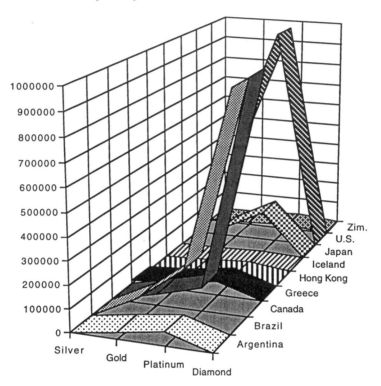

*Figure 14.8 Silver, gold, platinum, and diamond records hanging on a record executive's wall represent different levels of record sales in various countries. As an example, a gold record represents 500,000 units sold in the United States, 30,000 in Argentina, 100,000 in Brazil, 50,000 in Canada, 30,000 in Greece, 10,000 in Hong Kong, 3,000 in Iceland, 100,000 in Japan, and 10,000 in Zimbabwe. Most countries double gold sales levels to represent platinum certification. Platinum requires 1 million units sold in the United States, 60,000 in Argentina, 200,000 in Brazil, 100,000 in Canada, 20,000 in Hong Kong, 200,000 in Japan, and 20,000 in Zimbabwe. Iceland, with a population of approximately 300,000, requires 7,500 for platinum.[15]*

## Piracy

Just as the pirates of the Caribbean were the scourge of honest sailors in the 16th and 17th century, modern-day music pirates are loathed by the music and entertainment industry. Music pirates steal the profits of the creative and business participants of the industry. Making illegal copies of purchased albums or master tapes and selling them to the public is a crime.

Creative individuals who have often forgone secure monetary incomes to risk their creative efforts on careers in songwriting, singing, and musical recordings are victimized. Record labels who risk between half a million to a million dollars to create an album are also ripped off. It often takes years of dedicated work to develop the depth of talents and education required to make it in the music industry. It is a sad commentary on our society when the truly talented risk takers who have earned financial rewards through a hit recording are denied a portion of their earning because of piracy.

## Loss of Revenue due to Record Piracy

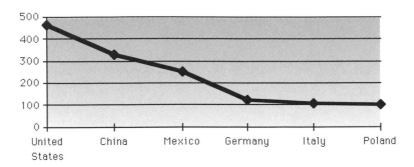

*Figure 14.9  Pirated Music in 1992 (latest figures) equaled $463 million in the United States, $330 million in China, $250 million in Mexico, $121 million in Germany, $105 million in Italy, and $102 million in Poland.[16]*

## Piracy Rate Per Country

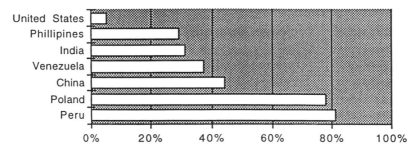

*Figure 14.10  Eighty percent of the records sold in Peru are pirated. Other countries include Poland, 78%; China, 44%; Venezuela, 37%; India, 31%; Philippines, 29%; and the United States at approximately 5.2%.[17]*

## Future Market Trends

Demographic changes may effect the future of consumer purchases. Five-year population trends project an increase in the U.S. population to 269 million by the year 2000. Yet, there will be decreases in the music-buying population of the 20-24 age group (-7.3%) and the 25-29 age group (-16.4%). There will be increases in the traditionally non-music-buying age groups of 40-49 (+35.8%) and 50+ (+16.84%). Forty-three percent of the population will be 40+ years old by the year 2,000.[18]

## Summary

The United States, Japan, Germany, The United Kingdom, and France totaled 70% of the world market recorded music sales in 1993. Secondary and much smaller markets include Canada, The Netherlands, Mexico, Australia, and Spain. The fastest growing markets are the emerging third-world countries including Turkey, Brazil, India, and Indonesia.

CDs are the most popular purchases followed by cassettes, DCCs and mini-disks. Vinyl albums have declined to less than 1% of sales in most countries. Worldwide sales of recorded music are approaching $35 billion annually. However, profits were reduced by high levels of piracy in the fastest growing third-world markets. Trends appear to suggest an aging American market, yet increases in recorded music sales by the mature consumers are predicted. Other major market countries are expected to continue to increase recorded music sales.

Break-even points are established by taking labels' share of a typical 40% retail, 20% distribution, 40% label split and dividing the unit figure (the average between the suggested retail list price of a CD and cassette) into the label's total debt on the project. Signatory labels to the AF of M labor agreement are also required to pay a Special Fund and Trust Fund Fee based on the amount of product sold (excluding free and promotional goods, and the first 25,000 copies).

## Chapter Footnotes

[1] Industry Sources (1996).

[2] "All You Need to Know About the Music Business," Donald S. Passman, Simon & Schuster (1994), p. 162.

[3] Ibid.

[4] Ibid.

[5] Music Business International (1993).

[6] Ibid.

[7] "World Music Figures Hit Flat Note," source IFPI as quoted in MBI (1994).

[8] Ibid.

[9] "World Music Figures Hit Flat Note," source IFPI as quoted in MBI (1994).

[10] "The New Music Biz," Paula Dwyer, Margaret Dawson and Dexter Roberts, Business Week (January 15, 1996), pp. 48-51.

[11] The RIAA is a Washington, D.C. based trade association whose label members create, manufacture, or distribute approximately 90% of all the legitimate sound recordings sold in the United States, RIAA News release (1994).

[12] RIAA (1996) and "RIAA Report Shows Stagnant '95 Shipments for Music, Videos," Paul Verna, Billboard Magazine (March 2, 1996).

[13] Ibid, and "Year To Date Overall Unit and Sales by Album Format Charts," Billboard Magazine (December 31, 1995).

[14] Ibid.

[15] "Cribsheet: What Does a Gold Disc Really Mean?" Source: IFPI as reported in Corporate Watch, Steve Redmond (editor) MBI (1994).

[16] MBI World Report (1994).

[17] Configured from the 1992 United States recorded music sales of $8.866 billion and pirated music sales valued at $463.4 million. Source MBI World Report (1994).

[18] Music Business International (1993).

# 15

# CREATING A SUCCESSFUL MUSIC BUSINESS CAREER

**Education**
**Practical Experience**
**Networking**
**Entrepreneurship**

The difference between being good at something and being great at something is called a "career." Many of us find the music and entertainment business glamorous and exciting. Of course, we want to make it our career. The question is "how?"

## Employment

The music business and entertainment industries combined with the recreation industries (amusement parks, etc.) have approximately the same number of employees as the vanguard of the American economy, the auto industry.

**Employment In The Music and Entertainment Industry**

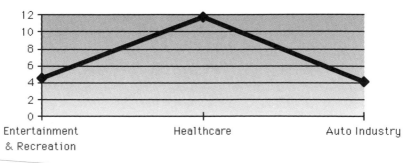

*Figure 15.1 The American entertainment and recreation industries employed approximately 4.5 million*

*workers in 1993; the auto industry, 4.3 million; and the health care industries, 11.8 million.*[1]

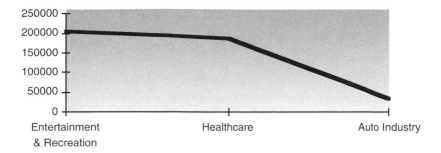

*Figure 15.2 The 204,000 new jobs created by the entertainment and recreation industries represents a 4.5% increase in employment compared to the 187,00 new jobs (1.5% gain) in the health care industry and the 33,000 jobs (0.7%) in the auto industry.*[2]

## Numbers and Realities

If you are a talented artist, musician, etc. and you're waiting to be discovered, you're in for a rude awakening. Professionals have assertively *earned their own success* by obtaining a quality education, meeting the right people, perfecting their artistic and business intellectual talents, and by being in the right place at the right time.

There are many reasons talented individuals want to be in the music business. Some want to be rich and famous while others just want to make people happy through the recordings and performances they create or help to sell. Some want it all. However, record labels are interested in one primary issue, making money. The reality is that the recording side of the music business is a much bigger gamble than rolling dice in Las Vegas or Atlantic City. Casino odds are slanted less than 1% toward the house. You can enter the game for less than one dollar and win money approximately 49% of the time. However, if you are an average player, over a period of time, you'll end up losing money because of the statistical odds in favor of the casino. Casinos make millions because the odds are in their favor and billions of dollars are being played.

In the music business, the odds of having a successful (profitable) recording career are much tougher. Less than 2% of all the recordings released sell enough units to be certified Gold or Platinum.[3] Labels spend hundreds of thousands of dollars just to get a recording completed and thousands more to press CDs and cassettes and often even thousands more to promote, market, distribute, and publicize the artist and their recordings.

The good news is that the industry offers many opportunities for creative and business-minded individuals other than the world of recording. For every recording artist, there are many other career opportunities. Artists need studio and tour musicians, record producers, audio engineers, managers, attorneys, booking agents, promotion agents, publicists, radio announcers, sales persons, financial managers, and many others to help them build their careers.

Here are some tips about the most noticed music industry careers and their employment opportunities:

## Songwriters

Songwriters can be employed as composers, arrangers, orchestrators, or music editors for television and movies. They provide songs for albums and music for commercials, jingles and advertisements. Talent is essential, but an excellent understanding of all forms of music, instrumentation, voicing, and musicianship is a must for long-term career success as a songwriter.[4] Communication and networking skills are also important for co-writing and industry networking opportunities.

## Musicians

Musicians have many career options and sources of income, including instrumentalists and or vocalists in rock, country, and jazz performance groups, concert bands, orchestras, and even in the armed forces. Recording opportunities include music soundtracks for TV shows, movies, commercials, jingles, and, of course, major artists' records. Additional opportunities include teaching music in public and private school systems.

Possessing musical talent is imperative if you want to be a recording artist or studio musician. A music education, an understanding of copyright law, music publishing, networking, the music business, and that "practice-practice-practice" ethic are important for success. Sight-reading is usually required for a musician to work quickly and effectively. Knowledge of the "number system" is required if you want to be a studio musician in Nashville and encouraged elsewhere.[5]

## Recording Artists and Vocalists

*Vocalists* find employment as soloists in choral groups, as opera singers, and in Broadway plays, theater, amusement parks, concerts, session background and harmony singers, recording artists, as well as singers on jingles, commercials, radio, TV, and movies soundtracks. Suggested skills and knowledge include superior vocal and musical talents, music theory education, a love of performing, people and showmanship, and practice-practice-practice. Also important are sight-reading, quick memorization skills, positive personality, knowledge of the copyright law, music publishing, accounting, marketing, publicity, business management, promotion, and the music business in general. Communication and networking skills are vital. Knowledge of a foreign language is often required for traditional vocal performances and opera.[6]

Obviously, to be on the creative side of the industry, the more courses taken in musicianship, music theory, voicing, diction, instrument pedagogy, French, German, Italian, conducting, English, and song literature, the better your chances of obtaining a music performance career. *But, to be a recording artist, it takes more than musical talent.* Focus groups of industry insiders indicate that in addition to having a great voice or musicianship, an *ideal recording artist* should be:

## Preferred Professional Characteristics

- DRIVEN
- SMART
- A VERSATILE WRITER AND PERFORMER
- ABLE TO COMMUNICATE THEIR IDEAS AND IMAGE
- BELIEVABLE
- EXCITING
- NON-THREATENING
- APPROACHABLE
- PERSONABLE
- UNIQUE
- FOCUSED
- CONFIDENT
- MARKETABLE
- A TEAM PLAYER WHO APPRECIATES THE INDUSTRY TEAM

*Figure 15.3 Recording artists are often seen by the public as having a "lifestyle of the rich and famous." Yet, they are often seen by record labels as "product" they are investing in to make a profit. The real person is often somewhere in between the two perspectives.*

The same focus groups also listed what they would *not* want to find in a recording artist. Comments included:

## Non-Professional Characteristics

- BE A FACELESS SINGER OR MUSICIAN
- BE CONTROVERSIAL
- BE IMMATURE
- BE UNATTRACTIVE OR HAVE A WEIGHT PROBLEM
- BE ARROGANT OR HAVE A BIG EGO
- BE OBNOXIOUS

- BE TECHNICALLY A GREAT SINGER, BUT NOT HAVE ANY PERFORMANCE EMOTION
- SING BAD MATERIAL
- BE A BORING PERFORMER
- NOT BE DEDICATED
- TALK TOO MUCH (TO PRESS)
- BE HIGH-MAINTENANCE
- TALK DOWN TO AUDIENCE
- EXPLOIT THEIR SEXUALITY[7]

## Record Producers

Suggested skills and knowledge include a passion for music, an understanding of music theory and sight-reading, and knowledge of the "number system." Producers also need to know copyright laws, music publishing, business finance and the music business sub-systems. Musicianship skills are essential for music producers. Successful producers communicate well with others, are decisive leaders, understand basic accounting skills for controlling budgets, and have strategic management skills for administration.

In addition, producers commonly have a consummate understanding of the recording studio - its acoustics, basic electronics, and equipment capabilities - and have an almost magical ability to "marry" the right song to the right recording artist. They meet other industry professionals through networking, showcases, parties, meetings, professional organizations, industry events, award shows, etc. Successful producers know the "movers and shakers" (the insiders and personalities who manage and control the industry), since that is where the majority of their work originates and these are the people who can get their products to the labels and ultimately to the consumers.

## Audio Engineers

Suggested skills and knowledge include a basic understanding of the music business systems, music theory, musicianship, copyright laws, music publishers, marketing, management, and business finance. Knowledge of computers, MIDI recording techniques, basic electronics, acoustics, recording equipment, and having a continuous desire to learn the latest technical advances in recording equipment and audio production are fundamental. Communication skills and the ability to work with highly creative individuals is crucial (for this reason the Number System is also strongly encouraged). Business courses are also required as most audio engineers are actually self-employed entrepreneurs. Most will own or lease a recording studio, own a music publishing company, and some will have their own independent record labels.

## Business Careers

Record label personnel, artist managers, marketers, promoters, publicists, and the other "business" careers in the industry often require basic business and computer skills. Education for *business professionals* includes marketing, management, finance, accounting, strategic management, computers, and business communications. Mass communication and broadcasting courses can be helpful. Knowledge of the music business, networking, copyright law, music publishing, and the ability to work with highly creative individuals is essential. Degrees in *Music Business* or business emphasizing marketing, management, accounting, computers, international business, and economics skills appear to be very helpful in obtaining a position in the music industry. *Music, Broadcasting,* or *Mass Communications* degrees with a *business minor* are also recommended.[8] Foreign languages are encouraged for those who want to work overseas or in international companies.

### Creative/Business Milieu

There are constant underlying philosophical conflicts between the creative and business sides of the industry. Successful industry professionals customarily accept the interface of creativity and structured global businesses as the key to success. Yet, when large sums of money are involved, adversarial attitudes often develop between the value of art versus the profits of business. Disagreements range from friendly discussions to lawsuits, which sometimes define the boundaries of the conversations and solutions to personal and financial conflicts.

### Business Professional Qualifications

For non-performance, career-minded individuals, a recent survey of industry professionals offers some insight into areas of knowledge that might help you become an industry success. Respondents were asked:

> *Which of the following "areas of knowledge" are the most important for building a successful career in your area of expertise? Assume the students have a basic knowledge of the structure and operation of the music business. Now, what else do they need to know?*

Four hundred and forty industry decision makers listed in the 1993 issue of Music Row's "In Charge" were mailed a survey. Respondents ranged from self-employed creative entrepreneurs to major label CEO's. Data was collected by return mail and correlated. Because of the high response rate of 39% a second inquiry and non-response bias verification was not conducted. Respondents were asked to rank 10 of 23 "areas of knowledge" they felt were most important for building a successful career in the music and entertainment industry. Twenty-six percent were employed in the creative and production occupations of songwriters, producers, etc. Thirty-five percent worked at a record label, 14% for music publishers, 5% at BMI, ASCAP, or SESAC, 5% at a music, film or television production company, 3% at a radio or television station, 11% were artist managers, 6% were publicists, and 20% listed other occupations including: 9% concert promoters and booking agents, 2% record producers, and 1% recording artists. Eighty-three percent of the respondents have worked in the music and entertainment industry for more than 10 years. Sixty-nine percent of the respondents were male, 31% female. Two percent were age 18-24, 11% were 25-34, 41% were 35 to 44, 29% were 45 to 54, and 16% were 55 or older. Sixty percent make more than $75,000 annually. Twenty-four percent hold graduates degrees, 55% have a bachelors and an additional 35% have completed some college education.

Results indicate positive support by industry professionals for expertise in communication, business classes, and entrepreneurship in addition to music knowledge and skills. The industry insiders high rankings of communication and thinking (cognitive abilities and skills) appears to infer writing and thinking abilities as important for a successful career. After all, it is the ability to creatively link entrepreneurial songwriters, producers, recording studio owners, etc. to the mega's marketing systems that ignites successful careers in the music industry. (See chart at right).

## Sage Window

"*My major (Music Business) gave me an overview of all the different aspects of the business, so when I tried to make a name for myself, I knew what questions to ask.*"[10]

**– Trisha Yearwood, MCA Recording Artist**

## Unions

There are several *unions* in the music business which represent the creative artists and workers. Unions are organizations formed by individuals in the same or similar profession who band together for increased representation with employers. They bargain for wages and set *scales,* which are the various levels of payments for different types of employment. There are several major music business and entertainment industry unions. As already stated, we know that the *American Federation of Musicians* (AF of M) represents arrangers' and musicians' performances in recording sessions, orchestras, night clubs, and other venues. The *American Federation of Television and Radio Artists* (AFTRA) represents singers, movie and television production sound effects artists, actors, and announcers who work in radio, television, and recording studios. The *Screen Actors Guild* (SAG) represents actresses, actors, recording artists, and other performers working on motion pictures, television shows (shot on film) and music videos. The *International Alliance of Theatrical and Stage Employees* (IATSE) represents audio engineers, lighting technicians, set designers and builders, and stage hands. The major labels, video producers, theaters, and Hollywood film studios

## Music Industry
## Preferred Professional Qualities

[1] = Responses Creative Sample      [4] = Responses of Other

[2] = Responses Management Sample      [5] = Totals

[3] = Responses of Marketing Sample      [6] = Rank on 100 Index Scale

| #1 | #2 | #3 | #4 | #5 | #6 | |
|---|---|---|---|---|---|---|
| 242 | 308 | 258 | 157 | 965 | 97 | Communication & Thinking |
| 172 | 278 | 216 | 135 | 801 | 80 | Writing Skills |
| 105 | 313 | 149 | 114 | 681 | 68 | Business Management |
| 101 | 223 | 174 | 59 | 557 | 56 | Business Marketing |
| 86 | 183 | 164 | 121 | 554 | 55 | Public Relations |
| 74 | 152 | 112 | 94 | 432 | 43 | Computers/Word Processing |
| 137 | 157 | 36 | 89 | 419 | 42 | Copyrights/Legal |
| 73 | 130 | 134 | 77 | 414 | 41 | Sales and Consumer Behavior |
| 128 | 131 | 82 | 58 | 399 | 40 | Entrepreneurship |
| 52 | 195 | 82 | 53 | 382 | 38 | Accounting & Finance |
| 104 | 143 | 44 | 74 | 365 | 37 | Music Publishing |
| 67 | 143 | 76 | 65 | 351 | 35 | Artist Management |
| 115 | 51 | 31 | 18 | 215 | 22 | Audio/Video Production |
| 48 | 77 | 47 | 50 | 222 | 22 | International Music Business |
| 65 | 33 | 70 | 171 | 185 | 19 | English Literature |
| 41 | 34 | 39 | 401 | 154 | 15 | History of Commercial Music |
| 78 | 39 | 19 | 18 | 154 | 15 | Music Technology |
| 104 | 14 | 5 | 9 | 132 | 13 | Musicianship |
| 57 | 12 | 00 | 21 | 90 | 9 | Knowledge of Instruments |
| 14 | 10 | 45 | 20 | 89 | 9 | Other: |
| 40 | 18 | 7 | 5 | 70 | 7 | Music Theory |
| 5 | 19 | 14 | 00 | 38 | 4 | Science and Math |
| 8 | 3 | 17 | 10 | 38 | 4 | Foreign Language[9] |

are union houses.[11] Most concerts by major recording artists are represented by union members, including the stagehands, sound and lighting people.

Several unions have also formed an alliance called the *Associated Actors and Artists of America*. Its union members are represented by the *AFL-CIO* and include *Actors Equity Association* (AEA), the *American Guild of Variety Artist* (AGVA) the *American Guild of Musical Artists* (AGMA) the *Screen Actors Guild* (SAG), and the *Screen Extras Guild* (SEG).[12] The AEA represents professional actors in plays and musicals; the AGVA represents live performance artists, such as singers and dancers at resorts; SEG represents extras in screen productions in Los Angeles, all other extras are covered by SAG; and the AGMA represents traditional musical artists and vocalists performing ballets, ensembles, operas, and other traditional forms of music.

## Professional Organizations

There are many *professional organizations* in the music and entertainment business. Most are organized by its members and function as a spokesperson to represent their profession. *Unions are considered professional organizations, however, most professional organizations are not considered unions.* Professional organizations serve as vital representative links to the creative and business sub-systems. Among the most well-known who represent songwriters and music publishers are: The *American Society of Composers, Authors and Publishers* (ASCAP), *Broadcast Music, Inc.* (BMI), and SESAC. In addition to being considered professional organizations, they are as we found out in previous chapters, *performance rights organizations* who collect song performance royalties for their members. The *Harry Fox Agency* and *Copyright Management, Incorporated* are both considered professional organizations and also *mechanical rights organizations* because they collect song mechanical royalties for their members.[13] The *American Symphony Orchestra League* (ASOL) represents orchestras and their organizations. The *American Record Producers Association* represents record producers, and the list goes on.

There are many professional industry organizations you can join or volunteer to help with social functions. Many cities have songwriter and other organizations that offer many opportunities for networking. Contacts are the name of the game, so don't forget the local radio, TV, and print "personalities." Most of them belong to a local professional organization and have some contacts with professionals employed by the major labels.

If you're a songwriter, producer, audio engineer, etc., get the attention of similar professionals in the business. Joining songwriting organizations leads to similar opportunities with successful, professional writers, producers, and music publishers. Audio engineers habitually start as "grunts" (carrying the heavy sound equipment) for touring bands or as second engineers in demo recording studios. A great place to meet the people who can give industry entry opportunities is a social function sponsored by the professional organizations.

## Salaries

Young professionals hold many of the better paying jobs in the music and entertainment industry.

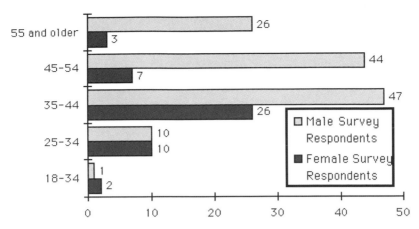

Figure 15.4 Many music business executives who earn premium salaries are young. Forty-one percent are between 35-44 and 70% are between 35-54 years old.[14]

Our recent survey of music industry executives found that 94% made more than $35,000 annually.[15]

*Figure 15.5 Eighty-four percent of music industry executives make more than $50,000 annually; 60% more than $75,000 annually. There are more males in executive positions in the music industry earning $75,000 annually than females. However, as women make inroads into the top executive positions, they are also receiving the $75,000-plus annual salaries.*

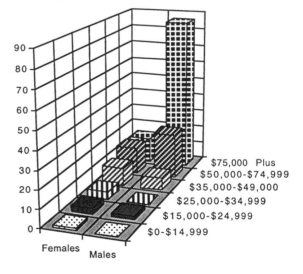

## Education

Procure an education, either in a Music Business program in your local university or through the school of hard knocks in the real world. Both are preferred. General college courses provide a stimulating foundation in the arts, humanities, sciences, and business. There are also many colleges and universities that offer a range of music business, film, and entertainment courses. Some offer actual degrees in Music Business, Commercial Music, Audio Engineering, and Record Industry Management, while others provide specific courses. In addition, take courses in an artistic area of interest, such as theater, mass media, communication, or within the School of Music. Business courses are also important. After all, it is the music *business* we are talking about. Prepare for a career by taking some fundamental business courses, including marketing, management, entrepreneurship, and accounting.

So, to be accepted into the artistic or business sub-systems, you'll need to be an educated person with artistic talents or appreciation and logical business wisdom.

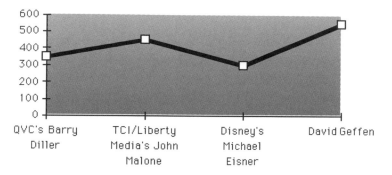

Figure 15.6 *Several entertainment executives are now listed by Forbes as being among America's 400 richest individuals. They include QVC's Barry Diller, net worth of $345 million; TCI/Liberty Media's John Malone, $450 million; Disney's Michael Eisner, $300 million.*[16] *David Geffen, producer of the film "Beetlejuice" and the Broadway plays "Cats" and "M. Butterfly," recently sold his Geffen Records to MCA for $550 million.*[17] *All together, the Forbes 400 have an estimated net worth of $328 billion, much of which is connected to the music and entertainment industry.*[18]

## Personality

*Successful music industry personnel seem to have a passion for both the music and the business.* You will want to have the same perspective. Industry insiders are proud of what they do. They are, in many cases, humbled by the experience of working with very talented musicians, songwriters, recording artists, producers, etc. and with the very bright business people who make it all happen. Many are honored by the fact that their artistic or business contributions to a recording are enjoyed by people all around the world. It is a privilege to be in a profession that provides music listeners with the recordings they can sing, laugh, or cry to when they hear your work. It's powerful when you are one of the persons who made it happen.

## Networking

Industry professionals customarily associate with other established music industry colleagues for commonalty, friendships, and to enhance their career opportunities. Nobody can make it in this business by themselves. Elvis needed Col. Parker, Axel Rose needed his record label, and everyone in the business needs the consumers to buy their recordings. It's just too big of an industry. You cannot do it on your own.

Joining together with others who have similar interests and talents is a common practice among industry professionals. It is a great way to introduce yourself to the industry insiders who can help your career. Music educators are frequently excellent initial contacts. Many are professionals, vocalists, musicians, audio engineers, music publishers, music and entertainment entrepreneurial businessmen and women, in addition to being teachers. Many local bands and musicians know somebody who is "somebody" in the industry. Get out there and get involved. Meet the people who can honestly help you become more successful in the business.

## Chauvinism

Successful music industry relationships are based on honesty, talent, and common goals. Solid artistic and industry business relationships are for the purpose of creating emotionally-stimulating, artistic, and financially-rewarding careers, not for negative purposes. Unfortunately, there are still some chauvinistic individuals who will take financial and/or sexual advantage of naive young people who want to be in the music business. Avoid all individuals who promise fame and fortune and then ask for your money or for you to participate in any unethical behavior.

## Creating a Local Buzz

If you want to make it in the music business, you'll have to "capture" the attention of someone in the business. If you're a band, get your act together, record an excellent demo, give it to the local station, put it on sale at the local record shop, and then invite local or national industry personalities to a showcase. If you're terrific, you may win over the support of the local radio stations music or program directors. They can give your demo some local airplay, and remember that most of them have contacts (through record promoters) with the major record labels. A referral by a local radio personality about a band that is "selling product" and is "getting airplay" on local radio stations will usually get "noticed" by major labels.

## College Internships

Artists managers, concert promoters, talent (booking) agents customarily start their careers as assistants working as road managers for local bands, radio station announcers, or college concert promoters. Others realize their first industry experiences and contacts through established college/industry internships and co-op programs. Most internships are non-paid and for college credit only. However, internships provide students with a valuable opportunity to experience the industry from the inside. They also provide industry professionals with a chance to check-out potential new employees before they offer them a job.

Internships are not for the types of individuals who want to acquire "stars'" autographs or schmooze with industry professionals. They are offered by the industry as an opportunity for students to "learn the business." In other words, college internships are a chance for students to make themselves *valuable* to the organization and industry by gaining knowledge about job specifics, qualifications, expectations, contacts, etc. Successful internships often lead to entry-level positions in the music and entertainment industry.

## Types of Businesses

Entrepreneurship appears to illustrate the business psychology of the music industry. A *sole proprietorship* is a business owned by one person, and in the music business, many songwriters and music producers are in business for themselves.[19] *Partnerships, joint ventures*, and *limited partnerships* are defined as businesses owned by more than one person.[20] Many bands, small record companies, and publishing companies are legal partnerships. *Corporations* bind the artists and business people together, and just as in any business, they bring their culture of artifacts, perspectives, values and assumptions.[21] Corporations have a separate entity and legal existence apart from the owners and stockholders.[22] They can be sued and taxed, just as a human being. However, legal action can only be filed against the corporation's assets, not the owners, who are typically record labels, artists, and stockholders. The corporation's business structure bestows on successful recording artists and entertainers a way to protect their personal assets from unjust claims.

## Entrepreneurship

A number of researchers have defined entrepreneurship as the recognition of an opportunity followed by the persistent exploitation of that opportunity.[23] It is an excellent way to describe the daily creative and business actions and mechanisms of the music industry. As an example, the mega entertainment corporations rely on entrepreneurial management processes to operate their labels. Bertelsmann Music Group has over 48,000 employees, 200 companies, and net revenues of approximately 9 billion dollars. Yet, the management and marketing scheme of the organization is a "decentralized divisional strategy based on the entrepreneurial spark of strong individual business units." Sony's attitude is to "find ways to stimulate consumer demand for music."[24]

The Atlantic Records group, a division of Time Warner, has boosted its revenues by marketing products to the "space between the elephant's toes." Niche marketing of exercise videos and audio books increased its net sales to 900 million dollars for 1994. In addition, Atlantic Records management has "recruited a group of young, trend-savvy music executives and encouraged them to take risks to find new talent." The result is a 9.4% market share of new releases.[25]

Time Warner's methodology is to <u>merge</u> with successful independent entrepreneurial entertainment companies and artists. In 1992, Time Warner paid 100 million dollars to the entrepreneurial businessman and recording artist, formally known as Prince, for his Paisley Park Enterprises. They also acquired a distribution deal (worth a reported 60 million) with entrepreneur recording artist Madonna to launch and fund her new record label Maverick.[26]

## Intrepreneurship

Record labels use *intrepreneurship* (entrepreneurship philosophy and methods applied to the inner operations of the company) to increase creativity and productivity. Examples include:

- ***Promotions:*** concentrate on radio stations that serve specific markets. This builds crossover potential and encourages good relationships and credibility with radio stations for future album releases.

- ***Marketing:*** Marketing reps correlate album typologies to specific retail outlets in order to increase shelf space where consumers are most likely to buy the product.

- ***Publicity:*** Both psychographic and demographic research provide insights into successful artist publicity.

- ***Publicity Department:*** uses the interface to predict which magazines, television shows, and movies to plant stories. Images are better defined or enhanced by predicting consumer attitudes and beliefs. Positive image characteristics are encouraged, negative ones are discouraged in publicity photos, biographies, image p.o.p. (point-of-purchase) displays, music videos, and publicity story lines.

- ***Art/Production:*** The Art Department uses image analysis to create a marketing plan for both the artist and the recorded product.

- ***A&R:*** Knowledge of which artists' and songs' consumers most enjoy, helps A & R concentrate on finding the types of artists and songs that are most marketable.

- ***Management:*** Corporate sponsorships and endorsements are correlated to image typologies.[27]

---

**Music Row Magazine**
1231 17th Ave. South, Nashville TN 37212
(615) 321-3617 (615) 329-0852 Fax

---

David Ross's <u>Music Row Magazine</u> bridges the gap between industry trade publications and the consumer press. It offers industry-related stories and research data. In addition, <u>Music Row's</u> "In Charge" annual directory provides pictures, addresses, phone numbers and job descriptions of industry professionals.

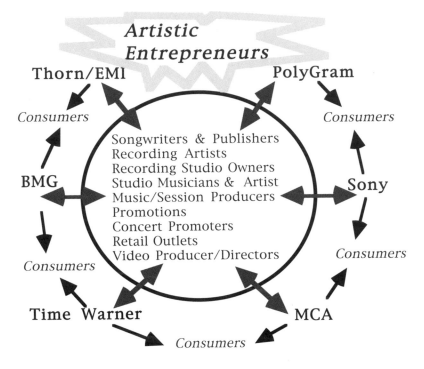

Figure 15.7 *The six mega entertainment corporations dominate the creative entrepreneur's success by controlling the financial, marketing, and lines of distribution of the majority of the global entertainment markets. The mega entertainment businesses need the entrepreneurial artists to create entertainment products (recorded music). The artists need the mega entertainment corporations to finance, market, and sell their recordings in order for them to make a decent wage.*

## Sage Window/Case Study:

*Mike Blanton and Dan Harrell have successfully exploited the interface between entrepreneurship and marketing to build several successful entertainment companies. In 1993, they estimated their companies are responsible for 75 million dollars worth of retail entertainment business. BMG was so impressed, they bought 50% of Blanton/Harrell artist management, 50% of the record label (Reunion Records), and 100% of the song publishing companies, Edward Grant, Inc. (ASCAP), Emily Booth Inc., (BMI), and Caroline, Inc. (SESAC).*[28]

*Harrell was pulled into the business. His sister in-law is popular recording artist Amy Grant. When concert promoters started to call Amy for concerts, the phone calls were redirected to Harrell, who at the time, was a Vice President of the Loan Department for a Nashville bank.*

**Harrell:** I was in the banking business and having a successful career. But I realized that this is not what I wanted for a lifetime career. I felt that it was a restrictive environment. It was a regulated business. It was hard to be compensated for the level of success you might contribute. I knew that at some point I was going to do something else. Amy Grant was my wife's youngest sister.

About three years into my banking career, when Amy was still in school, Amy's mom called and asked me to handle a phone call about a concert deal. So, I did. Her father is a doctor who handles cancer patients, so we didn't want to call him at the hospital. From that event, all the phone calls started coming to me.[29]

*As the business increased, the family decided to seek a manager for Ms. Grant.*

**Harrell:** I tried to find her a manager. I wanted out and didn't feel there was anyone we could trust or who understood what Amy was about. So, I came to the family and said, "Hey, I think I can do this."

*Michael Blanton, a dentistry student at a Christian University, toured the South Pacific as an assistant USO road manager. He changed his career to music, and in 1974 and 1975, worked as an artist manger at Opryland (a country music theme park in Nashville). For financial reasons, he dropped out of the music business and became the Executive Director of the Abilene Chamber of Commerce in Abilene Texas. In 1977, he returned to the music business working for Word Records in Waco, Texas. Later, he was transferred to Nashville as the Director of A & R.[30]*
*In 1980 Harrell left the bank and Blanton quit his job at Word Records to form Blanton/Harrell, Inc.*

**Harrell:** We just went for it blindly. We just said, "Hey, let's go do this." There was not a guaranteed pay check. There was a niche opportunity. There weren't any people in the management side of Christian Music, we felt, who were developing careers on a long-term basis. That's why many in Gospel music thought we were nuts. They would say, "Why does an artist need a manager?" Back in those days, artists didn't have managers, they had agent/managers. All we were going to do is try to earn a living off of advising a client "how to develop their career." Most of the people in the industry thought that was a luxury they could not afford.

*Blanton and Harrell believed they had a viable product in Amy Grant. They united their entrepreneurial venture with the marketing and distribution network of Word Records. Yet, their basic perception was that Ms. Grant had a broader potential market than the traditional Christian music audiences.[31]*
*To exploit the secular market, Blanton and Harrell had to accumulate the traditional retailing of Christian products through Christian bookstores with the marketing interface a secular record company would provide. They decided to portray their artists (Amy Grant, Kathy Troccoli, and Michael W. Smith) and corresponding images, songs, and recordings as popular culture entertainment that happen to be written from a Christian perspective. Secular methods of promotion, marketing, and retail distribution were established by pressuring Word Records, in 1985, to sign a co-distribution deal with Herb Alpert's A&M Records. As Harrell states: "A&M didn't understand the music, but Amy's*

album had gone platinum, and anytime someone sells platinum, everyone wants a piece of it."³²

The combined entrepreneurship and marketing efforts significantly increased profits for Blanton and Harrell. They managed Amy Grant to a very successful recording and concert performance career. She jumped from a contemporary Christian star to pop music superstar with her 1990 "Heart in Motion" album which sold 5 million-plus copies.

Blanton and Harrell founded Reunion Records in 1982 to market artists Michael W. Smith and Kathy Troccoli.

**Harrell:** "The Christian record labels liked Amy Grant, but they weren't interested in signing new talent. They thought Kathy Troccoli was too sexy and that Michael W. Smith couldn't sing. . . . So, out of necessity, we started Reunion Records and began producing albums. We talked Word Records into marketing and distributing the new label in their network of 4,500 Christian bookstores."³³

To increase Reunion's sales in 1991, Blanton/Harrell singed a distribution deal with Matsushita and Geffen Records (MCA records). Geffen's promotion budget and relationship with secular record stores helped Michael W. Smith become a pop star with "Place in This World" and "I will Be Here for You."³⁴

To market Troccoli, Blanton and Harrell used two separate press kits, one for the secular market which described her as a hot new soul pop singer, and another for the Christian market which stated how important it is for her to "stay within the sovereign will of God."³⁵ Troccoli had a pop hit with "Everything Changes."³⁶

Author Frank Peretti's first novel _This Present Darkness_ had sold 10,000 copies when Blanton/Harrell signed him to a book deal. Using the same strategy that had worked with Amy Grant and Michael W. Smith (treat it as a popular culture entertainment item that happens to be written from a Christian perspective), they boosted sales to over 1 million. Peretti's second book _Piercing the Darkness_ sold 1.2 million in three months.³⁷

Blanton and Harrell found a niche audience for their artists' music and changed the business of Gospel music in the process. They are predominantly responsible for Gospel music tripling its revenues from $180 million to $500 million annually.³⁸

**Harrell:** I think the real thing we had to do is to not listen to people who had done Gospel music a certain way for so many years. We didn't have any parameters or restrictions about how we thought about it as a business. We weren't categorizing our artists' music as Gospel music because we didn't grow up in Gospel music. We didn't understand all the "ins" and "outs," and probably some of the hardest things we experienced was that we stepped on a lot of people's toes. We didn't play by their rules. It wasn't that we weren't trying to do that, we just didn't know any better.

Why did they sell a portion of their companies? They needed to join their *entrepreneurial ventures with a global entertainment marketing corporation.*

**Harrell:** We made a decision two years ago that because of the cost of doing business, the risk, and the worldwide nature of the entertainment business, we had to get in with a big player to be competitive."[39] We want to grow into a full-line entertainment company. Which would include film and television. A media communications company that has a Christian philosophy behind it. It doesn't mean everything will be preaching. It doesn't mean that everything will have to have Jesus plastered on it, but it will be understood in our own minds that what we believe drives the kind of artist and art we create.

*The BMG merger appears to satisfy the entrepreneurial and marketing effort needs of both companies. Reunion's label acts are distributed by BMG through its RCA record label. According to BMG Ventures Senior Vice President Tom McPartland, "Our partnership with Reunion Entertainment Group and Blanton/Harrell fits perfectly into Ventures' commitment to diversified, entrepreneurial-driven entertainment companies."[40]*

*Through Blanton/Harrell, BMG Ventures expects to "launch into a number of diversified businesses that spring from their core strength. Areas such as sports management, film, and book properties."[41]*

**Harrell:** When I look back at what Mike and I did 15 years ago, we were absolutely nuts. Our original investment was about $20,000. The initial instinct of what makes a business go is "do you have the ability to create something people are going to go out and buy." We did have that instinct. We didn't necessarily understand that we did, but we did. All we really did was create things that became commercially viable. We had to be sure that our distributors understood what we were talking about and understood what the product was, because a lot of times marketing people, if they don't understand what it's all about (the real geniuses of it), then it doesn't have heart or feeling. So, we spent a lot of time putting together teams of people who believed in our vision and believed in what we were trying to accomplish.

*– Dan Harrell, Blanton & Harrell*

## Sage Window:

Photo courtesy Reunion Records

**Susan Shurtz**
**Music Business**
**Student/Recording**
**Artist**

**Q: Why do you want to be a recording artist?**

**A:** Whew! Big question. I just have a passion for it. I love music. I love the entertainment business. I love how it impacts people; how it influences people. So, part of it is the passion, and the other part is to influence people.

I think music is a powerful tool of communication. Whether it is "I got Friends in Low Places" or "Don't Worry, Be Happy," it can literally start a nation singing.

**Q: When did you discover that this is what you wanted**

**to do with your life?**

**A:** I was pretty young. Even when I was five or six, I was singing to Karen Carpenter in my room. I think it was in high school when I really knew I wanted to be in the music industry; be an artist and make records.

**Q: How did you make your dream into a reality?**

**A:** It's been a lot of fun, even as hard as it's been. I'm from Champagne, Illinois. It doesn't have the resources there for me to make it in the music business. I knew I needed to move to a city where the industry was happening. I decided to keep my ears open and to just learn how it all works. I didn't know anything about publishing. I made the most of school, using the studio time, taking music business classes, and getting work experience and contacts from my internships.

I did things on my own. I listened to famous artists and tried to emulate what I heard. Ultimately, I formed my own sound. I've done a million and one day jobs, and I've sung in night clubs just to be in front of an audience. I did some demo recordings, jingle work, and, eventually, started to write my own songs.

When I got out of school, it was a big shock to find out how hard it was to get work. I knew that it was not time yet. I think that you can be too anxious. I knew that I needed a few years just to grow up, get wiser, and better myself. I thought I would work for six months and then audition for a tour. Do that for a while and then get a record deal. None of that happened! I couldn't even get auditions, let alone get on a tour. It was very eye-opening. I had no idea that three and one half years later (after school) I would still be broke and struggling. But, I just kept on going.

My dad said something to me a long time ago, and it is really true: "We should never burn any bridges." It is amazing, someone sitting next to you in literature class in school who looks kind of geekie may someday be the guy working at a record company that you want to talk to. It is really true. It sounds corny, but we should really treat other people like we want to be treated. It really does pay off in the end. It all comes full circle. The guy who is signing me to a record deal is someone I met five years ago through a guy I was dating. So, we have known each other for years, and now he's the one who is giving me a deal.

**Q: When you select songs, what are you looking for?**

**A:** There are several things I look for in songs including the lyrics, melody, and the groove. I like lyrics that are very powerful and "get" people, but say it in a different way. Not just the old moon, spoon, June rhymes, but something that is said in a different, creative way. I'm a big melody person. The song needs to have a strong, memorable melody. The song should stand on its own, even before the production in the studio.

**Q: How important is your team of people who are going to help you become successful?**

**A:** Extremely important. Every piece of the puzzle is important - management, attorneys, my production team, and songwriters, publicist - everybody is extremely important. I am trying to move ahead with caution and to be wise by checking out people's track records and by trying to perceive their character.

**Q:** **What advice would you give to people who want to get into this business?**

**A:** (a) Learn as much as you can about the business.

(b) Network and meet as many people as possible in the business.

(c) Become the very best you can be at whatever your specialty or talent is.

(d) Be flexible, assume that things may not happen exactly the way that you planned, but persevere.

## MEIEA

Formal education provides an opportunity for life-long growth. Real world experience provides insights into the "systems" society has established for survival, communication, emotional, and financial rewards. There are the philosophical approaches to life and the practical. Attending college and trying your hand in the local music scene offers an opportunity to see if you really have the talents and desire necessary to attain a career in the music and entertainment industry. Talent, education, and persistence are the keys. Have a passion for the music and entertainment industry and an honest desire to contribute to it and to be part of it. Education and experience will provide the opportunities you will need to become successful.

There are many universities and community colleges offering courses in the music business. Try one, see if it's what you want to do. In addition, you may want to contact the *Music & Entertainment Industry Educators Association* for a listings of programs and schools near you.

**Music & Entertainment Industry Educators Association**
C/O Dr. Scott Fredrickson,
President of MEIEA
College of Fine Arts
University of Massachusetts Lowell
Lowell, MA 01854
(508) 934-3850  FAX ((508) 934-3034

## Summary

Most of the successful people in the music and entertainment business have created their own shot at success. Luck is important, but successful people often create their own "luck" by setting personal goals, developing creative and analytical talents, having a positive attitude, attaining excellent communicative skills, and by gaining as much knowledge as possible about the society or profession they want to experience.

Entrepreneurship may be the key to success in the music business. Creative artists are often sole proprietors who must fulfill the role of a business person or hire others to control the business aspects of their artistic creations. In other words, successful musicians, vocalists, songwriters, producers, etc. are, in addition to being a creative artists, businessmen and women who "put on another hat" in order to make a living from their musical and artistic talents. The mega entertainment corporations often fund and distribute the most successful of these creative entrepreneurs' products (songs, recordings, movies, etc.) in order to make a profit.

## Chapter Footnotes

[1] "The Entertainment Economy," Mandel J, (Et. al.) Business Week (March 14, 1994).

[2] Ibid.

[3] Gold records are issued for sales of 500,000 units, platinum for 1 million or more units sold.

[4] Career World, The Music Educators National Conference and The United States Department of Labor.

[5] Also known as the "Nashville Number System." It is a system of using relative numbers, instead of letters, to represent chords and note intervals; Noted by April Higuera, Platinum Heart Music/Black Puppy Publishing (1995).

[6] Career World, The Music Educators National Conference and The United States Department of Labor.

[7] Industry Focus Groups "What Makes a Recording Artist Successful," Wacholtz, Belmont University (1995).

[8] The Music Educators National Conference, The United States Department of Labor as reported in Career World, and Music & Entertainment Executive Survey by Wacholtz, Belmont University (1993).

[9] Wacholtz, Survey of the Music Industry class (1994).

[10] "Yearwood is singer/businesswoman," The Tennessean (September 16, 1994).

[11] A "union house" is a venue, studio, etc. that has signed a contractual agreement with the performance unions (AFTRA, AF of M, etc.) to allow only union workers (members) to be employed during the creation of various entertainment products. Most "Broadway theaters" musical performances "staged" in areas or sports complexes, and movies made in Hollywood, are considered "union jobs" made or performed in union houses. Exceptions include the production facilities in "Right-to-Work" states which often allow for non-union productions. However, in the music business, all the major labels have signed agreements with the performance unions that require all recordings distributed by the labels to pay the musicians and vocalists who created the recordings, union scale wages.

[12] Music Business Handbook & Career Guide, Baskerville (1990).

[13] See Chapter Three.

[14] Ibid.

[15] "Music Industry Executive Survey," Wacholtz, Belmont University (1993).

[16] "The Prince of Pay," Graef S. Crystal, Forbes (September 30, 1994), p. 92.

[17] "A Boffo Deal," Fortune (April 23, 1990).

[18] "There's No Business Like Show Business," edited by Seneker, et al., Forbes "400" (October 18, 1993), p. 110.

[19] Contracts will often include the sole proprietor's name and the term "Doing Business As" (DBA).

Source: David Maddox, Attorney Nashville, TN (1993).

[20] The Musicians Business & Legal Guide, Halloran (ed). (1991).

[21] Entrepreneurship Creativity and Growth, Donald L. Sexton and Nancy B. Bowman-Upton (1991), and E. Schein, "Coming to a New Awareness of Organization Culture," Sloan Management Review, (Winter, 1984). Corporations appear to have four levels of culture including: (1) artifacts, which may be verbal, stories, and myths; (2) perspectives which include various types of special dress, behavior, rituals, ceremonies, socially-shared rules and norms; (3) values which are defined as attainable objectives, goals, standards, and ideals; and (4) assumptions which are often described as "unconscious assumptions which determine how we think or feel."

[22] The Portable MBA in Entrepreneurship, William D. Bygrave (1994).

[23] Stevenson & Gumpert (1985), Stevenson & Sahlman (1986), Sexton & Bowman-Upton (1987).

[24] Music Business International (1992).

[25] Strodghill II & Grover "Atlantic's Sweet Listening Guy," Business Week (June 20, 1994), pp. 176-177.

[26] Music Business International (1992).

[27] Entertainment Media Research as suggested by Miller & Wacholtz (1994).

[28] Source: Billboard Magazine, Holly (1993).

[29] Telephone interview with Dan Harrell conducted by Wacholtz (1994).

[30] Blanton/Harrell bio packs as supplied by Blanton/Harrell (1994).

[31] Source: "Religious Conversions," Gubernick, Forbes, (February 14, 1994), pp. 128-9.

[32] Ibid.

[33] Ibid.

[34] Oermann, The Tennessean (1993).

[35] Source: "Religious Conversions," Gubernick, Forbes (February 14, 1994), pp. 128-9.

[36] Oermann The Tennessean (1993).

[37] McCall (1991).

[38] Ore (1993).

[39] Ibid.

[40] Oermann (1993).

[41] Holley (1993).

# APPENDIX
## Industry Related Books

The music and entertainment business change quickly. Read as much as possible to stay informed about the shifts in business strategies, advances in technology and daily business operations.

## Industry Related Books

All You Need Is Ears by George Martin, St. Martins Press (1982).

All You Need To Know About the Music Business by Donald S. Passman, Simon & Schuster (1994), 2nd. edition.

Acoustic Techniques for Home & Studio by F. Alton Everest, Tab Books (1984).

Audio In Media by Stanley A. Alten, Wadsworth, Inc. (1994).

Consumer Electronics Annual Review, by the Electronic Industry Association (1994).

Courtney Price Answers The Most Asked Questions From Entrepreneurs by Courtney Price, McGraw-Hill, Inc. (1994).

Entertainment Industry Economics by Harold L. Vogel, Cambridge University Press (1990).

Entrepreneurship Creativity and Growth by Donald L. Sexton and Nancy B. Bowman-Upton, MacMillian Publishing Company (1991).

Guerrilla P.R.: How You Can Wage An Effective Publicity Campaign, Without Going Broke by Michael Levine, Harper Business (1994).

Handbook of Recording Engineering by John M. Eargle, Van Nostrand Reinhold (1991).

Handbook for Sound Engineers: The New Audio Cyclopedia by Glen Ballou, (Ed.) Howard W. Sams & Company, (1987).

Hit Men by Fredric Dannen, Time Books, (1990).

How to Make and Sell Your Own Recordings by Diane Rappaport, Prentice Hall (1992).

Inside MTV by R. Serge Denisoff, Transaction Publishers, First paperback reprint (1991).

Inside Country Music by Larry E. Wacholtz, Billboard Books (1986).

Inside The Music Business by Michael Fink, Schirmer Publishing (1989).

Lights, Glamour, and BS Inside The Music Business, by Larry E. Wacholtz, Thumbs Up Publishing (1982).

Managing Your Band, Artist Management: The Ultimate Responsibility by Dr. Stephen Marcone, HiMarks Publishing (1995).

Marketing in the Music Industry, Charles W. Hall and
    Frederick J. Taylor, Simon & Schuster, (1996).

Modern Recording Techniques by Robert E. Runstein and
    David Miles Huber, Howard W. Sams & Company (1986).

More About This Business of Business of Music by William
    Krasilovsky and Sidney Shemel, Billboard Books (1994), 5th
    edition.

Music Business Handbook & Career Guide by David Baskerville,
    Sherwood Publishing 5th edition (1990).

Music in the Market, by Don Cusic, Bowling Green State University
    Popular Press (1995).

Music, Money, and Success by Jeffrey and Todd Brabec,
    Schirmer Books (1994).

Music On Demand: Composers and Careers In The Hollywood
    Film Industry by Robert R. Faulkner, Transaction Books
    (1982).

Music Sound and Technology by John Eargle, Van Nostrand
    Reinhold Publishing (1990).

Music Through MIDI: Using Midi to Create Your Own Electronic
    Music System by Michael Boom, Microsoft Press (1987).

Networking In The Music Industry: Making The Contacts You
    Need To Succeed In the Music Business by Jim Clevo and
    Eric Olson.  Rock Press Publishing (1994) Second Printing.

Principles of Digital Audio by Ken C. Pohlmann, Howard W.
    Sams & Company (1989).

Rockonomics: The Money Behind The Music, by Franklin Watts,
    The Entertainment Law Institute, University of Southern
    California (1989).

So You Want To Open A Music Store, by NAMM Publications
    (1994).

Sound Advice: The Musicians Guide to the Recording Industry
    by Wayne Wadhams, Schirmer Books (1989).

Sound Advice: The Musicians Guide to the Recording Studio by
    Wayne Wadhams, Schirmer Books (1990).

Successful Artist Management by Xavier M. Frascogno, Jr.,
    Watson-Guptill Publishing (1990).

The Billboard Guide to Music Publicity by Jim Pettigrew, Jr.,
    Billboard Books (1989).

The Beginner's Handbook of Electronics by George Olsen,
    revised by Forrest M. Mims, Prentice-Hall, Inc. (1977).

The Communication of Recorded Country Music: A Q-Technique
    Portrait of Seven Listener Types by Larry E. Wacholtz,
    UMI (1992).

The Copyright Law of the United States of America U.S.
    Government Printing Office 1993-342-582/80,038, (1993).

The Gold Book by The American Symphony Orchestra League:
    Washington DC (1994).

The Musician's Business & Legal Guide by Mark Halloran, (ed.)
    Prentice Hall (1991).

This Business of Artist Management by H. Lee Heatherington
    and Xavier M. Franscogna Jr., Billboard Books (1997).

This Business of Music by Sidney Shemel and M. William
    Krasilovsky, Billboard Books (1990) 6th Edition.

Understanding Copyright Law, by Marshall Leaffer, Matthew
    Bender Books (1989).

# ADDITIONAL PROFESSIONAL ORGANIZATIONS

## Trade Organizations

American Music Conference (AMC) 5140 Avenida Encinas, Carlsbad, CA 92008. 1-(800) 767-6266/(619) 438-7327 fax.

American Society of Music Arrangers (ASMA) P.O. Box 11, Hollywood, CA 90028.

Audio Engineering Society (AES) 60 E. 42nd Street, New York, NY 10165. (212) 661-8528/(212) 682-0477 fax.

Electronic Industries Association (EIA) 2003 I Street N. W., Washington D.C. 20006. (202) 457-4900.

Music Distributors Association (MDA) 38 W. 21st Street, 5th floor, New York, NY 10010. (212) 924-9175/(212) 675-3577 fax.

Music Industries Association of Canada (MIAC) 1210 Shepherd Ave. East, P.O. Box 20, North York, Canada, ONM2K1E3. (416) 490-1871/(416) 490-9739 fax.

National Association of Band Instrument Manufacturers (NABIM) 38 West 21st Street, 5th Floor, New York, NY 10010. (212) 924-9175/(212) 675-3577 fax.

The National Association of Music Merchants (NAMM) 5140 Avenida Encinas, Carlsbad, CA 92008. 1-(800) 767-6266/(619) 438-7327 fax.

Retail Print Music Dealers Association (RPMDA) 4020 McEwen, Suite 105, Dallas, TX 75244. (214) 233-9107/(214) 490-4219 fax.

## Additional Professional Associations

Academy of Country Music, 6255 Sunset Boulevard Suite 923, Hollywood, CA 90028. (213) 462-2351.

American Mechanical Rights Agency, Inc. (AMRA) 2112 Broadway New York, NY 10023 (212) 877-4077.

American Music Conference (ACM) 303 East Wacker Drive, Chicago, IL 60611. (212) 595-3050.

American Symphony Orchestra League (ASOL) 777 14th Street N.W. Suite 500, Washington DC (202) 628-0099.

Black Music Association (BMA) 1500 Locust Street, Philadelphia, PA 19102. (215) 545-8600.

Country Music Association (CMA) 7 Music Circle North, Nashville, TN 27202. (615) 244-2840.

Gospel Music Association (GMA) P.O. Box 23201, Nashville, TN 37203. (615) 242-0303.

Nashville Entertainment Association (NEA) P.O. Box 25309 Nashville, TN 37203. (615) 321-5662.

National Academy of Songwriters (NAS) 6381 Hollywood Boulevard, Suite 780, Hollywood, CA 90028. (213) 463-7178.

National Association of Record Merchandisers (NARM) 10008 F. Astonia Boulevard, Cherry Hill, NJ 08034. (609) 427-1404.

National Association of Independent Record distributors and Manufactures (NAIRD) P.O. Box 568, Maple Shade, NJ 08052. (609) 427-1404.

Recording Industry Association of American (RIAA) 1020 19th Street N.W. Washington DC 20036. (202) 775-0101.

Society of Professional Audio Recording Studios (SPARS) 4300 10th Avenue North, Lake Worth, FL 33461. (305) 641-6648.

The Songwriters Guild of America (SGA) 276 Fifth Avenue, New York, NY 10001. (212) 686-6820.

# INDEX